THE UNITY OF
KNOWLEDGE
AND ACTION

SUNY series in Philosophy
George R. Lucas Jr., editor

THE UNITY OF KNOWLEDGE AND ACTION

Toward a Nonrepresentational Theory of Knowledge

WARREN G. FRISINA

State University
of New York
Press

Published by
State University of New York Press, Albany

© 2002 State University of New York

For information, address State University of New York Press,
90 State Street, Suite 700, Albany, NY 12207

Production by Susan Geraghty
Marketing by Jennifer Giovani

Library of Congress Cataloging-in-Publication Data

Frisina, Warren G., 1954–
    The unity of knowledge and action : toward a
nonrepresentational theory of knowledge / Warren G. Frisina.
        p. cm. — (SUNY series in philosophy)
    Includes bibliographical references (p.) and index.
    ISBN 0-7914-5361-8 (alk. paper) — ISBN 0-7914-5362-6 (pbk.
: alk. paper)
    1. Knowledge, theory of. 2. Act (Philosophy). I Frisina,
Warren G., 1954– II. Title. III. SUNY series in philosophy.

BD161 .F69 2002
121.21—dc21

                                                                200104616

10 9 8 7 6 5 4 3 2 1

To Patsy

CONTENTS

ACKNOWLEDGMENTS

When a book has a long gestation it leaves the author with a responsibility to acknowledge a great many people who have contributed either directly or indirectly to its production.

It is perhaps fair to say that this book's roots reach all the way to my undergraduate days at the State University of New York at Purchase. As a philosophy major in the early 1970s I had the great good fortune to study with Robert C. Neville. He introduced me to the extraordinary insights of process thought and American pragmatism. He helped me to see value in the vast philosophical literature that existed outside of the American and European traditions. And, he taught me to trust my interest in religious questions, promising that by placing myself among thinkers interested in religion I would receive precisely the kind of much needed stimulation that was missing in professional philosophy. He was right about that. Even though this book has little to say about religion, I know that it would not have been written were I to have stuck to the narrower path of strictly philosophic training. And, although the specific ideas outlined in this book did not occur to me till some twenty years after my college graduation, the general contours of my thinking were established under Neville's tutelage and are a direct result of his influence.

Later, as a graduate student at the University of Chicago, Edward Ch'ien was my guide into the complex world of Chinese thought. With a healthy dose of the early Foucault, and a great deal of patience, he translated complicated and foreign sounding Chinese metaphors into a language I could grasp. He encouraged my comparative interests, and promised that the world needed more western philosophers who had an appreciation for the contributions of Chinese thought. It is hard to overestimate how much I learned as a result of the doors he opened for me. We all suffered a great loss with his early passing.

Langdon Gilkey was my advisor during my years at Chicago. His own interest in non-western traditions helped convince me that the path I was just beginning to mark out could be a fruitful one. I attribute to him my conviction that no matter what the area of investigation, the most important questions in that area will always turn out to have theological implications.

It is a Deweyan truism to note that like everything else books are the products of situations rather than individuals. There are a number of times when my "situation" provided the kind of support that is necessary to produce a book like this one. Early in my career I spent several years as a faculty member in the University of Houston's Honors Program (now College). There, under the careful guidance of Ted Estess (Dean) and Bill Monroe (Associate Dean), I learned a great deal about what it means to be a teacher, and how my teaching informs my scholarly work. I also caught a glimpse of the creativity and ingenuity that are needed to nurture an institution. Without their support, both personal and professional, it is hard to imagine how this book, or just about anything else I've written, would ever have seen the light of day.

Along these same lines, I owe a great debt to the American Academy of Religion and especially to its executive director Barbara DeConcini. Much of this book was written while I was the AAR's associate executive director from 1991–1996. In the Confucian tradition a chün-tzu is someone who has both the administrative and spiritual wisdom to provide the kind of leadership that helps a community to flourish. Given what she has done, there is no doubt that Barbara is a true chün-tzu. The AAR flourished under her care, as did I. Among her many great good deeds was arranging a six-month sabbatical for me. It allowed me to spend the time I needed to bring this project into focus. I'll always be grateful to her and to the AAR for all the ways I have been helped. I also want to acknowledge then-AAR staffers Ondina Gonzalez, Bradley Hurley, Steve Herrick, and the late Tammy Adams, who on countless occasions provided me with the support I needed to continue making progress on this project

These days I have the great good fortune of working with an extraordinary group of colleagues in the Philosophy and Religious Studies Department at Hofstra University where I've found intellectual stimulation from: Ralph Acampora, David Cernic, Terry F. Godlove, Jr., Robert Holland, Elliot Jurist, Amy Karofsky, Arvind Mandair, Eske Mollgaard. Anne O'Byrne, Ira Singer, and Kathleen Wallace. Extra-departmental colleagues who have contributed to my thinking include: John Teehan, Dan Varisco, Eduardo Duarte, and Jacques Berlinerblau. It is a glorious thing to go to work with friends who bring out the best in you.

Among my current colleagues, however, I do need to single out two for special mention with respect to this project. Anthony Dardis went the "extra mile" by reading through most of this manuscript when it was in its penultimate stage. I will always be grateful to him for his careful commentary and his encouragement. They were very helpful.

I also owe an extraordinary debt of gratitude to Terry Godlove, who has been my friend for more than twenty years. In countless ways, both professionally and personally, Terry's insight, kindness and good humor have helped to make this book possible. He generously read through and commented upon the earliest versions of most chapters in this book. His professional advice and assistance are singularly responsible for whatever success I am now enjoying. It also helped that he has for many years arranged things so that each summer his family and mine can enjoy a blissful week in Wellfleet on Cape Cod, where we do nothing but swim, build sand castles, drink gin and tonics and eat seafood. His friendship and encouragement have helped carry me through the difficult times and made the good times all that much better.

Having spent some time working in the executive office of a learned society and professional association I am perhaps more aware than most of the role such organizations play in nurturing research that simply would not have happened without them. Too often those contributions go unrecognized. I already mentioned the AAR, where the Confucian Studies group (led by John Berthrong and Mark Csikzentmihalyi) and the Pragmatism and Empiricism in American Religious Thought group (led by Thomas Byrnes and Jerome Soneson) have been especially helpful. I want to also acknowledge the American Philosophical Association, the International Society for Chinese Philosophy and especially the Highlands Institute for American Philosophical and Religious Thought (HIARPT). HIARPT has provided numerous opportunities for extended reflection on issues in American thought. I have extraordinary memories of weeks spent in the North Carolina mountains talking with HIARPT founder Creighton Peden as well as Nancy Frankenberry, Sheila Davaney, Del Brown, Bill Dean, Bill Hart, Henry Levinson, Don Crosby, Richard Bernstein, Wayne Proudfoot, Richard Rorty, Michael Raposa, Wesley Robbins and many others. I learned so much in those conversations, and am looking forward to many more to come. I also want to thank Gene Reeves and the Rissho Kosei-kai lay Buddhist association for giving me the opportunity to talk with an extraordinary group of scholars about knowledge, action and the Lotus Sutra in the mountains outside of Tokyo.

As a non-sinologist I've had to depend on a great many colleagues for help interpreting the Confucian and Neo-Confucian traditions. I'm especially grateful to Tu Wei-ming, P. J. Ivanhoe, Wu Kuang-ming, Steve Odin, A. S. Cua, Julia Ching, Cheng Chung-ying and the writing team David Hall and Roger Ames. Hall and Ames merit special attention for the extraordinary work they have done, for the help they've given me throughout my career, and to acknowledge how great a loss it was when David passed away this fall. We all miss him greatly.

I've learned a great deal from my many students over the years. I am especially grateful to Neil Adler for our conversations on the brain and the unity of knowledge and action.

No matter how long I extend these remarks I certainly will fail to acknowledge someone who has had a hand in the creation of this book. For that I apologize ahead of time.

But before bringing my thank yous to a conclusion, I need to acknowledge that without the love and care I received from my family, this book simply would never have appeared. While I may have learned to think about the "unity of knowledge and action" by reading Chinese and American philosophy I know that the deepest confirmation of the truth in that slogan has come from watching the growth and development of my two daughters, Kyle and Jessica. I know that they've taught me much more than I ever taught them.

My very last thank you brings me back to where these acknowledgements began, the State University of New York at Purchase, where I met and fell in love with a young woman from the Bronx named Patsy Cooper. Back then there was no way to predict that some 30 years later we would find ourselves parents of children approaching the age we were when we first met, and colleagues at a university where our students remind us daily of how we began and how far we have come. I simply do not have adequate words to explain to my readers the extent to which who I am and what I've accomplished is as much a result of her efforts as my own. For all she has done on my behalf, for all the sacrifices she has made, for all the love she has bestowed upon me, I will always be eternally grateful.

December, 2001
Hofstra University, Hempstead, NY

Earlier versions of some chapters have appeared in the following journals.

Chapter 2: "Davidson, Rorty and Religion: A Response to Wesley J. Robbins," *American Journal of Theology and Philosophy*, Vol. 17, no. 2, 1996, pp. 157–65. Copyright 1996 by American Journal of Theology and Philosophy. Reproduced by permission of the publisher.

Chapter 4: "Are Knowledge and Action Really One Thing: An exploration into Wang Yang-ming's theory of mind," *Philosophy East and West*, vol. 39, October, 1989, pp 419–447. Copyright 1989 by University of Hawaii Press. Reproduced by permission of the publisher.

Chapter 5: "Knowledge as Active, Aesthetic and Hypothetical: A study of the relationship between Dewey's metaphysics and epistemology," *Philosophy Today*, Vol.33, no. 3, 1989, pp. 245–63. Copyright 1989 by DePaul University. Reproduced by permission of the publisher.

Chapter 6: "Knowledge as Active, Aesthetic and Hypothetical: A pragmatic interpretation of Whitehead's cosmology," *The Journal of Speculative Philosophy*, Vol. 5, no. 1, 1991, pp. 42–64. Copyright 1991 by Pennsylvania State University. Reproduced by permission of the publisher.

Chapter 7: "Minds, Bodies, Experience and Nature," in *Pragmatism, Neo-Pragmatism, and Religion: Conversations with Richard Rorty,* ed. by Donald A. Crosby and Charley D. Hardwick, Peter Lang Press, 1998. Copyright Peter Lang Press, 1998. Reproduced by permission of the publisher.
Chapter 8: "Heaven's Partners or Nietzschean Free Spirits?" *Philosophy East and West,* Volume 45, no. 1, January, 1995, pp. 29–60. Copyright 1995 by the University of Hawaii. Reproduced by permission of the publisher.

INTRODUCTION

In 1926 John Dewey opened *Experience and Nature* with the observation, "To many the associating of the two words [experience and nature] will seem like talking of a round square, so ingrained is the notion of the separation of man and experience from nature" (1958, 1a). Some readers of this volume may have similar feelings about being called upon to make sense of a phrase such as the *unity of knowledge and action*. After all, most of us speak as if knowledge is prior to and separate from action. The maxim Look before you leap still neatly sums up the sense many have that the mind (however it is defined) first formulates a *mental* plan (or idea/concept/picture), which it uses to determine how and where the "bodily self" should leap.

Of course, things have changed since Dewey's time. Only a few philosophers still follow the Cartesian tradition of positing a separation of our mental and physical selves.[1] In the time since the publication of *Experience and Nature*, traditional dichotomies such as mind/body, mind/brain, experience/nature, natural/unnatural, organic/inorganic, intentional/mechanistic have all been blurred. Popular culture is even beginning to loosen its attachment to dualistic language as it assimilates scientific advances in medicine, neuroscience, and cognitive science that render in vivid terms the degree to which our thoughts, emotions, and feelings are intertwined with the brain's electrical and chemical processes.

In spite of these changes, however, most of us continue to use language that makes it seem as if knowledge and action are clearly separable. This book argues that we need to work harder at giving up this distinction. Letting go of the sharp knowledge-action distinction will make possible a more coherent theory of knowledge that is more adaptive to the way we experience one another and the world. It will also transform our philosophical anthropology, opening whole new ways to understand the self. When we treat knowledge as a form of action, knowing turns out to have less to do with an "inner" representation of immaterial ideas and more to do with refinements in the way we behave.

As Charles Taylor has pointed out, the modern understanding of the "knowing self" has a long and complicated history (1989). It stems, he claims, from a turn toward inwardness, an affirmation of ordinary life, and the romantic struggle to understand how human experience and values can remain connected to a world that science describes in mechanistic terms.[2] Late-modern and postmodern thinkers have been struggling for almost a century with the incoherent implications embedded within the modernist view of the self as a private knower. These include problems such as whether there are other minds, whether we really control our bodies, and whether our so-called inner thoughts connect at all to an externally verifiable world. Philosophers, anthropologists, and cognitive scientists, to mention but a few of the fields where the investigation of this topic is central, have all taken a whack at the modernist view of the self and its implicit theory of knowledge. Viewed from this angle then, this book is also a contribution to the broad contemporary effort to reconstruct our understanding of the self. I argue that an unthinking acceptance of the separation of knowledge from action creates an impediment to any attempt to overcome the problems implicit in the modernist notions of the self.

In sum, the central assertions in this book are that by taking seriously the notion that knowledge and action are really one thing, we will improve our theory of knowledge and our understanding of the self.

In order to understand why I focus such attention on the relationship between knowledge and action, it is important to recognize how this distinction is tied to a representationalist epistemology that is already under attack from many different quarters. Often ascribed to Descartes, who was himself transforming epistemological assumptions implicit in medieval and early Greek philosophy, representational theories typically portray knowledge as the apprehension and re-presentation of an aspect of the world within the so-called mind's eye. This position assumes the existence of an objective world that is *separate* from the knowing subject and *fixed* in some way so as to be capable of being known. As Donald Davidson (1973) and Richard Rorty (1979) have argued, representational assumptions such as these make human sight the primary metaphor for knowledge and typically posit a medium (often called "experience") between the knowing subject and the known world. Unfortunately, a number of paradoxes arise when metaphors such as the *mind's eye* are taken literally. For example, representationalism makes it difficult to understand how the ideas occupying an inner "mental self" connect with the so-called outer world. Representationalism also creates confusing questions about the human body. Is the body (especially the brain) part of the mind that knows? Or is it part of the world that is known? Moreover, representational theories of knowledge sometimes lead philosophers and scientists to describe the qualitative content of experience (e.g., its colors, textures, and values) as purely subjective impositions on an utterly valueless, materialistic, and mechanistic world. This paradoxical conclusion leaves us unable to articulate how the qualitative dimension of human experience relates to the so-called external or nonhuman world.

During the past thirty years, problems such as these have brought critiques of representationalism to a fever pitch. With attacks on representationalism coming from many different directions (including representatives from almost every philosophic school or faction), it is possible to describe the end of the twentieth century as an age of epistemological crisis. Despite the progress made by contemporary analytic philosophers, phenomenologists, and cognitive scientists, we do not yet have anything like a consensus on what an adequate nonrepresentational theory of knowledge might look like. Though it is easy to find reasons to criticize Cartesian dualism and representational theories of knowledge, the lack of a new nonrepresentational paradigm for knowledge has left us in the awkward position of speaking and acting in ways that appear contrary to our beliefs. We may deny representationalism in theory, but our common speech and even some sophisticated philosophic discussions (particularly in practical areas such as ethics) remain dependent on the very metaphors that reinforce it. I guess this shouldn't surprise us for, as Thomas Kuhn (1970) pointed out in his early work on scientific revolutions, no one willingly abandons a paradigm without having before him or her a fully plausible alternative that effectively removes or displaces the problems that had surfaced in the previous paradigm.

Part of the reason we have yet to succeed in constructing an acceptable alternative to the representational paradigm is our failure to take seriously the degree to which our description of knowledge would have to change were we to adopt a truly nonrepresentational position. This is especially the case with respect to the separation of knowledge from action. Old metaphors that portray knowledge as static and held apart from action (be they in a mind, a transcendental ego, or brain) effectively condemn us to reiterating the mistakes that have led to the current impasse. By translating talk about knowledge into talk about action, we create a new tool that will help us to escape the false dilemma of having to affirm either Cartesian dualism or mechanistic materialism.

To achieve this transformation of our understanding of the relationship between knowledge and action, we are all going to have to reach beyond the narrowly defined (one might even say factional) boundaries that have shaped philosophy for the latter half of the twentieth century. I am happy to say that we can already see this happening in the way that the work of phenomenologists, cognitive scientists, and language analysts seems to be converging around what I am calling the "quest for a nonrepresentational theory of knowledge." In this volume I am concerned to draw into this conversation three more traditions whose importance I believe has been underappreciated to date. They are American pragmatism, process philosophy, and Chinese Neo-Confucianism. I will speak briefly in this introduction about each one, leaving the detailed discussions for later chapters.

Most readers would readily acknowledge that Chinese philosophy has played only a marginal role in Western philosophic thinking. Recently, however, the consistent output of scholarly work on Chinese thought (e.g., translations, scholarly monographs, and articles by sinologists) is being supplemented with work by philosophers and others who are just beginning to appreciate the many ways that the Chinese intellectual traditions can contribute to contemporary philosophic discussions. In my own case, the very idea for this book was inspired by the philosophy underlying the Neo-Confucian scholar Wang Yang-ming's famous slogan *chih hsing ho-i* (the unity of knowledge and action). Though it sounds strange at first, I have come to believe that he meant us to take this slogan literally. For Wang, knowledge is a way of acting. To say that we know something is really a statement about how we interact with it. All of the analyses in the chapters that follow are my attempt to rethink our theory of knowledge and the self in light of Wang's insight.

While it is clear that Chinese thought is only just beginning to have a serious impact on Western discussions of knowledge and the self, process philosophy has had a more varied history. Viewed broadly, it is possible to argue that many forms of contemporary philosophic discourse have made the shift away from substantialist to some form of process thinking. Here I am thinking of certain strands within phenomenology, existentialism, and hermeneutics, as well process-oriented consequences that flow from the scientific discoveries of Einstein, Heisenberg and Bohr. When we speak of process philosophy as the more narrowly defined legacy of Alfred North Whitehead and his followers (e.g., Charles Hartshorne, John Cobb), however, the situation is more complex. At times, Whitehead's work has been at the center of contemporary philosophic discourse, though it is fair to say that the majority of contemporary philosophers now consider it less relevant. For the most part, Whitehead's style of systematic metaphysical speculation is ignored or considered a form of philosophizing whose time has passed except in the field of theology where speculative metaphysical questions retain some relevance. Obviously, I disagree with such judgments. In fact, I will be arguing throughout this book that one of the things hanging up our attempts to get past representational theories of knowledge is a refusal to address the basic metaphysical questions that fascinated Whitehead. Moreover, I believe that it was his willingness to explore these issues that made it possible for him to develop some of the resources we need to construct a nonrepresentational theory of knowledge.

Since American pragmatism has been at the center of many contemporary epistemological conversations (e.g., Quine, Putnam, Rorty), I should explain why I include it among a list of voices underrepresented in the quest for a nonrepresentational theory of knowledge. While it may be true that increasing numbers of philosophers have been talking about Dewey, Peirce, James, and Mead, many routinely ignore the so-called metaphysical (i.e., organismic or panpsychic) side of the pragmatic movement. One of the arguments running through this book is that metaphysical moves that are common to pragmatism, process philosophy, and (surprisingly) Neo-Confucianism will lead us toward a satisfactory resolution of the quest for a nonrepresentational theory of knowledge. In short, I believe that works such as Dewey's *Experience and Nature* have much to teach us about the unity of knowledge and action. Together with insights from process philosophy and Chinese Neo-Confucianism, pragmatism contains precisely the tools we need to break through faulty assumptions we have carried around since Descartes.[3]

This book sets our conversations about knowledge and the self in a much larger context. Part 1 examines the work of four contemporary philosophers who represent, in broad terms, some current trends in continental philosophy, analytic philosophy, postanalytic philosophy, and cognitive science. Specifically, I argue that Charles Taylor, Donald Davidson, Richard Rorty, and Daniel Dennett are engaged in the quest for a nonrepresentational theory of knowledge. Moreover, as I see it, these thinkers each make specific metaphysical assumptions (some explicit and others implicit) that prevent them from reaching that goal. In my discussion of each thinker, I go on to identify the nature of these metaphysical roadblocks and spell out how the pragmatic, process, and Neo-Confucian traditions could be helpful in removing them. Part 2 contains the argumentative heart of the book. In it I describe and put to use the pragmatic, process and Neo-Confucian insights that make it possible for us to see how knowledge and action are truly one thing. Part 3 defends these claims against some typical accusations and concludes by examining the work of two contemporary philosophers who are heading in the direction I believe we should be pursuing in our quest to develop a nonrepresentational theory of knowledge.

Having described the steps in my argument, I want to end this introduction by telling the reader something about *how* I intend to get to my conclusions. The work of the contemporary American philosopher Richard J. Bernstein shapes my approach to a significant degree. As readers of Bernstein will know, my book is not the first attempt to argue that a concern for our understanding of action is a common thread among seemingly disparate philosophic schools. In 1971, Bernstein showed in *Praxis and Action* how Marxism, existentialism, pragmatism, and analytic philosophy were all wrestling with the relationship between knowledge and action. In the introduction Bernstein said: "I intend to show that the concern with man as agent has been a primary focal point of each of these movements and further, that each contributes something permanent and important to our understanding of the nature and context of human activity" (1971, 1). Elaborating on this thesis Bernstein goes on to say: "The felt difficulty experienced by many contemporary philosophers within the mainstreams of modern philosophy and even earlier philosophy has been that the conception of man which we have inherited is a distorted one. It has been distorted not only by the preoccupation with man as knower, but by a certain view of what knowledge is or ought to be—one that is 'incorrigibly contemplative'" (Ibid., 7). Through a careful analysis of paradigmatic figures in four philosophic schools—Marx and Hegel, Kierkegaard and Sartre, Peirce and Dewey, and an assortment of analytic philosophers— Bernstein discussed the ways in which each school criticizes the Cartesian characterization of knowledge and offered alternatives that place a greater emphasis on the linkage between knowledge and action. I agree completely with Bernstein's assessment. I agree with his instinct that the root of the problem can be found in an overly mentalistic definition of knowledge. Most important, I am impressed with the way Bernstein built his argument. Seeing each of the figures lined up side by side makes it easy for me as a reader to recognize the patterns Bernstein wanted to illustrate.

Twelve years later, in what could be described as a companion to *Praxis and Action,* Bernstein took his argument further. In *Beyond Objectivism and Relativism: Science, Hermeneutics, and Praxis,* he presented evidence that a new paradigm for knowledge was beginning to emerge among philosophers. Philosophy, he claimed, has long operated under the thrall of a "Cartesian anxiety." We have been afraid that without a secure foundation for knowledge, we would eventually drown in the chaos of uncertainty (1988, 16–19). According to Bernstein, advances in hermeneutics, philosophy of science, and praxis theory are moving the conversation beyond the traditional dilemma of having to choose between a foundationalist objectivism on the one hand (to preserve a sense of order) and a subjective relativism on the other (to preserve a sense of human freedom). In place of the Cartesian focus on the individual, European and American philosophers were turning to the community, beginning to see experience, rationality, and knowledge from within the context of broader communicational systems or language games. Viewed from this perspective, the focus of epistemology is less on information processed by an individual mind (Descartes's primary concern) and more on the way communities establish ideals, make choices, and accomplish their goals. In short, Bernstein sees in recent philosophy a shift away from the view that knowledge is contemplation and toward the view that knowledge is best understood within the context of *phronesis*, or practical wisdom.

As was the case in the earlier book, Bernstein built the arguments in *Beyond Objectivism and Relativism* via a careful analysis of paradigmatic figures. In this case, his focus was on Arendt, Habermas, Rorty, Gadamer, Kuhn, and others. By juxtaposing the claims of each in relation to the other, Bernstein could point to the changes that were already underway while at the same time indicating the changes that he thought we ought to be pursuing.

One point of connection between my own work and Bernstein's efforts is our mutual appreciation for the importance of the American pragmatic tradition, especially John Dewey. Both Bernstein and I see Dewey as a key figure in the effort to reconstruct our attitudes about knowledge and action. Nevertheless, as I mentioned above, I come to Dewey from a different direction than that taken by Bernstein. It was the sixteenth-century Neo-Confucian Wang Yang-ming's slogan *chih hsing ho-i* (the unity of knowledge and action) that set the context for my rereading with new eyes Dewey's *Quest for Certainty: A Study of the Relation of Knowledge and Action* and Whitehead's *Process and Reality*. Therefore, unlike Bernstein, who focuses almost exclusively on American and European philosophers, my analysis draws upon Chinese thinkers, especially from the Confucian and Taoist traditions.

The establishment of an on-going Confucian-Pragmatist conversation is a recent phenomenon.[4] As I see it, this conversation represents a new front in the battle marked out by Bernstein, one that I assume he would welcome. By including in the conversation voices that are not saddled with modernist and postmodernist assumptions, those of us who engage with Chinese thinkers hope to gain access to new insights that will help us to reshape the context for epistemology (Neville, 1992; Hall and Ames, 1987, 1995).

The second difference in my approach from that of Bernstein may represent an area where there is potential for substantive disagreement between us. I am convinced that a change in our attitudes about the relationship of knowledge and action must be coupled with adjustments in the cosmological and metaphysical presuppositions that support our thinking about minds, bodies, experience, and nature. If there is a flaw in Bernstein's books (and it is surely best seen as a sin of omission rather than commission), it is that he does not acknowledge the extent to which his analysis calls for a rethinking of traditional metaphysical assumptions. Bernstein may not have a problem with the metaphysical direction I will be taking. There is evidence in *Praxis and Action* that he would find such an approach congenial. For example, he favorably cites Whitehead as a philosopher who might be included in a longer study of changing attitudes about praxis and action (1971, p. 8). In *Beyond Objectivism and Relativism*, the situation is more ambiguous since Bernstein's focus is largely limited to figures who express either little interest in, and in some cases antipathy for, the speculative metaphysical issues that I feel must be raised once one claims that knowledge and action are really one thing. Among Bernstein's heroes in *Beyond Objectivism and Relativism* are Thomas Kuhn, Hans Georg Gadamer, Richard Rorty, Jürgen Habermas, and Hannah Arendt. Of course, not all of these figures have presented themselves as unalterably opposed to metaphysical reflection. Nevertheless, it is certainly the case that in *Beyond Objectivism and Relativism*, typical Deweyan concerns, such as the relationship between experience and nature, the generic traits of existence, and so on all take a back seat to what Bernstein considers more pressing issues. The argument of this book builds upon an appreciative analysis of the metaphysical and cosmological insights of Neo-Confucianism, pragmatism, and process philosophy. Of course, when I pursue metaphysical issues, I do so as a pragmatist, someone for whom human inquiry is always hypothetical and speculative rather than deductive or a priori.

I have taken time in this introduction to spell out my relationship with Bernstein's work because there is a way in which his *Praxis and Action* and *Beyond Objectivism and Relativism* have served as models for what I try to do in this book. Instead of building independent arguments on the central philosophic questions that he addresses, Bernstein weaves together disparate strands of complicated philosophical positions taken by other major philosophical figures. When it is done well the reader is led to a brilliant new way of viewing a seemingly intractable problem. I adopt a similar strategy in this book. I work largely by exposition, juxtaposition, and reconstruction to make the case for the unity of knowledge and action. Sometimes it really *is* helpful to stand on the shoulders of those who came before you.

Part I

PRELIMINARY REMARKS

Since the publication in 1979 of Richard Rorty's landmark work *Philosophy and the Mirror of Nature*, many American philosophers have been struggling to understand what knowledge might be if it is not a mental representation of an external world. In that book, as in all of his subsequent writings, Rorty champions what he calls "anti-representationalism." He identifies Dewey, Wittgenstein, and Heidegger as precursors to this position and Derrida's deconstructionism as a later variation on it. Rorty also points to Donald Davidson as a crucial ally in this same struggle to cultivate an antirepresentational understanding of knowledge. Davidson's critique of the scheme/content dichotomy, his literalist understanding of metaphor, and his holistic approach to meaning are all key elements of Rorty's antirepresentationalism (Davidson, 1973; Rorty, 1979).

I am very sympathetic to many of the themes implicit in Rorty's antirepresentational theory of knowledge. Nevertheless, I have arrived at my position by a different route. In my intellectual biography, it was not Dewey, Wittgenstein, Heidegger, Davidson, or even Derrida who led me to take seriously the possibility of a nonrepresentational theory of knowledge. Rather, it was a sixteenth-century Chinese scholar-general Wang Yang-ming.

As a graduate student reading Chinese intellectual history in the 1980s, I was amazed to discover in Wang a thinker whose talk about knowledge seemed to resonate with Rorty's antirepresentationalism. Though his concerns were different from Rorty's, Wang's famous slogan, *chih hsing ho-i* (the unity of knowledge and action), seemed similarly opposed to an unfortunate tendency toward mentalistic descriptions of knowledge. In the backwash of excitement surrounding the publication of Rorty's *Philosophy and the Mirror of Nature,* I realized that the Cartesian-based spectator theory of knowledge that Rorty and his heroes were struggling against had no parallel in a world where

9

knowledge and action are truly "one thing." A Cartesian spectator stands outside the flow of things in order to grasp them with what Rorty calls the "mind's glassy essence." Wang, by contrast, described human cognition as always already in the flow of things. From Wang's perspective cognition cannot be separated from acting because there is no sense in which our cognitive faculties (if that is what we should call them) are apart from the world.

Despite these similarities, I also understood the many ways Rorty's position differs from Wang's. Where Rorty argued for an *anti*representational theory of knowledge to combat Platonic and Cartesian assumptions, Wang developed what should more properly be called a "*non*-representational" position, one that reaffirmed what he took to be central insights of the Chinese tradition. Thus, while Rorty saw himself struggling against the entire history of Western philosophy, Wang thought he was drawing upon and confirming essential metaphysical insights that were part of his Chinese heritage. This difference intrigued me, especially as I read further and discovered in the Neo-Confucian assimilation of Confucian, Taoist, and Buddhist metaphysical insights important parallels with what I took to be the most interesting aspects of American pragmatic and process metaphysics. As scholars have noted many times, there are key similarities among the organicist and process metaphors that are central to Whitehead's work and those that are operative in Chinese thought, especially Confucianism (Needham, 1956, 279ff; Schwartz, 1985, 356). More recently, scholars have begun to recognize similar parallels with metaphysical positions taken by Dewey, James, and Peirce (Hall and Ames, 1987; 1995).

The apparent concord among Neo-Confucianism, pragmatism, and process philosophy around metaphysical issues led me to see Dewey and Whitehead in a new light. By beginning with Wang's assumption that knowledge and action are truly one thing, I was able to see more clearly the antirepresentationalism and perspectivalism that Rorty claimed were present in Dewey. I also realized that despite his somewhat rationalistic-sounding language, Whitehead was actually much closer to Dewey on epistemological issues than is usually acknowledged. Most important, the fact that Wang's nonrepresentational theory of knowledge is deeply dependent upon broader Neo-Confucian metaphysical beliefs helped disconfirm one of Rorty's most controversial claims. As most readers know, Rorty's description of Dewey as an antirepresentational hero comes at a severe price. He rejects out of hand most of Dewey's metaphysical assertions as holdovers from an older style of thought that Dewey was actually working to overturn (Rorty, 1994; 1995). Thus, Rorty presents a truncated Dewey, one that jettisons talk of experience, nature, the generic traits of existence, in short, just about all of Dewey's magnum opus, *Experience and Nature*. My encounter with Wang helped me to see why such a restricted reading of Dewey is counter-productive and unnecessary. In fact, it was by reading Dewey with Wang's slogan in mind that I realized the extent to which Dewey's metaphysics lays the groundwork for and ultimately makes possible the antirepresentational claims that Rorty prefers. Moreover, I had a similar experience when I went back to review Whitehead's process philosophy. The whole process epistemology fell into place for me once Wang made me see, in a concrete way, that we could talk sensibly about the unity of knowledge and action.

All of this information about my route into the issues dealt with in this book sets the stage for part 1 of this volume. I am convinced that the quest for a nonrepresentational theory of knowledge is a broad movement cutting across the battle lines that often divide philosophers. I want to illustrate this by reviewing the work of a few contemporary philosophers who are struggling to develop alternatives to what representationalism has bequeathed to us. The main point of part 1 will be to mark out the extent to which these independent quests fit within a broad field of inquiry where the work of analytic philosophers, phenomenologists, cognitive scientists, pragmatists, process philosophers, and Neo-Confucians intersects.

With this goal in mind, I will begin with a discussion of Charles Taylor's remarkable work *Sources of the Self: The Making of Modern Identity* (1989). It is useful to start with Taylor's book because it develops a persuasive description of the steps leading from the classical to the modern understanding of selfhood. Since the negative consequences of a strict separation of knowledge and action only become fully clear with the arrival of the modern self, I intend to use Taylor's analysis to help set the stage for the Neo-Confucian, pragmatic, and process alternatives that I find persuasive. I feel justified in using Taylor in this way because Dewey and Whitehead would agree with Taylor's complaint that modernity has led us up something of a blind alley with respect to our understanding of the self. Moreover, as I see it, many of the criticisms Taylor levels at the modern understanding of the self simply do not apply to process and pragmatist descriptions of the self and knowledge.

In taking this position I am agreeing with Robert C. Neville, who has argued forcefully that pragmatists and process thinkers took a "high road around modernism" effectively avoiding many of the pitfalls that have led modern thinkers into the situation that Taylor bemoans (1992). Along these lines it is interesting to note that Taylor's comprehensive study of the history and development of the contemporary understanding of the self never mentions the American pragmatic and process traditions. While some Americanists might complain that Taylor's history looks myopically toward Europe and away from American contributions to philosophic discourse, I think Taylor's omission makes perfect sense considering that both pragmatic and process thinkers have been complaining about the modern description of the self for almost one hundred years! Thus, as I read them, Whitehead and Dewey are useful allies in Taylor's effort to construct a theory of the self that does justice to the role value plays in human experience. Moreover, Wang's theory of the unity of knowledge and action lends additional support, helping us to redefine knowledge in a way that lifts up the extent to which knowledge always entails a qualitative or valuative dimension. In short, by showing how "purely cognitive states" are always already active engagements with the world, Wang, Dewey, and Whitehead go a long way toward overcoming the corrosive effects of the modern subject/object and fact/value dichotomies that Taylor roundly criticizes.

CHAPTER 1

Knowledge and the Self: Charles Taylor's Sources of the Self

Charles Taylor's *Sources of the Self* has at least two objectives. On the one hand, it traces the historical sources of the modern understanding of selfhood. On the other hand, and perhaps more important, *Sources of the Self* aims to contribute to the *reconstruction* of that same understanding of selfhood. Specifically, it promotes the view that our description of the self should be radically revised so as to take seriously the interdependent claims that values have objective reality and that our moral sensibilities play a central role in determining who we are and what it means to be a self.

Though most readers are likely drawn to *Sources of the Self* by the historical promise implied in its title, Taylor signals the importance of his second objective by prefacing the historical analysis with a one hundred–page defense of the claim that to be adequate *any* description of the self must acknowledge the extent to which human identity is deeply intertwined with our understanding of the good. Rather than appealing to historical sources to defend this claim, Taylor develops a phenomenological argument that lifts up the extent to which human experience is inevitably colored by our capacity (he might even say need) to engage in qualitative judgments. "My identity is defined by the commitments and identifications which provide the frame or horizon within which I can try to determine from case to case what is good, or valuable, or what ought to be done, or what I endorse or oppose. In other words, it is the horizon within which I am capable of taking a stand" (1989, 27). Viewed from this perspective appetition is at the heart of what we mean by life, and the desire to be rightly related to what we take to be good is among those core cravings that constitute life as human (ibid., 44).

VALUE AND THE SELF

Taylor considers it reductionistic to attempt to view the self from a perspective stripped of its moral/aesthetic framework. We live by assessing the *qualitative* dimensions of things in our world, including ourselves. This constant sifting and measuring is a component of every action and supplies the rationale behind almost every decision.

> One could put it this way: because we cannot but orient ourselves to the good, and thus determine our place relative to it and hence determine the direction of our lives, we must inescapably understand our lives in narrative form, as a "quest." But one could perhaps start from another point: because we have to determine our place in relation to the good, therefore we cannot be without an orientation to it, and hence must see our life in story. From whichever direction, I see these conditions as connected facets of the same reality, inescapable structural requirements of human agency. (Ibid., 51–52)

Because he views the self as emerging from within the context of a moral/aesthetic framework, Taylor rejects the claims of those who would identify the self with a set of core cognitive functions. Our moral/aesthetic frameworks are complicated constructions that combine broad cultural inheritances with dense mixtures of abstract reasoning and the immediacies of concrete experience. Thus in defining the self Taylor turns away from cognitive function and toward narrativity and metaphors such as the *quest for the good* in order to preserve the nuances, ambiguities, and complexities that we bring to bear on all of our qualitative assessments about the world and our selves.

Taylor contrasts this approach with the tendency among modern thinkers to distill the moral self through a few abstract principles, such as the categorical imperative (Kant) or universal justice (Habermas). "In both these cases, and in many others, the 'moral' encompasses a domain significantly narrower than what ancient philosophers define as the 'ethical'" (ibid., 64). As Taylor sees it, "our tendency to limit the range of human moral reflection parallels the rise of natural science and its elimination of the language of final causes, its concomitant dismissal of qualitative distinctions from scientific descriptions of the natural world, and its objectification of all things including the self. Followed to its natural conclusion, science has rendered us 'inarticulate' about the basis for our moral judgments" (ibid., 53–91). There is literally nowhere to stand from which we could explain or justify who we are and why we respond to the world in the way that we do. This has led us to speak as if we could identify a self absent of those values that, though hidden from view, continue to give direction to our ownmost feelings, thoughts, and actions. For Taylor such a claim is an illusion. He argues instead that our very identity is tied up with the values that give structure and direction to our lives.

Taylor goes on to say we should not be surprised or dismayed to learn that natural science fails to discern anything like the qualitative distinctions that animate human life. After all, science is a form of inquiry whose objective has been to describe things from a perspective freed of anthropocentric conceptions. It is "an unjustified leap to say that [notions of good and right] therefore are not as real, objective, and non-relative as any other part of the natural world" (ibid., 56). Against such scientistic reductionists, Taylor pointedly asks the following rhetorical question:

> What better measure of reality do we have in human affairs than those terms that on critical reflection and after correction of the errors we can detect make the best sense of our lives. Making the best sense here includes not only offering the best, most realistic orientation about the good but also allowing us best to understand and make sense of the actions and feelings of ourselves and others. For our language of deliberation is continuous with our language of assessment, and this with the language in which we explain what people do and feel. (Ibid., 56–57)

Taylor's defense of the language of values should not be confused with sixteenth- and seventeenth-century obscurantists who fought feverishly against the natural sciences in an effort to preserve a theological basis for human dignity. He gives natural science free rein to construct whatever languages seem appropriate to its pursuits. What he objects to is the tendency to generalize such languages to cover *all* dimensions of human life, arguing that it is possible to do so only if we ignore or deny aspects of life that are central to making it human.

> Theories like behaviorism or certain strands of contemporary computer-struck cognitive psychology, which declare "phenomenology" irrelevant on principle, are based on a crucial mistake. They are "changing the subject," in Donald Davidson's apt expression. What we need to explain is people living their lives; the terms in which they cannot avoid living them cannot be removed from the explanandum, unless we can propose other terms in which they could live them more clairvoyantly. We cannot just leap outside of these terms altogether, on the grounds that their logic doesn't fit some model of "science" and that we know *a priori* that human beings must be explicable in this "science." This begs the question. How can we ever know that humans can be explained by any scientific theory until we actually explain how they live their lives in its terms? (Ibid., 58)

Thus, as Taylor sees it, even those who promote scientific reductions of the human to mere mechanical processes do so only while operating within the context of the very values which their theories claim to unmask as epiphenomenal. In short, there is no way to climb out of the framework of human reflection, a framework that is always partly structured by valuative thoughts, feelings, and goals. Scientists who claim to have more accurately described the world without the qualitative dimension are "changing the subject" and describing an imagined world, one where human experience simply does not exist.

In light of all this, it is possible to read part 1 of *Sources of the Self* as raising the following pointed question: Why should we continue to allow ourselves to take seriously modern descriptions of the self that seem to render incomprehensible the kinds of activities that form the substance of human experience? The long answer as to *how* this situation came about is contained in four hundred pages of analysis, in which Taylor traces the complicated history of the West's description of the self. The short answer, however, is that we have allowed a particularly powerful form of discourse (natural science) to extend its range beyond the tasks for which it was designed. "Of course, the terms of our best account [of human life] will never figure in a physical theory of the universe. But that just means that our human reality cannot be understood in the terms appropriate for this physics. . . . Our value terms purport to give us insight into what it is to live in the universe as a human being, and this is a quite different matter from that which physical science claims to reveal and explain" (ibid., 59).

Taylor, however, is interested in more than just detailing how we got ourselves into this awkward situation. The reader who takes part 1 of *Sources of the Self* seriously should see the book as a call to reject the Enlightenment-inspired assertion that qualities and values are epiphenomenal subjective illusions that we impose upon a value-neutral, mechanistic universe. Viewed from this perspective the rest of the book is designed to lift up what has gone into the construction of the modern understanding of selfhood in order to point forward toward the possibility of a newly reconstructed discourse about the self, one that affirms the objective reality of qualitative distinctions and values.

Though *Sources of the Self* points toward a reconstructed discourse about the self, it does remain largely a historical text. Taylor does not present his own fully reconstructed philosophy of selfhood. Nevertheless, he does make a few suggestions that point in the direction he believes new approaches to the self ought to follow. For example, early on he coins the term *hypergoods* to refer to the background values that set the stage for all of our moral and aesthetic judgments. Though typically hidden behind a veil of inarticulacy woven by the modern understanding of selfhood, hypergoods are "goods which not only are incomparably more important than others but provide the standpoint from which these must be weighed, judged, decided about" (ibid., 63). Thus, hypergoods are components of the moral/aesthetic framework that we inherit and modify. They serve to orient us to ourselves and the world around us. Without hypergoods it is hard to see what we might mean by human identity. For, as Taylor sees us, to be a self at all is to have the capacity to take an evaluative position with respect to the things we confront in our world.

In light of Taylor's quest to restore talk of values and qualities, as well as his constructive description of hypergoods, it is interesting to note that both Whitehead and Dewey built their entire philosophic projects around variations on the assertion that to make sense of ourselves and the way we relate to the world, value must be given ontological status. For Whitehead it is a truism that all organisms are oriented toward maximizing the intensity of experience, a trait he defines in aesthetic/moral terms. Similarly, Dewey points to a line of continuity that stretches from the amoeba's quest for satisfactory physical transactions to the exquisitely complicated satisfactions that culminate in higher-order human experiences.

Some might complain that by describing human values as a subset of these broader organic tendencies, Whitehead and Dewey effectively reduce human experience to a more complicated version of something that animals enjoy. The fear behind such accusations is that both thinkers are engaging in a naturalistic reductionism whose aim isn't far from the scientistic reductionisms that Taylor roundly criticizes. But Dewey and Whitehead argue that efforts to protect the integrity of human ends by elevating and separating them from ends-in-nature can lead only to confusion. As Taylor shows, the Western tradition moved directly from a Platonic vision that locates value outside the human realm to the modern scientistic conclusion that values are epiphenomenal, subjective impositions on a mechanistic universe. Dewey and Whitehead, by contrast, both argue in favor of a form of continuity that is not guilty of scientistic reductionisms. They claim that human values are continuous with those that regulate less complicated organic processes in order to provide an ontological basis for asserting their reality. There is nothing unreal or subjective about the Deweyan and Whiteheadian understanding of value. Value, in all its forms, has an ontological status that, as Taylor shows, many modern philosophers have wanted to deny.

Thus, in affirming the ontological status of value, both Whitehead and Dewey anticipate essential themes in Taylor's analysis even as they reaffirm a commitment to nonscientistic forms of scientific discourse. In fact, one advantage both have over Taylor is the conviction that it is possible to develop a naturalistic position that is not reductionistic. There are instances in the early chapters of his book where Taylor seems to equate naturalism with scientistic reductionism. Since he does not consider either the pragmatic or process traditions, which both affirm a nonreductionistic naturalism, it isn't clear from the text whether he would find the Deweyan or Whiteheadian options amenable routes toward restoring value language.[1] As we will see in chapters 4 and 5, pragmatists and process thinkers are able to resurrect value language because they undertake the metaphysical and cosmological arguments that are necessary to make the case for recognizing the ontological status of value. Taylor, who avoids metaphysics in *Sources of the Self,* is on shaky ground when he calls for a reconstructed discourse about the self without explaining what the ontological status of value ought to be. Absent a metaphysical argument, all Taylor can do is rely upon the phenomenological argument that we cannot imagine ourselves operating in the world without engaging in a continual evaluative process. As Dewey and Whitehead make clear, however, to develop a description of the self that takes seriously the role value plays in formulating our identities, just about everything having to do with our understanding of knowledge and action must be rethought. We have to recast our description of matter so that value is restored to it. This leads us to redescribe knowledge in a way that removes any trace of the Platonic and Cartesian notion that knowing is a state of mind. In its place, we need to begin imagining knowledge as a way of relating to something, as a kind of action.

Of course, the denial of ontological status to value is a notion that would be perceived as utterly foreign (and perhaps even barbaric) by most Chinese thinkers. Throughout his life, Wang Yang-ming adhered to the traditional Mencian position that every human is born with an innate awareness of and tendency toward the good. This tendency, if nurtured properly and given a chance to develop, eventually blossoms into a full-fledge moral sensibility, one that is truly human. Thus, according to Confucius, Mencius, and Wang, we are raised up into our humanness *(jen)* by families, teachers, and communities, who have a responsibility to develop in us a more finely tuned responsiveness to values that are inherent in the very nature of things. Like all good Confucians, Wang would automatically reject modern Western efforts to ascribe human selfhood to something that could exist apart from these innate moral feelings and responsibilities. Moreover, like Dewey and Whitehead, Wang draws upon a much broader set of metaphysical arguments to create a context within which it makes sense to claim that human values are interwoven with values that underlie the whole of things. While such talk may sound to modern ears like a form of wishful thinking, I hope to demonstrate in chapter 3 why we ought to pay close attention to thinkers such as Wang whose work emerges from a tradition where the fact/value and subject/object dichotomies have not played the same destructive role that Taylor shows them to be playing in Western intellectual history.

INTERIORITY AND DISENGAGEMENT:
OVERCOMING THE MODERN SELF

As I said at the beginning of this discussion, Taylor's primary objective in *Sources of the Self* is to create the intellectual space necessary for exploring alternatives to the traditional description of selfhood. By showing that contemporary attitudes about the self are a modern construct, Taylor opens us to the possibility of alternative formulations. Rather than experiencing the structures of selfhood as a given, we are freed to seek remedies to the problems and anomalies that those structures entail.

For example, Taylor examines in considerable detail the sources of our attachment to the metaphors of "inwardness." In phrases such as *I know it in my heart*, we sometimes reveal a prereflective conviction that each of us enjoys a purely private realm of immediate subjective experience that is the locus of our "real inner self." This "inner experience" or "interior space" is often perceived as the *only* place where our true identity can be found. It is the one thing that, if taken away, would surely entail the destruction of what we call the "self."

Taylor points out, however, that this very notion of interiority has rendered confusing how we relate to the so-called external world. It also makes anomalous the status of our bodies, which serve a mediating role between the inner self and the world around us.

> But strong as this partitioning of the world appears to us, as solid as this localization may seem, and anchored in the very nature of the human agent, it is in large part a feature of our world, the world of modern, Western people. The localization is not a universal one, which human beings recognize as a matter of course, as they do for instance that their heads are above their torsos. Rather it is a function of a historically limited mode of self-interpretation, one which has become dominant in the modern West and which may indeed spread thence to other parts of the globe but which had a beginning in time and space and may have an end. (Ibid., 111)

Human beings did not always view themselves in this way. In fact, as Taylor shows, it took more than two thousand years, roughly the time from Homer to Locke, to create and then occupy this purely inner world where selves enjoy the pleasure of complete autonomy and yet are also forced to suffer the terror of solipsistic isolation.

Metaphors of interiority are particularly important for my argument because of the role that they play in legitimating the separation of knowledge from action. By locating mental states within a so-called inner space, knowledge is lifted clean out of the realm of action. The mind's "inner eye" seems to observe the external world from a metaphysical distance, and the vital link between knowledge and action becomes obscure. As Taylor makes clear, the way to escape from this situation is to become self-conscious about the route that led us to our current confusion over the relationships among self, world, knowledge, and action so that we can begin to consider alternative paths.

Many have remarked on the West's growing sense of interiority from Homer to Plato through Augustine and on up into Descartes and Locke. Homeric poetry exhibits little sense of an interior self, relying instead on the assumption that selves grow large through brave deeds and sumptuous living. Plato, by contrast, shifts attention away from actions and toward the ideas that he says ought to be directing actions. According to Taylor, however, Platonism exhibits only a very thin sense of interiority. In the Platonic tradition, the focus is typically on our ignorance of ideas rather than the self. Ideas are viewed as objective markers of what is real and important. They reveal a rational order that transcends any particular knower, an order we can use to guide us in our actions. Thus, in both the Homeric and Platonic traditions, the emphasis is on the actual living of life, rather than on the self that lives it.

Things change, however, with Augustine, who turns a self-reflexive eye upon the actions that make up our lives.[2] Suspicious of his unconscious motives and hyper-attuned to differences between his own first-person accounts of experience and accounts given by others, Augustine translates Socrates' concern for the unexamined *life* into an anxiety over the unexamined *self*. As Taylor reads him, Augustine's quest to locate the sources of his own sinfulness led him to the conviction that the route back to the divine is through the purification of his subjective impulses. Thus, Augustine shifts the focus to purification of the will and away from the acquisition of knowledge. He moves away from transcendent ideas to a new level of reflexive awareness. Ultimately, Augustine's fascination with the motivations that lay behind his actions required that he posit within each of us a *realm* where such motives could be observed and a *capacity* to stand apart from those motives so that one is capable of modifying them.

Though the moves from Homer through Plato to Augustine all contributed to the interiorization of Western consciousness, they are still a long way from the remarkable transformations that appeared with the advent of modernity. In Descartes, Taylor claims, there is a tremendous shift as Augustine's reflexivity is hitched to a new Galilean cosmology and radicalized to a degree that Augustine could not have imagined. Once we see nature as a vastly complicated mechanism, it transforms everything about human experience and human values. The Platonic interweaving of science and morals is immediately unraveled, and scientific knowledge, now disjoined from phronesis, is redefined as *represen-*

tation. "To know reality is to have a correct representation of things—a correct picture within of outer reality as it came to be conceived. And this conception of knowledge comes to seem unchallengeable, once an account of knowledge in terms of self-revealing reality, like the Ideas, was abandoned" (ibid., 144). By supplanting ancient and scholastic teleological assumptions, the new science effectively redefined knowledge and emptied the natural world of its intrinsic value.

Of course, the shift to a mechanized view of nature involved more than merely giving up residual faith in a Platonic moral order. Taylor points out that after Descartes, it is no longer tenable to assert that the qualitative characteristics of experience are aspects of nature. "We have to cease seeing the material universe as a kind of medium, in which psychic contents like heat and pain, or the supposed Forms or Species of the scholastic tradition, could be lodged or embodied or manifest themselves" (ibid., 146). The toothache is no longer in the tooth but rather in one's mind. Pain is not a part of objective reality but rather is the mind's way of translating a specific organic state into an experiential one. In this way, the qualitative content of our sensory data shifts from the world into the mind. Consequently they are viewed as largely deceptive and confusing and in need of carefully reasoned controls in order to ensure that we do not lapse into error.

Thus, to gain control over our lives, Descartes adopted what Taylor calls a "disengaged" perspective, one that enables us to separate ourselves from the immediacies of everyday experience so as to be capable of thinking critically about the ideas and sensations that occupy our minds. "To bring this whole domain of sensations and sensible properties to clarity means to grasp it as an external observer would, tracing the causal connection between states of the world or my body, described in primary properties, and the 'ideas' they occasion in my mind. Clarity and distinctness requires that we step outside ourselves and take a disengaged perspective" (ibid.). From this perspective, the interior knowing subject objectifies everything. Even the body is viewed as an object capable of being observed, sifted, and measured by an immaterial subject who employs rational procedures in order to discern truth from error, fact from fiction.

Though Taylor doesn't emphasize it, the link between Descartes's disengagement and the separation of knowledge from action should be obvious. By requiring that reason disengage from the immediacies of subjective experience, Descartes effectively removes our cognitive faculties from the realm of action. The certainty that he craves could be attained only by suspending immediate experience and limiting rational judgments to an interior realm that is not subject to the changing conditions of daily living. In short, to make it possible for us to attain certainty,

Descartes posits an entirely inner, nonmaterial dimension to subjective experience, one that is necessarily separate from the realm of action where uncertainty is a structural necessity.

Nevertheless, Descartes was interested in more than establishing a certain foundation for rationalist sciences. As Taylor reads him, his whole moral philosophy was also built around the impulse to disengage reason from the hurly burly of immediate subjective feelings. Since Descartes counseled disengagement from subjective experience as essential to clarifying thinking about the natural world, it is not surprising that he applied the same technique in seeking control over the self. According to Descartes, each of us should step back from our passions in order to allow our own rational faculties to give guidance and coherence to our lives. Viewed this way, our rational faculties function from within an inner sanctum separated from the passions and therefore capable of modifying them when the situation calls for it. While this may sound like a reiteration of Platonic and Augustinian themes, Taylor insists there are important differences that mark the shift from the ancient to the modern paradigm for selfhood.

With respect to Plato it is immediately clear that Descartes has expanded the internal life of the subject and internalized the very objects of knowledge that Plato urged us to seek. "For Plato, to be rational we have to be right about the order of things. According to Descartes, rationality means thinking according to certain canons. The judgment now turns on *properties of the activity of thinking* rather than on the substantive beliefs which emerge from it" (ibid., 156; italics added). From this perspective, Descartes follows Augustine's lead by internalizing Plato's Ideas and making them a product of reasoning rather than a facet of the objective world. Nevertheless, Descartes also differs from Augustine with respect to the end toward which this disengaged reason aims.

> For Augustine, the path inward was only a step on the way upward. . . . [The] thinker comes to sense more and more his lack of self-sufficiency, comes to see more and more that God acts within him. . . . In contrast, for Descartes the whole point of the reflexive turn is to achieve a quite self-sufficient certainty. . . . God's existence has become a stage in my progress towards science through the methodical ordering of evident insight. . . . The centre of gravity has shifted. (Ibid., 156–57)

Descartes's disengaged reason suggests we have a level of autonomy that simply was not imaginable for Augustine. By disengaging from the immediacy of its own subjective feelings, it objectifies its "inclinations, tendencies, habits of thought and feelings so that they can be *worked on,* doing away with some and strengthening others, until one meets the desired specifications" (ibid., 159). Thus, Descartes's disengaged self is able to take a purely instrumental view of itself.

This Cartesian instrumentalism is carried forward and extended by Locke, according to Taylor. In fact, as Taylor tells the story, Locke represents something of a culminating moment in the history of the West's understanding of the self. For it is Locke who transforms Descartes's disengaged subject into what Taylor calls the "punctual self."

> To take this stance is to identify oneself with the power to objectify and remake, and by this act to distance oneself from all the particular features which are objects of potential change. What we are is essentially none of the latter, but what finds itself capable of fixing them and working on them. This is what the image of the point is meant to convey, drawing on the geometrical term: the real self is "extensionless" it is nowhere but in this power to fix things as objects. (Ibid., 171–72)

In order to see why Locke feels compelled to go beyond Descartes it is important to note the role of Locke's antiteleological commitments. In an effort to put behind him any remnants of the scholastic sciences, he was impervious to assertions that natural objects and human beings might have a natural tendency toward either the true or the good. In fact, given the plurality of our habits and the murkiness of the sources of our passions, whatever tendencies we have are most likely plagued by error and confusion. Our task, he claims, is to clear away such cognitive habits of mind in order to locate those "rock bottom" ideas, which are secure by virtue of having *not* been influenced in any way by our own subjective activity. Having found a foundational starting point, we would then be free, in Cartesian fashion, to build up again the structures of knowledge and morals. However, unlike Descartes, whose foundation was located in a self-reflexive awareness of his own thought processes, Locke's "ultimate stopping place is the particulate ideas of experience, sensation and reflection. And these are to be taken as rock bottom, because they *aren't the product of activity at all*" (ibid., 166; italics added). Thus, for Locke, the starting point of all cognitive activity is the *purely passive* reception by the mind of mechanical impressions made by objects in the external world. He characterizes these ideas as interchangable building blocks, only accidentally associated with a particular mind and easily transferable from one mind to another. Once the mind is stimulated by these impressions, the "real Lockian self," that part of us that is fully and completely autonomous, steps in to work the ideas into coherent thoughts, plans, and projects. But the starting point is always impressions made by the world on a purely passive, immaterial mental substance.

Thus, Taylor sees in the history of the West's understanding of the self a progressive disengagement from the immediacy of lived experience. Beginning with Augustine's self-reflexive gaze and continuing through Descartes's objectification of our subjective states, the process culminates in Locke's reification of the self and his identification of it with the *capacity* to control our "inclinations, tendencies, habits of thought and feelings." From the perspective of a book on the unity of knowledge and action, it is easy to see how Taylor's story contains a parallel tale involving the growing separation of knowledge from action. With each step inward the links between knowledge and action grow more tenuous. By the time we get to Locke, for whom knowledge is founded on ideas that are imposed upon a passive mind, there is a complete separation. Lockian ideas begin as simple impressions, a form of purely passive mentality lacking any inherent qualitative or valuative content. Whatever qualities or values come to be attributed to them are the result of the habits of our own thought processes and not the things in themselves. Thus, the interiorization of the self as Taylor describes it has led us to the point where ideas are viewed as insubstantial, valueless, qualityless, mental atoms that are the building blocks from which mentality is constructed.

Taylor, of course, is deeply dissatisfied with the direction taken by Descartes and Locke. He points out that it is not obvious that the best route to knowledge is through disengagement. Oftentimes, the quest for greater control in a situation can only be attained through more engagement rather than less. Sometimes in everyday life the better route is to "lose oneself" in an experience. For example, critical distance is only one among a number of approaches to performing music or dancing or making love. Of course, someone might retort that these examples are hardly instances of "knowledge." Such a response, however, raises precisely the issue this book is seeking to examine. Why should we feel the need to draw such a sharp distinction between knowledge and activities such as music, dancing, and making love? As Taylor says,

> The point of this contrast is to see that the option for an epistemology which privileges disengagement and control isn't self-evidently right. It requires certain assumptions. If the great age of rationalism and empiricism launched itself on the "way of ideas," it was because it took certain things for granted. Epistemically, it was based in part on a belief in mechanism as against the universe of meaningful order, or the ontic logos. . . . It was [also] powered by a radical rejection of teleology, of definitions of the human subject in terms of some inherent bent to the truth or to the good, which might give justification to an engaged exploration of the true tendencies of our nature. (Ibid., 164)

While a "belief in mechanism" and a "rejection of teleology" were important tools contributing to the rise of natural science, it may be a mistake to think that those assumptions should be treated as cornerstones for the cultivation of *all* knowledge about ourselves and the world around us. As Taylor points out these are useful for getting at the truth from a perspective that examines the world in abstraction from human experience. If, however, we are interested in cultivating our understanding of the world that includes our genuine joys, terrifying saddnesses, and sublime beauty, then we need to look beyond science's faith in mechanism and its antiteleology. Constructing epistemological and cosmological theories that reduce such experiences to mere illusions or epiphenominal impositions has precisely the opposite effect from that which is intended. Instead of giving us greater control over our lives, it gives us less. In sum, the interiorization of human consciousness has led us up what feels like a blind alley where our so-called inner life seems disjoined from our physical surroundings. It is a place where some form of dualism seems like the only alternative capable of preserving both our faith in natural science and our conviction that human life is meaningful.

Throughout the rest of his book Taylor explores responses to the crises engendered by the interiorization of the self and the triumph of the natural sciences. He points, for example, to intellectual movements that affirm everyday life, to the romantic reaction to rationalism, and to a variety of other late- and postmodern strategies. All attempt to negotiate some compromise between a fully objectified, mechanistic world and an interior life where the self is equated with pure autonomy and knowledge is separated from action. In this book, however, I am struggling to lift up a line of response not included among those Taylor considers. As I mentioned earlier, the pragmatic and process movements play no role in Taylor's book. This is an interesting omission because thinkers such as James, Peirce, Dewey, and Whitehead argued that reason must remain "engaged" if it is to be capable of working on or improving the self. In other words, for these thinkers, disengagement from one's immediate subjective feelings would be precisely the wrong route to take if we are seeking greater control of ourselves and the world around us. Instead of cutting us off from nature, they called upon us to recognize the extent to which human cognitive experience is an outgrowth of processes in nature. As Dewey said, "experience is both *of* and *in* nature" (Dewey, 1958, 4a).

The key to understanding the pragmatic approach to these issues is in its willingness to recognize the extent to which experience is not limited to cognition alone. Dewey, for example, argued in *Experience and Nature* that philosophers who focus their attention upon cognitive activities often fall victim to what he called the "intellectualist fallacy." They confusedly assume that the secondary higher-order levels of experience are primary. In effect, such philosophers tend to eliminate from consideration those dimensions of experience that are the bases for our qualitative and valuative sensibilities. Sensory data, for example, is sometimes taken to be the starting point for knowledge. As we have seen, Locke described the acquisition of knowledge as a process whereby objects in the physical world impress themselves upon a passive mind and only later are worked upon by higher mental processes. This is all a muddle as far as Dewey is concerned. "For things are objects to be treated, used, acted upon and with, enjoyed and endured even more than things to be known. They are things *had* before they are things cognized" (ibid., 21). It is in the "having," Dewey claims, that experience is clothed with qualitative content.

On this issue Whitehead is in agreement with Dewey. Like Dewey, he also divides experience into two modes that he calls "causal efficacy" and "presentational immediacy." While a detailed description of what Dewey and Whitehead mean by both of these modes will have to wait until chapters 4 and 5, respectively, it is important to note here that primary experience (Dewey) and causal efficacy (Whitehead) are both designed to fill the epistemological gap that Taylor has uncovered in his analysis of traditional theories of knowledge and the self. Rather than allowing such theories to effectively rule the qualitative and valuative dimension out of experience, Whitehead and Dewey suggest that we reimagine what we mean by experience. Like Taylor, their goal is to describe experience so that it is inclusive of those things without which it would be difficult to make sense of our lives. For Whitehead, qualitative and valuative feelings are the basis for higher-order cognitive activity. Instead of trying to fit them in after the fact, after the mind has formed its Lockian impressions, Whitehead argues that those feelings are embedded in the process from the beginning. In fact, in an ironic twist, Whitehead's magnum opus, *Process and Reality*, contains what contemporary literary theorists might call a "strong misreading" of Locke. In a discussion of Locke's *Essay concerning Human Understanding*, Whitehead finds evidence leading in precisely the opposite direction from that attributed to Locke by Taylor (Whitehead, 1978, 51–60). Instead of confirming Descartes's move toward the disengaged subject, Whitehead sees Locke providing us with empirical ammunition to support the claim that cognitive experience is always fully engaged in the processes that surround it. He says that Locke "gives the most dispassionate description of those various elements in experience which common sense never lets slip. Unfortunately, he is hampered by inappropriate metaphysical categories that he never criticized. He should have widened the title of his book into 'An Essay Concerning Experience'" (ibid., 51). Whitehead suggests that had Locke shifted from a discussion of understanding, with its limited focus on higher-order cognition, to a discussion of experience, which is much broader and inclusive of the noncognitive organic processes that are essential to the understanding, he would have been in position to develop an epistemology that includes those valuative and qualitative aspects of experience that seem so anomalous under traditional Lockian assumptions.

Of course, it would have done Locke no good merely to shift his epistemological theories so that they were inclusive of quality and value. As Whitehead's statement suggests, Locke needed to criticize the metaphysical categories he inherited from Descartes and others. For experience to begin with qualitative and valuative feelings, things have to *be* valuable and quality-laden. Nevertheless, this is precisely what the move to mechanism and antiteleology ruled out. Dewey and Whitehead explore alternative metaphysical theories that replace traditional mechanistic metaphors with organic ones. For each, the goal is to develop a nondualistic ontology that is capable of handling value. In pursuit of this goal, both adopt a naturalistic approach to epistemological issues. Both describe mind as emerging directly from natural organic activities. This allows them to maintain that actual values and qualities inherent in the world can when properly criticized spawn the qualitative and valuative feelings engendered by a fully engaged consciousness.

As helpful as they are on these issues, Whitehead and Dewey still do not often address in a direct way one of the key issues motivating Taylor's historical study. The crisis engendered by the history of Western thinking about the self is more than a philosophic problem. It is, Taylor claims, a moral/religious problem as well. We find ourselves living at a time when the traditional categories for thinking about the self have made us strangers to ourselves and to the world around us. Taylor's ultimate mission is to contribute to the creation of a context where our first-person experience does not seem unavoidably estranged from other people and the world around us. His goal is to initiate conversations that lead away from chronic feelings of false isolation and anomie and toward a greater appreciation of the extent to which our lives are (for better and worse) interconnected and both aesthetically and morally rich.

On this issue Wang Yang-ming has a tremendous advantage over Whitehead and Dewey, neither of whom spent much time writing about these issues from a first-person perspective. In fact, there has been significant debate among scholars over whether Dewey and Whitehead even have coherent theories of the self. The reason for such debate is likely two-fold. First, their metaphysics and cosmologies are so different from traditional modernist approaches to these issues that a process or pragmatist self does not look like what we've traditionally called "the self." Second, neither Dewey nor Whitehead wrote much about self-transformation except in abstract terms. Despite an interest in religious issues, and even a couple of small books written by each on the subject, neither developed a full-fledged philosophical anthropology. Both Dewey and Whitehead did write on education, of course. But for them the focus is less on self-transformation and more on the learning process. Wang Yang-ming, by contrast, built his whole philosophy around his understanding of selfhood and self-transformation. In fact, throughout his career Wang focuses almost exclusively on the religious implications of certain important Confucian metaphysical and onto-logical ideas. Thus, with respect to Taylor's project, Wang is a near perfect partner, offering as he does a window into how the self might be understood were it to have developed outside the pernicious effects of the West's fact/value and subject/object dichotomies. As we will see in chapter 3 Wang's assumption that knowledge and action are truly one thing is rooted in a theory of the self where interiority is not tied to disengagement. As Wang describes it, cultivation of this inner self is the cultivation of a more comprehensive connectedness to the things around you. This is what Wang means by "forming one body with the whole of things."

By beginning with a discussion of Taylor's *Sources of the Self*, I hope to have accomplished a few goals simultaneously. First, I want Taylor's analysis to lift up the extent to which our understanding of knowledge and action is rooted in our understanding of selfhood. Second, building upon Taylor's critique of traditional Western descriptions of the self, I want to highlight inadequacies in our typical understanding of the relationship between knowledge and action. If, as Taylor suggests, the West's traditional understanding of the self is flawed, and if, as I have suggested, our understanding of knowledge and action is tied directly to that theory of the self, then we need to look outside traditional assumptions in order to navigate our way out of the "blind alley" into which Descartes and Locke have led us. This has led directly to my third and final goal, namely, to begin developing my case for presenting Wang Yang-ming, John Dewey, and Alfred North Whitehead as plausible conversation partners who have thought long and deeply about the issues that currently occupy Taylor.

At this point, I would like to turn away from Taylor's concerns with selfhood and look directly to the topic of antirepresentationalism. Specifically, I intend to look at the late/postanalytic philosophies of Donald Davidson and Richard Rorty, who both are struggling to reverse the trend toward greater interiorization of consciousness. They argue that we should drop altogether the notion of an interior mind that is dependent on a mediating structure such as "experience" to give it access to the external world. Surprisingly, we shall see that in some instances the proposals by Davidson and Rorty resonate well with certain strategies employed by Wang, Dewey, and Whitehead. As was the case in the previous section, one of my principle goals will be to demonstrate why it is that I am convinced Dewey, Whitehead, and Wang belong in these contemporary discussions about mind, knowledge, and the self. The full description of the Neo-Confucian, pragmatist, and process positions will be reserved until later chapters.

CHAPTER 2

Antirepresentationalism in
Late- and Postanalytic Philosophy:
Donald Davidson and Richard Rorty

CLOSING THE GAP BETWEEN
THE KNOWER AND THE KNOWN

According to Donald Davidson, Cartesianism's deepest problem isn't merely the separation of minds and bodies (Davidson, 1973). Rather, it is Descartes's willingness to describe the mind as a generator of internal conceptual objects and categories for organizing raw experience into a system of beliefs or representations about the world. This separation of our internal mental life from our direct encounter with the world—raw experience, causal efficacy (Whitehead), primary experience (Dewey), *liang chih* (Wang), or immediate subjective experience—you may choose your favorite philosophical term for the buzzing, blooming, confusion—leads to the dualism of scheme and content, which Davidson says is central to many of our most basic confusions about ourselves and knowledge. The dualism of scheme and content creates a three-fold structure that includes an objective world, experiential content, and mental representations or schemes to organize the content. This three-fold structure, like Descartes's pineal gland, is designed to bridge the gap between an objective/external realm and a purely subjective/internal realm.

As an alternative, Davidson argues that we need to collapse the dualism of experiential content and conceptual schemes. He asks us to let go of the notion that meaning and belief systems are private and determined "in the head" and drop our traditional understanding of subjectivity. Rather, he claims we should view meaning and belief systems as the direct product of the public circumstances in which words are learned. There is, therefore, no need for inner *representations* of the way the world is. Our beliefs are tools for coping with a world we encounter directly.

To interpret our beliefs Davidson suggests that we need an understanding of what went into their development, something like a "natural history of what is in the head." We also need a sense of how languages work and what it means to make sense or be rational. For Davidson, none of these entails a mediating structure that explains how an independent and internal subject connects to a fully public and relational outer world. He counsels us to drop the whole notion of inner selves that are separate from the world and acknowledge that belief systems "derive their meaning from the objects and the circumstances in which they were learned." There is no pure subjectivity to connect with a pure objectivity.

After laying out the gist of his argument about the need to avoid the dualism of scheme and content Davidson says:

> Instead of saying that it is the scheme-content dichotomy that has dominated and defined the problems of modern philosophy, then, one could as well say it is how the dualism of the objective and the subjective has been conceived. For these dualisms have a common origin: a concept of the mind with its private states and objects. I have reached the point to which I have been leading up, for it seems to me that the most promising and interesting change that is occurring in philosophy today is that these dualisms are being questioned in new ways, or are being radically reworked. There is a good chance they will be abandoned, at least in their present form. The change is just now becoming evident, and its consequences have barely been recognized, even by those who are bringing it about; and of course, it is, and will be, strongly resisted by many. What we are about to see is the emergence of a radically revised view of the relation of mind and the world. (1990, 163)

By dropping the inner/outer distinction, the subject-object dichotomy, and the whole notion of experience as a medium for carrying information between a fully external objective world and a fully internal subjective self, Davidson describes us as relating directly to one another and the things that make up our world. Experience does not mediate between the world and us. If we want to explain *how* we arrive at a particular set of beliefs, we need only point to the actual interactions that led to those beliefs. This is what Davidson means by giving an account for what is going on "in the head."

In this context, however, the term *belief* has taken an unusual turn. Since there is no inner self to own the mental concepts, Davidson cannot mean to describe beliefs as internal mental pictures of the way we take the world to be. Rather, he must mean to identify beliefs with patterns or habits that guide our interaction with the things that make up our world. Such a view of mentality puts him not very far from Wang's notion that knowledge and action are really one thing. It also brings him within range of my understanding of Dewey's redescription of experience and Whitehead's "reformed subjectivist principle."

The main difference in each case seems to be one of context rather than contradiction. Davidson's position is rooted in language theory, theories of rationality, and his own effort to overcome the Western tendency to posit an ontological divide between subjectivity and objectivity. Wang, by contrast, is struggling to make the religious and philosophical practices of his day consistent with his understanding of Confucian ontological assumptions. Despite the difference in focus, both refuse to dichotomize knowing and acting, subject and object, inner and outer. Moreover, both present an image of the self as *directly* responsive to the world without need for an intermediary level of subjective activity. Similarly, Dewey works throughout *Experience and Nature* to overcome the same subject/object duality by suggesting that *situations* rather than individuals form the most basic experiential units. Redefined this way, experience is *both* "of" and "in" nature. Experience for Dewey is not a medium between the subject and the object; it is the activity that produces subjects and objects. Finally, rejection of the traditional subject-object dichotomy is the starting point for the entire Whiteheadian project. Everything about Whitehead's description of bipolar organic entities reflects his desire to overcome the Cartesian formulation of subject-object duality that Davidson cites as among the root causes for the separation of scheme from content.

J. Wesley Robbins, however, has argued that traditional and radical empiricisms deriving from Dewey and Whitehead actually preserve rather than overcome the separation of mind and the world that mind represents (1996). By positing a distinction between primary experience (causal efficacy) and secondary experience (presentational immediacy), he believes they slide over the unbridgeable gap between the subjective and objective realms. Thus, on Robbins's reading, empiricists and radical empiricists who use Whiteheadian or Deweyan language see cognitive activity as the organizing of so-called primary experiences into representational systems. They are, therefore, not much further along in their efforts to overcome the dualisms that infect the modern understanding of subjectivity and are still subject to Davidson's critique.

As I read them, however, Whitehead and Dewey struggled with the very issues that occupy Davidson today. To explain what I mean, I would like to concentrate for a moment on Whitehead's understanding of causal efficacy and then turn to a much briefer discussion of Dewey's use of the phrase *primary experience*. In both instances, I claim that they redefine experience in a way that evades Davidson's concerns.

When I first read the long passage cited above, where Davidson highlights the connection between the scheme-content dichotomy and the dualism of the objective and the subjective, I immediately turned to the chapter in Whitehead's *Process and Reality* titled "The Subjectivist

Principle" (1978, 157–67). There, Whitehead provides a detailed discussion of what he called his "reformed subjectivist principle." Of course, the key word in the phrase is *reformed*. Throughout the discussion Whitehead is very clear that he is rejecting the traditional Cartesian approach to subjectivity. He claims that after Descartes, thinkers who subscribe to what he calls the "subjectivist principle" and the "sensationalist principle" have dominated philosophy. He argues that both principles are incoherent and in need of reform. I will take them in turn.

Whitehead ranks the subjectivist principle as Descartes' greatest discovery and his most pernicious error. It entails the assertion that "those substances which are the subjects enjoying conscious experiences, provide the primary data for philosophy, namely, themselves as in the *enjoyment of such experience*" (ibid., 159; italics added). According to Whitehead, the rise of the subjectivist principle entailed a shift in philosophy. Instead of asking about the world, philosophers began asking about our *experience* of the world. He sums up his example in two different conclusions philosophers might draw about a gray stone. Before Descartes philosophers could easily draw a conclusion such as This stone is gray, without concern for the experiencing subject. After Descartes such statements were inevitably translated into 'My *experience* of the stone is gray.' From that point on, Whitehead claims, we have been obsessed with a desire to know more about this thing called "experience" that seems to stand between us and the world. From this brief summation of the way Whitehead introduces the issues, it should be easy to see that his construction of the problem bears some familial resemblance to Davidson's concerns. Both are uncomfortable with the way subjectivism separates the self from the world and entails the insertion of a medium of exchange to connect them again.

Whitehead goes on to point out that, once the "subjectivist principle" gains prominence, the "sensationalist principle" is not far behind. For we need the doctrine of sensations to help explain what it is that the mind is processing. For a subjectivist like Descartes the mind deals in abstract universals such as grayness that are derived somehow from our sensations, which in turn take them from actual concrete stones. That raises the question, How does the notion of grayness make it from the stone into the mind? Whitehead points to Hume's reformulation of Lockian simple impressions as one possible explanation. "But this is an entire muddle, for the perceiving mind is not gray, and so gray is now made to perform a new role. From the original fact 'my perception of this stone as gray,' Hume extracts 'Awareness of sensation of grayness'; and puts it forward as the ultimate datum in this element of experience. He has discarded the objective actuality of the stone-image in his search for a universal quality" (ibid., 159). Alternatively, in Davidson's terms,

Hume substituted mental schemes and categories for a direct encounter with the world and positioned sensation or experiential content in the middle. Whitehead offers an entirely different approach to the theory of knowledge, one that is dependent on different metaphysical hypotheses but that has the virtue of allowing us to conceive of subjectivity and objectivity in other than representational terms. According to Whitehead, the object is included in the very constitution of the subject. On the deepest level possible, there is no separation of subjectivity and objectivity. Such an approach effectively removes the occasion for the problems that Davidson says have bedeviled our epistemological theories from the beginning of the modern period.

I do not want to take this line of argument too far. I am not saying that Whitehead is making exactly the same moves that Davidson is making. Instead, I merely want to argue that in order to see whether Davidson's claims undermine a process epistemology, as Robbins suggests, it is necessary to ask, Is Whitehead's *reformed* subjectivist principle subject to Davidson's critique? In response to that question, I would first repeat my observation that Whitehead and Davidson seem to be concerned with the same family of issues, though they approach them from very different directions. Davidson approaches his critique of subjectivism via a careful analysis of language and an attempt to identify those linguistic behaviors that tend toward incoherence. Whitehead approaches his critique of subjectivism from the perspective of metaphysics and cosmology. He was especially concerned to develop a theory of mind that was continuous with the organic world and consistent with what science tells us about organic activity.

Second, it seems reasonable to conclude that if Davidson is right in calling on us to "give up on the mind with its private states and objects" and to put in its place a conception of mind that is in direct contact with the world, then a host of metaphysical and cosmological consequences will ensue. Whitehead's entire project is an effort to explore the metaphysical implications that follow on his Davidsonlike rejection of the subjectivist principle. For Whitehead, however, it is not enough to assert that we should give up subjectivism; that very assertion is the occasion for the whole Whiteheadian project. He wants to know *how* organic activity in general sets the context for and gives rise to that specific form of organic activity that is language. Given the notion that the mind is not separate from the world, Whitehead asks, What are the continuities linking us to the organic and inorganic realms? What are the evolutionary steps from mere organic activity to the complicated nuances of human art, music, and philosophy? How should we describe what it means to be something if we are to describe ourselves as directly connected to the natural world in the way that Davidson seems to suggest? The point is not to suggest that Whitehead supplants Davidson but rather to argue that he is involved in exploring consequences that stem from the same late modern critique of subjectivism. Moreover, there is nothing implicit in Davidson's critique of scheme-content dualism that would prevent the exploration of such consequences.

Some of what I am merely asserting here will be substantiated in chapter 6, when I describe epistemological consequences that stem from a careful examination of Whitehead's "metaphysics of experience" and in chapter 7, where I defend pragmatic and process forms of panpsychism against the claim by Rorty and Robbins that they lead directly to a representationalist epistemology. As I read them, Whitehead's causal efficacy and Dewey's primary experience should be considered theories of *causation* (a way of accounting for the transfer of energy from place to place and through time) rather than as a medium standing between subjects and objects. Prehending entities, to use Whitehead's language, do not produce mental pictures of past entities during the process of concrescence. Rather, they *incorporate the objective reality* of that which preceded them. In fact, in contrast to Robbins, I suspect there is embedded in Whitehead's notion of causal efficacy a host of resources for extending and making more sense of Davidson's claim that minds are in direct contact with the world.

Finally, to address directly Robbins's claim that causal efficacy is equivalent to the experiential content Davidson seeks to discredit, it is important to remember that Whitehead's division of experience into causal efficacy and presentational immediacy does not mark an ontological divide between two different orders of being. The whole point of Whitehead's project is akin to Davidson's effort to remove the notion that inner subjects stand apart from the physical processes that constitute them. For Whitehead, the goal is to see subjectivity as continuous with and an outgrowth of organic processes. Higher-order cognitive activity, according to Whitehead, is the outcome of the same cosmological processes that regulate causal efficacy. Granted, human cognition is more complicated. It is not the case, however, that causal efficacy is mere data for some real subject, who is hiding behind the curtain of presentational immediacy. Instead, according to Whitehead, the subject emerges (comes to be) because of organic processes that begin at the level of causal efficacy and make possible even more complicated processes. Ultimately, Whitehead's is a *reformed* subjectivist principle, one that retains the notion of subjectivity without conceding the need for either a subject-object dualism or a dualism of scheme and content. To accomplish this, Whitehead felt compelled to rethink the most basic ontological metaphors, a move that led him to hypothesize that we need a shift away from the metaphors of substance and inorganic entities toward processes and organisms. These moves do not contradict Davidson's insights. In fact, they can help us to see some of the consequences that ensue from Davidson's rejection of the dualism of scheme and content.

Having explained in some detail why Whitehead's causal efficacy is not subject to Davidson's critique, I can say rather quickly that similar arguments apply to Dewey's primary experience. Like Davidson and Whitehead, Dewey rejects subject-object dualism. He is akin to Whitehead in that his metaphysical and cosmological speculations are an effort to understand the consequences that flow from such a rejection. Moreover, Dewey posits a similar shift in basic metaphors away from substances in favor of processes and organisms. Thus, for largely the same reasons, it is possible to say against Robbins that Dewey's primary experience is not equivalent to Davidsonian content. Although Dewey retains empiricist language by continuing to talk of "experience," that term simply does not refer to a medium serving to link the subjective and objective realms. It is the organic activity out of which subjects and objects emerge. There is no subject apart from such activity, so the activity itself cannot serve as a medium between the subject and its world. Moreover, as with Whitehead, Dewey envisions a line of continuity linking the activities that mark primary experience to those that constitute secondary experience. In this way, the terms *primary experience* and *secondary experience* operate analogously to Whitehead's causal efficacy and presentational immediacy. In both cases, the shift they describe is accomplished by increasing complexity rather than crossing an ontological divide.

THE RELATIONAL SELF

To this point, we have seen some of the ways in which Wang, Dewey, and Whitehead all have an interest in issues related to Davidson's antirepresentationalism. Where they differ from Davidson is in their ability to grasp the metaphysical and ontological implications of a Davidsonlike call to reconstitute our understanding of subjectivity. Having explained briefly why Wang, Whitehead, and Dewey would find much to appreciate in Davidson's effort to overcome scheme-content dualism, I want to look next at two ways in which Richard Rorty builds upon and extends Davidson's position. I turn to Rorty because he is the one most responsible for establishing a link between Davidson and Dewey around the quest for an antirepresentational theory of knowledge. Since my present aim is to continue demonstrating how the unity of knowledge and action connects with contemporary epistemological discussions, my exposition of Rorty's positions will be relatively brief. I will, however, return to Rorty in more detail in chapters 7 and 8.

Davidson, of course, does not always agree with the particular spin Rorty places on the themes I have outlined. Nonetheless, for those who know Rorty's work, all of the issues discussed above should be familiar territory. The first extension that Rorty introduces has to do with his a-rational understanding of language. According to Rorty, it should be clear to Davidson's followers that language has no universal aim or purpose. Drawing upon Nietzschean presuppositions, Rorty claims that if we give up the distinction between scheme and content, and with it the notion of an inner self that presents to itself mental images of an external world, then language should be seen as a fully *contingent* creation, one that has no telos other than to serve as a tool for helping each of us to achieve a constantly shifting series of personal goals.

Thus, Rorty follows Davidson in denying that language is a medium for carrying information about an external world to a fully private mental self. He argues that there is no "inner self" to bring that information to and no reason to believe that the so-called objective world breaks itself up into sentencelike chunks or facts. Moreover, he counsels us to let go of our tendency to equate *true* with mental duplication of an objective world. Drawing on James and Dewey, he argues that we typically award the accolade *true* to particular sentences when they better enable us to cope with a given situation. While some see different languages fitting together like a jigsaw puzzle, with each representing a different perspective on the universe, Rorty sees languages as nearer to a collection of tools in a toolbox. Each is designed to accomplish a different end, and there is no reason to assume, as would be the case with a jigsaw puzzle, that all languages fit together into a coherent representation of the whole of things.

Instead of viewing us as creatures that use language to represent to ourselves a fixed external world, Rorty prefers to describe us as creators of metaphors. As Rorty sees them, metaphors do not represent things. They are organizing patterns. Human spontaneity and creativity are manifest in the endless stream of metaphors we spew forth and use to give shape and texture to our world and ourselves. Rorty's focus on metaphoric spontaneity and denial of an overarching telos or universal purpose to language places him relatively close to the Taoist sage Chuang Tzu (399 B.C.E.), who also insisted that our linguistic constructions are utterly contingent. Both Rorty and Chuang Tzu counsel us to let go of the effort to describe the world "as it is" and to enjoy the unmitigated pleasure of creatively playing with metaphors that we use to constitute ourselves and the world around us. According to Rorty, language has no representational responsibilities and therefore no particular telos toward which it aims.

Talk of reshaping the self via new metaphors brings me to a second way in which Rorty extends Davidson's antirepresentationalism. In addition to the contingency of language, Rorty believes that the antirepresentational understanding of mental activity and knowledge leads to a contingent conception of the self, one that is drastically different from Platonic-Cartesian-Lockian descriptions. Rorty describes the self as a contingent web of beliefs that we continually rewcave as we adjust our relations to those things that we encounter. By beliefs Rorty is not pointing to cognitive representations of the way things are. Relying on a combination of his understanding of Davidson and his own somewhat unique reading of Freud, Rorty is pointing to the way we construct ourselves and our world by weaving together partially conflicting, always contingent narrative/metaphoric streams. As was the case with Davidson, these beliefs are best understood in nonrepresentational terms as patterns or habits of interaction rather than mental images. By bringing in Freud at this point, Rorty reminds us that the beliefs/habits that constitute our "selfhood" are contingent upon historical events. In a particularly helpful summation of his position Rorty says: "The strategy is the same in all these cases: It is to substitute a tissue of contingent relations, a web which stretches backwards and forward through past and future time, for a formed, unified, present, self-contained substance, something capable of being seen steadily and whole" (1989, xiv). In short, Rorty is an antiessentialist in all things, including the self. The relationships we form determine who we are. Peel away the relationships, and there is nothing left.

Viewed from the perspective of this inquiry into the unity of knowledge and action, what are we to make of Rorty's "extensions" of Davidson's antirepresentational positions? For example, how would Wang relate to Rorty's assertion that language is fully contingent and without any particular telos? At first, it might seem that Rorty is pointing to an amoral position, where it is not possible to tell better from worse. After all, if Rorty is right and language is fully contingent, there are no transcendent values (e.g., such as truth, beauty) to aim for, and it would seem that "anything goes." This seems diametrically opposed to Wang's Confucian sensibility wherein *everything* we do is ultimately moral and set within a context where it is possible to discern better from worse. As I see it, however, by rejecting the tendency we have to exaggerate their positions, we can bring Wang and Rorty together.

Though Rorty is often characterized as an amoral Nietzschean, I think that is a mistake. As his later writings make clear, he is a deeply moral thinker, preoccupied with the problem of how we are to establish a moral language in a post-Nietzschean world. Rorty's emphasis on empathy through heightened sensitivity to the pain others experience resonates nicely with Wang's demand that we should act so as to "form one body with all things." This is no small point since the Confucian idea that we should form one body with all things forms part of the rationale for Wang's epistemological assertion that knowledge and action are truly one thing. Thus, on a spectrum between classical Confucianism and classical Taoism, I place Rorty near the Neo-Confucian middle. As we will see in chapter 8, he is attuned to the role of spontaneity and perspectivalism (Taoist traits that reinforce his antirepresentational epistemology), but he is also convinced that humans have a responsibility to one another (a truly Confucian premise).

If we sometimes overstate Rorty's amorality, we also tend to overstate Confucian moralism. It is true that Wang goes so far as to claim that our first response to things is always moral/aesthetic. Nevertheless, as we will see in chapter 4, we should not confuse Wang's Confucian faith in our moral sensibilities with the notion that we must first "know" transcendent moral principles before we can act. Rather, Wang's doctrine of *liang chih* (primordial awareness) points to the creative partnership Confucians believe we enjoy with Heaven and Earth. According to Wang, when we take up our appropriate role in this holy trinity, we actually contribute to the *creation* of those moral principles that make life truly human. Thus, one way to see that knowledge and action are one thing is to recognize how the act of creating meaningful order involves us in the establishment of the very principles that we use to measure the quality of our actions. From Wang's perspective, all of our actions are moral, yet there is no place where we can stand and know ahead of time what moral principles should be applied in a given situation. The apparent paradox is resolved, in part, by giving up the distinction between knowledge and action.

Where I find Rorty and Wang particularly close is in Rorty's metaphor of the self as a contingent web of beliefs. If belief is, as I've suggested above, a way of being in relation to something rather than an internal image of it, then Rorty and Wang share a sense that the self is ultimately constituted by relationships that are largely contingent. We are born into a particular context that sets the stage for what we become and at the same time defines its outer limits. Our creativity is all tangled up in what we do with the world we are given. For both Wang and Rorty there is no perspective from which to view the self as a "a formed, unified, present, self-contained substance, something capable of being seen steadily and whole" (Rorty, 1989, xiv) because we are constantly engaged in the task of remaking ourselves in response to the changes in our situation.

Of course, Rorty's metaphor of the self as a tissue of contingent relations also works nicely for Dewey, whose own description of the self is wedded to his view that selves are embedded in and emergent from "situations." As I mentioned above, Dewey urges us to give up the tendency to view the self as an atomic unit that comes into relations with others, in favor of a relational model. According to Dewey, the self is best described as a set of transactions that share certain commonalities but that are also continuous with the transactions constituting the self's broader environmental context. Just as it is difficult to discern where one's bodily self leaves off from the environment that provides it with its food, water, and air, so is it the case that the borders of selfhood are diaphanous and difficult to define. Dewey suggests that selfhood extends precisely to those things over which the self can claim ownership. This aligns nicely with Rorty's use of Freud, whose therapeutic method has sometimes been interpreted as providing patients with the opportunity to take control over aspects of their lives by rehearsing and taking ownership of the various narrative streams that constitute their current situation.

Having lifted up a few of the points where Dewey and Wang have affinities with Rorty's nonrepresentational approach to knowledge, language, and the self, it is important to note where the differences are. Rorty is quite explicit in rejecting the metaphysical side of the pragmatic tradition, especially Dewey's interest in anything approximating panpsychism. He believes such thoughts are a holdover from a style of philosophizing that Dewey was engaged in overthrowing and ought to be left behind. At its core, Rorty's fear is that metaphysics is inherently representational and therefore incapable of sustaining itself in the face of Davidson's critique. One of the main goals of this volume is to demonstrate why those fears are mistaken. Moreover, I aim to go further by showing how metaphysical reflection can actually lend crucial support to Rorty's antirepresentationalism. Of course, there are metaphysical theories that are inadequate and should be dropped. Part of what has contributed to our metaphysical confusion has been a dependence on representational metaphors to describe what we mean by knowledge. In short, I believe that our metaphysical theories would look and sound quite different if we began with the hypothesis that knowledge and action are truly one thing. This, in fact, has been my approach to reading Dewey and Whitehead, an approach that was originally inspired by my reading of Wang and later reinforced by what I learned from Taylor, Rorty, and Davidson. My hope is that readers who have been raised with a late-modern prejudice against metaphysical reflection will be inspired by comments in this volume to take a second look at the very idea of metaphysics. Once the unity of knowledge and action is rendered plausible, and once it is shown how important metaphysical reflection is for clarifying our understanding of the self, metaphysics should have renewed relevance.

To this point, I have explored the works of Charles Taylor, Donald Davidson, and Richard Rorty from the perspective of Wang's claim that knowledge and action are really one thing. Moreover, Taylor's critique of modern conceptions of the self and the Davidson/Rorty critique of representationalism have both been shown to intersect at key points with the thinking of Dewey and Whitehead. There are differences, of course, but my main goal has been to begin marking out the borders of a common field of inquiry. As I see it, things would appear clearer within this common field of inquiry if we all began with Wang's hypothesis that knowledge and action are truly one thing. Before turning to a detailed discussion of the Neo-Confucian, pragmatist, and process articulations of this claim, there is one more area of contemporary philosophic investigation that seems important to discuss. Cognitive science, that field of inquiry focusing on the relationship between brain and mind, is an area of inquiry where such a shift in metaphors would be very effective. It is difficult to imagine what the cognitive sciences would look like had they been operating under Wang's hypothesis that knowledge is an activity rather than an immaterial representation of reality. As cognitive scientists (and the philosophers they influence) struggle to find a way to talk sensibly of the relationship between "mind states" and "brain states," the temptation has been typically to take the easy route and simply reduce the former to the latter. This leads almost inevitably to the description of mental states as mere epiphenomena. As I see things, the temptation to such reductionisms would be greatly reduced were scientists to begin with an entirely different set of metaphors for describing knowledge. To demonstrate why I think this is the case, I turn next to a discussion of Daniel C. Dennett's popular book *Consciousness Explained* (1991).

CHAPTER 3

Minds, Bodies, and Consciousness: Daniel Dennett's Consciousness Explained

I should begin this discussion by indicating why I think Dennett's efforts connect with those of Taylor, Davidson, and Rorty. As I have tried to show, all three are engaged in a battle with Cartesian assumptions about selfhood and knowledge. Each rejects the Cartesian notion of a fully formed, internal, immaterial self that is clothed in a material body. Approaching this battle from the perspective of cognitive science and artificial intelligence, Dennett too struggles against our tendency to believe in the existence of what he calls the "Cartesian theater." Interestingly, Dennett does not limit his criticism to traditional dualists and Cartesian materialists. Rather, he sees remnants of Cartesianism embedded in the basic metaphors that govern the thinking of almost all cognitive scientists. He believes this leads them to feel that there must be a central processing place within the brain, a place where "it all comes together" and a conscious self emerges. As an alternative, Dennett argues that we should give up our Cartesian assumptions about the nature and function of knowledge and consciousness. Instead, he claims we need a new theory, one that does not assume the existence of an "internal witness."

Dennett's theory of consciousness effectively dissolves the very notion of interiority that we have seen Taylor chronicle and Davidson and Rorty criticize. It suggests that the brain is a multitasking system and that consciousness is the product of interlocking decentralized processes. By eliminating the inner Cartesian screen and replacing it with a decentralized collection of processes, Dennett reinforces the antirepresentational positions developed by Davidson and Rorty. After all, Cartesian and Lockian representational theories of knowledge cannot be right if there is no inner screen on which to project the representations.

At the same time, however, Dennett brings his own problems to the quest for a nonrepresentational theory of knowledge. Sometimes he seems not to recognize the antirepresentational implications of his position and lapses into what can only be described as confusing representational language. More seriously, toward the end of his study, he seems to take a reductionistic approach to describing human experience that only makes sense if you accept his materialist metaphysical claims. For example, Dennett seems to take delight in saying that all human experience is "just a combination of electrochemical happenings in [the] brain" (1991, 410). He even has a chapter titled "Qualia Disqualified," in which he explains why his theory of consciousness effectively reduces the qualitative dimension of human experience to mere epiphenomena.

Taylor, of course, would reject this aspect of Dennett's project. As we have seen, *Sources of the Self* aims at *restoring* our ability to talk sensibly about the objective reality of nonmaterial qualities and values. When Taylor complains that "certain strands of contemporary computer-struck cognitive psychology are based on a crucial mistake. They are changing the subject" (1989, 58), he could easily be referring to Dennett. Though I agree with Taylor's complaint, my own position is that a genuine defense of the objective reality of qualities and values requires more than Taylor offers. It calls for a revision of the metaphysical and ontological assumptions that structure our understanding of knowledge. Like Rorty, Davidson, and Taylor, Dennett also seems disinclined to pursue this dimension of the antirepresentational quest. Wang, Dewey, and Whitehead, however, have no such timidity. All three are able to point us toward a nonrepresentational theory of knowledge because they are unfettered by traditional metaphysical assumptions. Thus, where Dennett is pleased to announce that his theory explains away the qualitative content of mental states, Wang, Dewey, and Whitehead present us with alternative positions that could be used to preserve most of Dennett's position while also retaining the commonsense conviction that there is something real about the world's colors, textures, tastes, smells, and values.

Dennett divides *Consciousness Explained* into three parts. Part 1 is a survey of the problems of consciousness and a discussion of some of the methodological moves that are necessary to talk sensibly about consciousness. Part 2 contains the argumentative heart of the book, a description of what he calls his "multiple draft" theory of consciousness. In part 3 Dennett uses the multiple draft theory to attack traditional puzzles that have haunted those whose understanding of minds and bodies have been shaped (either wittingly or unwittingly) by Cartesian assumptions.

THE PROBLEM OF CONSCIOUSNESS

Dennett opens part one of *Consciousness Explained* by arguing that current ideas about consciousness usually presume the existence of a *sub-*

ject who is capable of witnessing what we take to be the *objects* of consciousness. The problem with this view, of course, is that events in the brain, much like events in the liver, seem to proceed quite nicely with no sign of any such witness (ibid., 26–29). From Descartes's time to today, researchers have asked, How can a collection of unwitnessed physical transactions taking place within the brain ever be equivalent to, or the source of, the phenomena we call "consciousness"?

Dualistic attempts to solve this problem have always had to face what Dennett considers an insurmountable problem. A nonmaterial, subjective, or otherwise purely mental substance seems unable to have contact with or any impact on the objective, physical realm. If dualism is correct, and mentality is truly outside the system of material causes and effects, then there is no way it could contribute to physical processes. The fact that Cartesian dualism seems at all plausible to us is a sign indicating how deeply dependent we are on the notion that consciousness entails a single, unified, witnessing "self." After all, how else could we account for our attraction to a theory that at its base contains such a fundamental contradiction? Our deep attachment to the notion that consciousness is at some basic level a witnessing of internal and external events is the source of dualism's plausibility.

Most scientists, of course, have tried to go the materialist route and give up the comforts afforded by the irrationality of dualism. But materialism has its own problems. If mind is really nothing more than a series of electrochemical processes, as materialism suggests, what are we to do with our felt conviction that witnessing is an essential component of consciousness? Where in the series of electrochemical processes does this witnessing occur?

According to Dennett, most researchers simply ignore such questions. He tells us that neuroscientists, psychologists, and artificial intelligence researchers "postpone questions about consciousness by restricting their attention to the 'peripheral' and 'subordinate' systems of the mind/brain, which are deemed to feed and service some dimly imagined 'center' where 'conscious thought' and 'experience' take place" (ibid., 39). Dennett goes on to argue that failure to face these questions leads to a "theoretical myopia that prevents theorists from seeing that their models still presuppose that somewhere, conveniently hidden in the obscure 'center' of the mind/brain, there is a Cartesian Theater, a place where it all comes together and consciousness happens" (ibid.). As an alternative strategy, Dennett urges his readers to embark with him on a project designed to dismantle our understanding of consciousness. In its place he hopes to present a description of consciousness that makes witnessing a second order by-product of consciousness rather than its primordial starting point.

To some, this suggestion might not appear radical or new. After all, if he describes consciousness as an outcome of purely physical transactions, isn't he merely postponing the question of consciousness until the end, just like all the researchers he criticized? Dennett, however, thinks his approach makes all the difference because it relieves him of the need to find a "place" in the brain where consciousness is happening. On Dennett's model, consciousness is not in any one place within the brain. It is a product of the whole brain, an outcome that stems from the sympathetic interaction of innumerable subroutines, all of which are operating in concert but with no overarching witness or coordinator. In short, the witness is the end product, rather than the starting point of consciousness.

My sense is that Deweyans should be especially comfortable with this aspect of Dennett's position, since Dewey regularly says that the self emerges from the situation as a product rather than as a starting point.

METHODOLOGICAL ISSUES:
HOW IS IT POSSIBLE TO STUDY CONSCIOUSNESS?

Before turning to the question of how a multitasking brain might produce conscious effects, Dennett raises some important methodological issues. It is not immediately apparent how to study consciousness since most of the data about consciousness must come from descriptions of subjective experiences that researchers cannot record firsthand. There are, of course, first person accounts of experience. But Dennett rules out of hand the Cartesian (and by implication Kantian) "subjective turn," noting that first-person reports are hardly the reliable starting point we once took them to be. Having said this, however, Dennett goes on to label as "overly scrupulous" those researchers who argue that there is nothing that science can say about mental events that we don't observe directly. Experimental psychologists, neuroscientists, and behaviorists often rely upon this claim to justify their refusal to talk about mental events. While Dennett concedes that we cannot observe mental events directly, he also points out that the same can be said of black holes and genes. The fact that we cannot experience them directly does not keep us from using observable scientific data to develop perfectly good theories about them (ibid., 71).

What kind of scientific data are appropriate for developing a theory of consciousness? In response to this question, Dennett proposes the "heterophenomenological method." Drawing on his well-known earlier work *The Intentional Stance* (1987), Dennett argues that like everyone else researchers must begin their investigations by presuming that language speakers are rational agents whose words are linked to actual intentions. This presumption is "the price we must pay for gaining access to a host of reliable truisms we exploit in the design of experiments" (1991, 77). Taking such a step leaves us open to the risk that we might be dealing with "zombies" or "androids," creatures that walk and talk like humans but have no so-called "inner" life. But without it we would be blocked from any inquiry into the nature and meaning of consciousness.

At first, Dennett's heterophenomenology may seem uncontroversial. After all, isn't he merely saying that to study consciousness, we have to talk to people whom we take to be conscious? Opponents will point out, however, that there is no guarantee that a subject's description of an experience will turn out to be the best account of what was happening during that experience. Natural scientists, who usually operate via third-person descriptions, normally do not allow their subjects authority over the investigation. Even if we were to concede that a particular subject is reporting truly how things *seemed* to her, that *seeming* could be an elaborate fiction, one that was created without her even being aware of its fictional status.

In response to such criticisms, Dennett points out that although something may be fictional, we still can say some things that are reliable about it. We interpret fiction every day. We can do so because even within fiction there are certain things that are "facts of the matter" and other things that simply cannot be denied even though they are not objective in the traditional sense. Dennett gives as an example a Sherlock Holmes story, which, though fictional, simply would not work were there not certain definite things that could be said about it. As Dennett puts it: "The heterophenomenological method neither challenges nor accepts as entirely true the assertions of subjects, but rather maintains a constructive and sympathetic neutrality, in the hopes of compiling a definitive description of the world according to the subjects" (ibid., 83). Moreover, Dennett points out that such descriptions are only the starting point for the analytical process. While awarding the subject authority over how things may *seem,* the investigator retains the right to use this data in conjunction with data derived from other sources to create a "theorist's fiction, the subject's heterophenomenological world." "If we were to find the real goings-on in people's brains that had enough of the 'defining' properties of the items that populate their heterophenomenological worlds, we could reasonably propose that we had discovered what they were really talking about—even if they initially resisted the identifications" (ibid., 98). Dennett's heterophenomenological method investigates characteristics in the stories subjects tell about their experiences. By critically examining and interpreting what people say, he is able to draw conclusions without having direct access to first-person experiences. In this way, Dennett claims to have legitimated the scientific character of investigations into consciousness, forcing open a door that many in experimental psychology, neuroscience, and behaviorism believe is closed to them.

In the main, I agree with Dennett's methodological moves. I do, however, have two concerns. Dennett says that a researcher should strive for "sympathetic neutrality" when listening to a subject's description of an experience. While I agree that we should aim to minimize the extent to which biases or presuppositions influence our reception of the data, I am suspicious as to whether we can attain neutrality. The search for such neutrality in the social sciences has been akin to the quest for the holy grail. Everyone wants it, but we have no proof that it actually exists. All researchers carry biases and assumptions into their projects, and this includes assumptions as to whether the subject is capable of describing what is really happening. The important question is whether our assumptions distort the data in a *significant* way. I have no complaints regarding Dennett's willingness to assume such things as the intentionality of his subjects. Nevertheless, later on in *Consciousness Explained*, Dennett does seem to be guilty of assuming rather than proving that his subjects' claims about qualia are merely subjective fictions. I will argue toward the end of this chapter that Dennett's materialist metaphysical assumptions make it impossible for him to take seriously his subjects' claims in this area. Of course, it would be inefficient and ultimately useless to try to eliminate all presuppositions before beginning a line of inquiry. Therefore, it is understandable that Dennett takes for granted metaphysical assumptions that he shares with most of his colleagues. Nevertheless, one of my goals is to demonstrate why researchers such as Taylor, Rorty, Davidson, and Dennett would benefit by exploring metaphysical options that resolve some of the anomalies that crop up when efforts to achieve a nonrepresentational theory of knowledge are circumscribed by traditional materialist assumptions.

The second issue that concerns me about Dennett's methodology also has to do with the problem of reductionism. In the academic study of religion scholars are particularly sensitive to the tendency to assume that the only *real* explanation is one that reduces the phenomena (in this case religious beliefs and practices) to something other than they claim to be. Thus, there have been a parade of explanatory descriptions that have told us that religion is *really* an expression of economic, psychological, political, or sociological forces. While some in the field of religion bewail the absence of a universally accepted "theory of religion," most are simply willing to acknowledge that religion is a complicated phenomenon that can be illuminated by a variety of methods, but that seems always misdescribed when it is reduced to a single explanatory theory.[1]

I suspect that similar things can be said about theories of consciousness. Thus I reject Dennett's methodological claim (cited above) that coordinating brain activity with phenomenological descriptions of what things seemed like during those brain events would automatically tell us what our subjects were *"really talking about—even if they initially resisted the identifications."* I do not doubt that every mind state can be coordinated with a "brain state." I do think, however, that mechanistic materialism is not the only way to approach the description of brain states. Surely we can and should appreciate the mechanics of brain activity. But doing so does not mean we must rule out of hand our ability to talk about the objective reality of things such as qualities and values.

When it comes to assessing explanations, I follow pragmatic thinkers such as Dewey and Peirce. A good explanation is not necessarily one that reduces a complicated phenomenon to something simpler. A good explanation gives us more power and control over ourselves and the world we experience. Brain research has helped us discover a host of things that give us more control and power over ourselves and the world around us. It goes awry, however, when it claims to have unmasked as unreal the things that make lives human. The color red can be partially described as the movement of energy at a certain rate of frequency. That does not mean that we have fully explained redness in a way that eliminates the reality of the qualitative experience (the phenomenology) of redness.

My hesitancy here is akin to Taylor's argument (cited in chapter 1) that natural scientists presuppose the very human values that they claim to transcend in their quest for absolute objectivity. Dennett thinks that by creating a distinction between the way the world seems to his subjects and his description of the way it actually is, he has sufficiently protected his subjects' integrity while allowing himself to proceed to develop an objective description of the way things are. I suspect, however, that what he has really done is create a protected space wherein his assumptions about the basic structure of matter can operate unfettered by what his subjects actually say about the world they experience. This leads to the paradoxical situation where Dennett, and others like him, tell us that they can describe our world via materialistic metaphors and that when we experience colors, pains, or values, what we are *really* experiencing is the movement of this matter. I would suggest that while it is useful to be reminded of the fact that experience always involves the movement of matter, we have good reason to suspect that such a description is neither complete nor sufficient for understanding the phenomena. As *organisms,* we ignore qualities and values at our peril. Moreover, if it is possible to construct a theory that is capable of encompassing Dennett's mechanistic assumptions and at the same time preserving our sense that qualities and values are in some sense real, then we would have in hand a far more sophisticated tool for interpreting both ourselves and our world.

I should end this discussion of Dennett's methodological claims by reiterating that for the most part, I find his discussion of consciousness persuasive and helpful. As I said earlier, by removing the Cartesian theater, Dennett effectively dissolves the "interior" self, thereby contributing to the elimination of the very metaphor that gave plausibility to representational theories of knowledge. As I see it, if we could put representationalism behind us, the theory that knowledge and action are really one thing becomes much more plausible. With this in mind it is time to turn to an examination of Dennett's actual description of the rise of consciousness.

DENNETT'S MULTIPLE DRAFTS THEORY OF CONSCIOUSNESS

Dennett begins his analysis of consciousness by reminding us of the extent to which we define consciousness as equivalent to having a point of view: "Wherever there is a conscious mind, there is a point of view. This is one of the most fundamental ideas we have about minds—or about consciousness. A conscious mind is an observer, who takes in a limited subset of all the information there is. An observer takes in the information that is available at a particular (roughly) continuous sequence of times and places in the universe" (ibid., 101). Dennett goes on to lift up three corollaries from this premise. First, to have a point of view seems to entail that there be a single unified viewer who takes in and responds to what comes into view. Second, it presumes that somewhere (somehow) there exists within the brain/mind a mechanism that serves as the functional equivalent of a stage or screen on which the events are projected for this single observer to "witness." Finally, all of this entails the existence of a single "two-lane" passageway for all of the incoming and outgoing data relevant to consciousness.

Though I have put these claims rather crudely, Dennett argues that something like them continues to govern most attempts to talk about consciousness, including the efforts of many cognitive scientists. According to Dennett, the recent quest by cognitive scientists to locate a region in the brain dedicated to conscious activity is the materialist's equivalent of a search for the Cartesian theater. It assumes that if we could locate the physical matter that contains the "images of consciousness," we would have found the nearest physical equivalent to a Cartesian subject. Recent brain research, however, undercuts the notion that there is any one place in the brain where consciousness occurs. In light of this, Dennett suggests that we see consciousness as a product of the whole brain rather than any single subsystem.

To demonstrate how the idea of a Cartesian theater leads to confusing paradoxical explanations of our experience, Dennett describes an experiment that explores the well-known phi-effect, which creates in subjects the appearance of motion by flashing a series of still images on a screen (ibid., 114). In this version of the experiment, subjects were shown a sequence of two *differently colored* dots of light in rapid succession and a short distance apart from one another. The subjects reported that they experienced a single moving dot that changed color about *midway* through its movement. That the two dots became one moving dot is not surprising. This effect is the basis for our experience of all "moving pictures." What is surprising, however, is that the subjects claimed the color of the dot changed midway through its movement. This seems to indicate that the subjects were able to predict the color change *before* the second dot was illuminated. After all, if they experienced the change midway through the dot's motion, they were claiming to be conscious of the second color before it actually flashed on the screen (ibid.)!

In order to explain away the paradox, most of us adopt what Dennett calls either an Orwellian or a Stalinesque stance. The Orwellian response supposes that subjects unconsciously "rewrite" the history of their experience by inserting into the sequence of their memory illusory experiences of the second color at a point that is earlier than when it was actually experienced. He calls this explanation "Orwellian" because it assumes that in an effort to "make sense" of what is consciously felt, the subject literally reconstructs memory the same way Orwellian historians rewrote history in response to changing political circumstances. On this theory when incoming data does not make sense, the subject's mind works overtime to create for consciousness the most sensible *outgoing* reports possible. The Stalinesque alternative explains the early color change by presupposing that each subject operates under the equivalent of a preconscious timed delay, the kind of thing that radio talk show hosts use to ensure that obscene outbursts aren't broadcast to their audiences. On this theory, there is a "lag time" between what happens and the conscious experience during which the brain creates illusory images that effectively "fill in the gaps" when the incoming data doesn't make sense. Eventually, this "touched-up" product is delivered to consciousness. Thus, according to the Stalinesque explanation, the *incoming* data is manipulated, and the subject's outgoing report is an accurate rendition of how the information actually *seemed* to consciousness, even though the touched up version was based on false initial data.

The Orwellian claim is that data are distorted in the *outgoing* phase of consciousness, while the Stalinesque claim is that the data are reshaped on the *incoming* phase. They have in common the assumption that a single preexistent conscious subject receives and responds to information that is channeled to it from various bodily sources, including subsystems within the brain. They also assume that in order for the processing of that information to make sense, the information must be strung together for the subject in a single serial order (or stream) that reflects the actual order of events, as best they can be reconstructed. Dennett asks whether we need to presume the existence of a unified subject and a single stream of consciousness in order to account for what is happening in this experiment? Why can't the brain's subsystems simply be making discriminations as quickly as possible but not in precisely the same sequence as the actual events? Why would the stimuli have to be channeled to a single place in the brain when it is just as easy to imagine parts of the brain responding directly without such an intervening step?

From Dennett's perspective, the illusion of the change in color is not the product of an attempt to render information coherent for a pre-existing conscious subject. Rather, it is simply evidence that the brain processes information in a relatively loose, disjointed fashion. The scientists and those who read about the experiment know the *actual* order of events. We have no reason to assume that the subjects' brains process all of the data in precisely the same order. Data comes into the brain via a variety of channels and is processed at varying rates of speed. That there might be some disjunction between the order of production and our ability to report on the experience is "paradoxical" only if we *presume* that the universal substrate for human experience must be a single subject who is enjoying a single sequentially ordered stream of consciousness. In short, those who call upon either Orwellian or Stalinesque explanations do so because of assumptions they make about the nature of consciousness. If we let go of those assumptions, there is nothing paradoxical about the fact that in this experiment the brain seems able to take in and respond to color changes more quickly than it can handle the processing of "apparent" motion.

Granted, we still need to account for consciousness. Dennett is suggesting, however, that we should not begin that process by saddling ourselves with the notion of a preexistent homunculus somewhere in the brain. After all, we don't need to identify a centralized self to understand how the brain regulates organic processes such as respiration and digestion even though some of those processes can, with some effort, be lifted into conscious control (e.g., yogis who learn to regulate their heartbeats). By letting go of the presupposition that consciousness requires a preexistent subject, we remove the paradox motivating both the Orwellian and Stalinesque descriptions of consciousness, and we find ourselves in need of an alternative description of consciousness.

Dennett, of course, is anxious to provide this alternate description. He calls it the "Multiple Drafts" model of consciousness: "According to the Multiple Drafts model, all varieties of perception—indeed, all varieties of thought or mental activity—are accomplished in the brain by parallel, multitrack processes of interpretation and elaboration of sensory inputs. Information entering the nervous system is under continuous 'editorial revision' (ibid., 111). If nothing else, recent brain research has demonstrated that the brain is a multitrack system capable of simultaneously coordinating an indeterminate number of input and output routines. Sometimes these routines operate in relative independence of one another, and at other times they knit together in codependent subsystems. Though we know more about the brain than ever before, no one has yet found anything close to a single regnant subsystem that is capable of distilling and responding to the vast amount of information that contributes to conscious experience. Therefore, though consciousness feels like a single stream of incoming data and outgoing intentional responses, such feelings might be the illusory product of subsystems interacting in a particular manner.

The multiple drafts model simply drops the assumption that the brain represents things to an inner-witnessing subject. "[T]he brain does not bother 'constructing' any representations that go to the trouble of 'filling in' the blanks. That would be a waste of time and (shall we say?) paint. The judgment is already in so the brain can get on with other tasks!" (ibid., 128). Statements like these are what led me to see a link between Dennett's project and the antirepresentational efforts of Rorty and Davidson. Like them Dennett is arguing that we should discard the layer of experiential "content" that used to seem essential for mediating between the supposed experiencing subject and its objective world. In place of the old subject/object structure, Dennett is promoting what I prefer to call (following Dewey) a "transactional model," one that takes a naturalistic approach to understanding the relationship between the mind/brain and its environment. Dennett wants us to see the mind/brain as a dynamic interactive system, one that is in direct contact with its world and that has no need for a cognitive loop where data is re-presented to an interior self. He calls this the "multiple drafts" theory because the brain is constantly taking in and adjusting to data from an indeterminate number of sources. Each adjustment is itself a "draft response" to the environment. Thus on Dennett's view there is no universal point of view regulating all of the subroutines. Instead, the brain is constantly adapting at many different levels, all simultaneously.

If we follow Dennett's lead, we must shift the basic metaphors we use for describing consciousness. In place of Cartesian visual metaphors (e.g., the mind's eye), he suggests we think of the mind/brain as a mechanism for predicting and adjusting an organism to its constantly shifting environment. Viewed this way, the main task of the brain is not representing something to consciousness. It is rather to "gather information . . . and use it swiftly to 'produce the future'—to extract anticipations in order to stay one step ahead of disaster" (ibid., 144). More than anything else the brain projects an organism forward into a hypothetical future, one that may or may not turn out as its actions anticipate. *Everything else about the mind/brain, including consciousness, is subordinate to this fundamental organic task.* Descartes and his followers mistakenly allowed a centuries-old metaphorical association between thought and visualization to obscure these basic truths about the role the brain plays in all organisms, including humans. As Dennett, Davidson, Rorty, and Dewey all argue, these visual metaphors render it almost impossible for us to understand how a so-called inner subject relates to its so-called objective world. This confusion forced philosophers to posit a medium to bridge the unbridgeable chasm separating the subjective and objective realms (Dennett, 1991; Rorty, 1979).

All of this disappears if we simply let go of the visual metaphors and the assumptions that go along with them. Instead of the static representational descriptions of knowledge, Dennett substitutes dynamic, process-oriented descriptors. For example, he describes consciousness as a "mode of action rather than as a *subsystem* of the brain" (Dennett, 1991, 166). It is the product of a whole range of subsystems interacting with one another, all aiming toward an ever-developing set of objectives. This makes consciousness an *outcome* rather than the starting point for experience. It also makes it difficult to determine the line between conscious and unconscious processes since no one process, when taken alone, is conscious.

> If one wants to settle on some moment of processing in the brain as the moment of consciousness, this has to be arbitrary. One can always "draw a line" in the stream of processing in the brain, but there are no functional differences that could motivate declaring all prior stages and revisions to be unconscious or preconscious adjustments, and all subsequent emendations to the content (as revealed by recollection) to be post-experiential memory contamination. The distinction lapses in close quarters. (Ibid., 126)

Thus, Dennett describes the mind/brain as a vastly complicated site of organic responsiveness that periodically gives rise to what we call "conscious experience." Consciousness is a flickering culmination of all this dynamic activity rather than a constant substrate. As we will see in subsequent chapters, Dennett's description resonates easily with Dewey's approach to knowledge and consciousness. For example, in *Experience and Nature* Dewey says, "Consciousness . . . is that phase of a system of meaning which at a given time is undergoing re-direction, transitive transformation" (1958, 308). Moreover, like Dennett, both Dewey and Whitehead reject the old visual metaphors that have guided philosophic talk about knowledge, consciousness, and mind in general. Consequently, their positions are largely free from the kinds of mistakes that Dennett roundly criticizes throughout his text.

CONSCIOUSNESS AND EVOLUTION

Describing consciousness, however, is only part of the task Dennett sets for himself. He also aims to provide an account of how it arises and why it takes on the specific forms that it does. While acknowledging that there will always be a speculative dimension to such theories, he claims that once we have toppled the "dictatorial idea of the Cartesian theater," we are freed to see how evolutionary theory can help us to understand both how and why organisms developed this relatively unique adaptation.

Dennett begins his evolutionary account of the rise of consciousness with a Darwinian rewrite of the opening verses in Genesis: "In the beginning, there were no reasons; there were only causes. Nothing had a purpose, nothing had so much as a function; there was no teleology in the world at all. The explanation for this is simple. There was nothing that had interests. But after millennia there happened to emerge simple replicators" (ibid., 173). Dennett offers no explanation for the emergence of replicators. They simply appear as a result of random combinations of causal interactions. Once on the scene, however, everything changes. Viewed from the perspective of a replicator's interests, the cosmos suddenly becomes the site of goods and evils. "If replicators want to continue to replicate, they should hope and strive for various things; they should avoid the 'bad' things and seek the 'good' things" (ibid.).[2] Things that enhance the chances of replication are counted as good, and those that do not are bad. In short, the arrival of replicators introduces purpose and value into what was previously a purely causal system.

Dennett's use of Darwin as the jumping off point for his description of consciousness may seem unremarkable. After all, he merely wants to explain how the universe moved from a purposeless causal sequence to a cosmos containing both purposes and values. However, he wants to accomplish this without violating his own commitment to mechanistic materialism. This becomes evident as Dennett spins off seven corollaries that he argues are implicit in the very notion of an organism. Three are particularly important for my purposes. First, he argues that wherever there are organisms, there must be clear boundaries. "Any agent must distinguish 'here inside' from 'the external world.'" Second, he claims that all early organisms accomplished their basic tasks (i.e., survival and replication) through a myriad of "'blind, mechanical' routines." This seems commonsensical since few of us are willing to speculate that early mold spores could do much more than generate new mold spores! Third, he notes that all early organisms pursued their interests without benefit of a "Higher Executive or General Headquarters" inside the defended boundary (ibid., 176). Simple organisms respond directly to changes in their environment and in most instances do so without relying on a centralized nervous system to coordinate those responses. With respect to this third corollary, I think it is fair to say that Dennett believes we have been taken in by the very metaphor of a "centralized nervous system." We've assumed that a central nervous system needs to have a centralized subject who is the recipient of all the information coordinated by the central nervous system.

With these three corollaries in mind, it is not hard to see why Dennett's appeal to Darwin and his introduction of replicators are very important steps in his argument. It lays the groundwork for his description of brains as more complicated versions of these early organic forms of responsiveness. Since a great deal rides on the way Dennett initiates his description of consciousness, I would like to stop for a moment to consider how Dewey and Whitehead might respond. After all, they also saw themselves as heirs to Darwin and spent a fair amount of energy thinking about how best to describe the origins of human organisms.

Dewey puts a different spin on the Darwinian story. In *Experience and Nature* he begins by making the metaphysical point that all things are patterned movements within the larger dynamic network that is the natural world. Viewed this way, the distinction between organic and inorganic patterns is the former's capacity to restore the equilibrium of its movement when that equilibrium is disturbed (either by internal changes or changes in the wider environment). A rock smashed by a hammer is forever in pieces, its equilibrium dispersed. A plant, by contrast, interacts with and is dependent upon its environment. It has the flexibility to recover from ecological shocks such as a mild drought and responds to abundant water and nutrients by flourishing. Thus, Dewey's organisms are transactional systems.[3] They are fully integrated with and dependent upon their broader environment. They are like Dennett's replicators in that they introduce interest and value into an otherwise purely causal system. However, Dewey places a greater emphasis on an organism's integration with its environment. The boundaries defining an "individual" organic process over against its environment are much less rigidly drawn than seems to be the case for Dennett who said: "Me against the world—this distinction between everything on the inside of a closed boundary and everything in the external world—is at the heart of all biological processes, not just ingestion and excretion, respiration and transpiration" (ibid., 174).

Despite their difference in emphasis with respect to the boundaries that define organisms, Dewey and Dennett both seem to agree that there is no real accounting for the transition from inorganic to organic entities. The emergence of organisms is simply a product of random juxtapositions. Whitehead, by contrast, is bothered that followers of Darwin could think of randomness as an explanation for the rise of anything. He argues that randomness is never an "explanation" in the technical sense. It is, rather, the admission that no explanation is possible (Whitehead, 1958, 3–34). In place of this a-rational impulse, Whitehead suggests that we consider another, more radical possibility. To put it in Dennett's language, Whitehead argues that *all* things are replicators, even subatomic particles. Whitehead's philosophy of organism substitutes basic biological metaphors for the metaphors of Newtonian physics and develops a description of the world that portrays the transition from so-called inorganic to organic patterns as a result of gradual development rather than random combinations. For Whitehead, then, interest and value are already operative throughout the cosmos long before the rise of complicated organic forms. Stated baldly like this, Whitehead's speculations are hard to take seriously because they sound so fantastic. But seen in the context of Dennett's effort to introduce interest and value into a valueless, mechanistic universe, they have at least the virtue of greater simplicity. After all, Dennett and Dewey find themselves forced to talk about crossing what some might see as an ontological divide. First there are random systems. Then there are organic/replicator systems. One has no interests; the other does. Whitehead, by contrast, suggests that all things are organic. Everything has interests. At the low end of the spectrum, the interests are simply the continuation of a relatively "fixed" pattern. At the high end, we find human beings whose interests and values include art, music, and intellectual life.

With respect to the issue of boundaries, Whitehead strikes a balance between Dewey and Dennett. Complex organisms, that is organisms made up of subsets of organisms, are fully immersed in and dependent upon their environment. Therefore, as with Dewey, the line between these complex organisms and their environment is not easily drawn. At the same time, however, Whitehead claims that *all* things are organisms. Since for Whitehead, as for Dennett, to be an organism is to be in pursuit of a specific set of goals or objectives, "self"-interest, what Dennett calls the "me against the world" attitude, extends all the way down to subatomic particles. While Whitehead might not be happy characterizing the biological impulse as inherently selfish, it surely is the case that for Whitehead *all* things have needs that they aim at satisfying.

The point of this brief excursion into Dewey's and Whitehead's interest in the origins of organisms is to set their accounts within the same context as Dennett's Darwinism and to initiate a line of criticism that I will be carrying throughout my discussion of Dennett's position. Though Dennett doesn't spend much time on it, a tremendous amount of work is accomplished in his simple announcement that "there happened to emerge replicators." After all, he needs replicators to introduce interest, value, good, and bad into a cosmos that he claims is otherwise devoid of such qualities. Without these qualities, there is no way, other than divine intervention or Cartesian dualism, for Dennett to get from inorganic molecules to conscious human beings. I do not begrudge him this move. Dewey and Whitehead are motivated by similar impulses. Both are seeking a naturalistic understanding of human cognitive activity. Moreover, both hope to develop a position that avoids the unbridgeable dichotomies that we have seen criticized subsequently by Taylor, Davidson, Rorty, and now Dennett. But Dennett wants to make this move and still preserve a preexisting commitment to mechanistic materialism. As I mentioned above, Dennett claims as the second corollary of his description of early replicators that they go about the business of replicating via "blind mechanical routines." In that seemingly benign phrase, Dennett is trying to have his cake and eat it too. After all, he knows he has to introduce the notion of purpose and value into the cosmos in order to make any sense out of conscious experience. By labeling simple organic processes blind and mechanical, he thinks he can preserve his mechanistic commitments as well. Eventually, he intends to extend this description to the chemical reactions that constitute brain activity, arguing that there is no need to look further for an explanation of human consciousness. Having already described them as purely mechanical processes, he preserves his materialism. At the same time, however, he is compelled to acknowledge that these processes are also organic expressions of purposes, needs, desires, or values. Well, which is it? Are they mere blind mechanical routines, or are they expressions of an organism's pursuit of simple goals? By mixing metaphors and calling simple organisms blind mechanisms, it seems like Dennett is behaving no better than Descartes did when he introduced the pineal gland as a way of bridging the mental and physical realms!

So far, I have given Deweyan and Whiteheadian responses to two of the three corollaries that I cited from Dennett's list of things that stem from the appearance of organisms. The first was that even the simplest organisms require clear boundaries separating them from the external world, and the second was that simple organisms accomplish their tasks through "blind, mechanical routines." Dennett's third corollary was that early organisms pursued their interests without the benefit of a "higher executive or general headquarters." In other words, when organisms with more than one response system appeared, they managed to coordinate the information from these multiple sensors without having to call on a single universal processor (or subject). This third corollary points to the *big* issue underlying his entire argument. If he can convince readers that the human mind is capable of functioning without such a central processing place, then he will have gone a long way in his effort to rid us of the Cartesian subject and its accompanying theater. To do this, Dennett needs to demonstrate that the way humans process information is analogous to the way simpler organisms process information. All of this leads Dennett into a discussion of representation and what it means when organisms with more complicated brains take in, hold onto, and make use of information over extended periods of time.

Dennett titles this step in his description of the evolutionary development of consciousness "New and Better Ways of Producing Future." This phrase nicely sums up the main advantage enjoyed by organisms that have more sophisticated nervous systems. It equips them to project themselves much further into an indeterminate future.

> The fundamental purpose of brains is to produce future. . . . In order to cope, an organism must either armor itself (like a tree or a clam) and "hope for the best," or else develop methods of getting out of harm's way and into the better neighborhoods in its vicinity. . . . The primordial problem that every agent must continually solve [is]
>
> Now what do I do?
>
> In order to solve this problem, you need a nervous system, to control your activities in time and space. (Ibid., 177)

Withdrawal-approach responses found in the simplest organisms are activated by direct contact (i.e., touch). Eventually, these primitive responses were surpassed as organisms evolved sensory systems capable of noting and responding to distant dangers and advantages. Dennett speculates that as organisms layered complicated sensory systems onto one another, each system attains a kind of preeminence within its own area of specialization. Thus, given certain aromatic signals, an antelope will take flight without waiting around for its ears or eyes to provide any more details about the danger lurking in the nearby bushes.

> At the minimalist extreme, then, we have the creatures who represent as little as possible: just enough to let the world warn them sometimes when they are beginning to do something wrong. Creatures who follow this policy engage in no planning. They plunge ahead and if something starts hurting, they "know enough" to withdraw, but that is the best they can do.

> The next step involves short-range anticipation—for instance the ability to duck incoming bricks. This sort of anticipatory talent is often "wired in." (Ibid., 178)

Beyond short-range anticipation lie the complicated tracking and avoidance responses of animals that are prey or hunters as well as the sophisticated navigational systems used by birds and butterflies.

What I find most interesting (and troublesome) in Dennett's description is the way he labels more sensitive response systems such as smell and sight as forms of representation. At first, it might seem uncontroversial to use representation in this way. After all, most of us would be comfortable saying that a lion's scent *represents* the lion (and all of its accompanying dangers) to antelopes who break into a run whenever they catch a whiff of it. There is, however, something confusing about using the term in this way. Not many of us would argue that the antelope has an "idea" or an "image" of a lion in its mind/brain, though that is usually what we mean when we talk about representation in humans. Most of us (and here I include Dennett) would likely say that antelopes have evolved sensitivities to minute changes in their environment, which give them something of a head start at avoiding danger, especially when the wind is right. Since we do not feel a need to posit a knowing subject in the antelope, the representational language is not necessary.

Dennett is sensitive to the ambiguity in his language. He points out that technically speaking, primitive organisms do not represent, but they react to things that touch them. Only when organisms are capable of responding to things at a distance (either temporal or spatial) does he feel pressed to use the language of representationalism.

> Until this point, I have tried to avoid speaking of simpler nervous systems as *representing* anything in the world. The various designs we have considered, both plastic and hard-wired, can be seen to be sensitive to, or responsive to, or designed-with-an-eye-to, or to utilize information about, various features of the organism's environment, and hence in that minimal sense might be called representa-

tions, but now we should pause to consider what features of such complex designs should lead us to consider them as systems of representations. (Ibid., 191)

Why this waffling over such a hot-button word? What is it that Dennett is trying to do here? Given all that Dennett has already said in the earlier parts of his book, it is surprising, to say the least, that he lapses into this representational language so easily.

As I see it, Dennett is struggling to establish and sustain a line of continuity between the simple stimulus-response mechanisms of primitive organisms and the sophisticated "representational systems" that animals (including humans) use to keep track of things in their world. This continuity is important because it supports Dennett's larger claim that we do not need to posit a central processing place (a Cartesian theater and subject) in order to understand the human mind. The logic of Dennett's position can be summed up in the following sentence: If we can use the language of representation to describe animal behavior, and yet we do not feel the need to posit within animals a Cartesian subject capable of witnessing such representations, then perhaps we don't need to assume that human representations require a Cartesian subject as their witness.

Evidence to support my reading of Dennett's intentions can be seen in the following statement, where he makes explicit the line of continuity between lower- and higher-level representations: "The beginnings of real representation are found in many lower animals (and in plants), but in human beings the capacity to represent has skyrocketed" (ibid.). Thus, according to Dennett, we might even extend our use of the term *representation* to what plants do in tracking the sun. But is this really what we mean when we speak of representational systems? While some of his readers might have been willing to accept his assertion that higher-order organisms like mammals are capable of some form of representation, how many would willingly adopt such language to describe the actions of plants?

Dennett uses the term *representation* in a way that seems stripped of all the epistemological baggage that has traditionally been associated with it. In this context, representation is perhaps better understood as an organism's ability to adjust to changes at either a temporal or a spatial distance. In fact, if I take his association of plant actions and human actions literally, it is hard to see why he uses the term *representation* at all. Why not just stick to the language of causal interaction? Plants, higher mammals, and humans all respond to changes in their environment. They are not representing anything to an internal subject; rather, they are just adjusting themselves to changes, taking advantage of the good things and avoiding those that are troublesome.

Dennett's reliance on the term *representation* seems largely rhetorical. It serves as a device to help his readers feel the connection he is trying to establish between the simple information processing of lower organisms (where everyone is comfortable talking mechanistically) and the information processing of the most complicated animals, human beings. If animals can represent things without being witnessing subjects, then so can humans.

I have no objection to Dennett's efforts to establish a line of continuity between humans and the rest of the animal kingdom. That kind of naturalistic instinct also runs through Dewey, Whitehead, and (for different reasons) Wang Yang-ming. Moreover, as I have tried to make clear throughout this text, my own project aims to contribute to the over-arching effort among contemporary philosophers to dismantle the last remnants of the Cartesian subject. Therefore, I agree with what I take to be the rationale behind Dennett's move. My concern, however, is that the language of representationalism is part of the problem. If Davidson and Rorty are right, we need to be looking for a nonrepresentational theory of knowledge. It is confusing to be in the midst of such a project (as I take Dennett to be) and then have Dennett rely on representational language to make the point. In both common language and technical philosophical jargon, representation always seems to involve some kind of witnessing, and that is precisely what Dennett and the rest of us are trying to avoid. Rather than redefining representation in the way that Dennett does, we need to drop it altogether. Let's not talk about plants representing and instead talk about the complex ways in which they respond to changes in their environment. Antelopes and lions don't represent images of one another to their "mind's eye." An antelope's defensive systems are activated whenever a lion's scent is detected, just as a lion's offensive systems are activated when it scents food. And, if we are to take seriously Dennett's multiple drafts theory of consciousness, human beings do not represent images of an external world to a Cartesian subject; rather, our brains are constantly responding directly to changes in the world.

Aside from Dennett's occasional lapses into representational language, there is much about the rest of his description of the evolution of consciousness that resonates nicely with what Dewey and Whitehead have to say on the issue. For example, Dennett, like Dewey, describes human behavior as stemming from a combination of mechanized routines, habitual patterns, and spontaneous efforts at problem solving. Mechanized routines are hardwired into the brain and direct things such as respiration, digestion, and involuntary movements such as ducking. Habitual patterns are learned responses that we pick up by imitating other creatures (both human and nonhuman) or through our own efforts at problem solving. As Dennett points out, our brains have evolved sufficient plasticity so that they require intense periods of training in order to inculcate a particular set of habits.

> One of the first major steps a human brain takes in the massive process of postnatal self-design is to get itself adjusted to the local conditions that matter the most: it swiftly (in two or three years) turns itself into a Swahili or Japanese or English brain. . . . It doesn't matter for our purposes whether this process is called learning or differential development; it happens so swiftly and effortlessly that there is little doubt that the human genotype includes many adaptations that are specifically in place to enhance language acquisition. (Ibid., 200)

Following Richard Dawkins, Dennett looks at the content of these learned responses through the lenses of contemporary genetics and sees in them all the basic traits of an evolutionary system. "Once our brains have built the entrance and exit pathways for the vehicles of language, they swiftly become parasitized (and I mean that literally, as we shall see) by entities that have evolved to thrive in just such a niche: memes" (ibid.). Memes are complex cultural ideas (Dennett suggests we think of things like language, clothing, calculus, and chess). They are called memes because, like genes, they replicate as they pass from person to person via language and culture. They also adapt to changing circumstances and attain a kind of immortality so long as they continue to be passed on from one person to another.

Neither Dewey nor Whitehead could draw upon the language of contemporary genetics to describe the transmission of these cultural units. Nevertheless, both would find the Dennett-Dawkins description of memes plausible. Dewey's emphasis on learning as the acquisition of habits fits nicely with Dennett's model, though Dennett's tendency to describe memes as ideas is a bit too static. Following Dewey it is perhaps better to describe them as patterned responses that can be passed around and serve as a kind of shorthand by brains facing similar problems. Moreover, Whitehead's Neo-Platonic discussion of "eternal objects," if read the right way, can also be seen as pointing to the same capacity that we have for cultural transmission. The key to seeing the connection with Whitehead is to downplay the transcendental tone embedded in the language he uses to describe the so-called "realm of eternal objects" and focus instead on his claim that entities literally become what they are by inheriting patterns from one another. This more pragmatic approach to Whitehead's epistemology is precisely the interpretive reading I will press in chapter 6.

Ultimately, Dennett distills his position in the following hypothetical description of how consciousness evolves:

> Human consciousness is itself a huge complex of memes (or more
> exactly, meme-effects in brains) that can best be understood as the
> operation of a "von Neumannesque" virtual machine implemented in
> the parallel architecture of a brain that was not designed for such activ-
> ities. The powers of this virtual machine vastly enhance the underlying
> powers of the organic hardware on which it runs. (Ibid., 210)

It is now a commonplace to liken the brain to computer hardware and
learning to the software that gives the brain instructions as to what
operations it should perform. But Dennett makes a distinction that people who compare our brains to computer chips sometimes ignore. Computers operate serially, funneling all their data through a single central
processor. There is only one channel through which all input and output must pass. A computer's power comes from the speed at which it
can process information serially. Its single processing unit is a bottle-
neck, but the raw calculating power of the chip makes up for that limitation. Brains, by contrast, are parallel processors. At any given time, a
human brain is simultaneously processing an indeterminate number of
responses to its environment. Thus, the power of the brain stems from
its capacity for true multitasking. As a result, Dennett claims it is a mistake to liken brains to computers. Brains are not single-track calcula-
tors; consciousness is. It is consciousness that operates via a single
stream of sequential events, a single channel for input and output.

This raises the question: How does a brain that operates in parallel
give rise to a consciousness that seems to be serial? Dennett claims that
it is all in the "software." Specifically, he argues that a "single track
meme" is overlaid onto the parallel architecture of the human brain.
That meme (pattern of responsiveness) operating within the space made
available by the brain's incredible plasticity, creates a *virtual* serial
machine (von Neumenesque). The key word, of course, is *virtual*. There
is no hardwired serial machine anywhere in the brain. There is, however, a virtual machine, one that exists only so long as the brain is capable of sustaining the fiction. Ultimately this meme is passed from brain
to brain as we each learn from one another how to make our brains act
as if there were a single "captain" who is directing all of our activities
when in fact almost all of our responses operate independently of one
another (ibid., 210–20).

With respect to raw processing power, the single-channel software
called "consciousness" is largely inefficient when compared to the
overall processing power of our serial hardware (the brain). The virtual
self has none of the raw processing power needed to overcome the bot-
tleneck of a serial processing unit. Moreover, the virtual self must be
laboriously constructed from data provided by competing subsystems.
Thus, according to Dennett, the so-called captain is really only a cipher

representing whichever of our response systems happens to be regnant at a particular time. Depending on the situation, visual stimuli dominate our consciousness; at other times it is hearing or touch. To maintain the illusion of unity, a great deal of information is continuously pushed into the background.

Dennett's software metaphor raises two important questions. First, if consciousness is not hardwired into the brain, then how is this "software" transmitted from one person to another? How do we learn to be conscious? Second, what good is it? After all, if Dennett wants to provide an account of the evolution of consciousness, he needs to explain the adaptive advantages of this particular meme.

With respect to the first question, Dennett argues that the habits of consciousness originated in and are passed on via language. In Dennett's speculative reconstruction, early human vocalization habits (which likely resembled those found in contemporary chimpanzees and gorillas) were designed to transmit basic information and to elicit a specific response from those who hear them. Animals that live in social groups routinely call on one another for assistance, as when one in the group is assigned to scan the horizon for danger. That individual reports by the tone and sound of its voice whether to be concerned. Dennett points out, however, that creatures capable of generating such vocalizations are simultaneously capable of hearing them as well. This fact leads him to suggest a possible explanation for the origin of self-consciousness: "Then one fine day (in this rational reconstruction), one of these hominids 'mistakenly' asked for help when there was no helpful audience within earshot—except itself! When it heard its own request the stimulation provoked just the sort of other-helping utterance production that the request from another would have caused. And to the creature's delight it found that it had just provoked itself into answering its own question" (ibid., 195). In short, Dennett is suggesting that "the practice of asking oneself questions could arise as a natural side effect of asking questions of others" (ibid.).[4] Viewed this way, there is no need for supernatural explanations of the origins of consciousness. Consciousness is a natural outgrowth of a tendency already embedded in animal behavior. All that is needed is a social animal that is dependent on vocal signals and that has a brain large enough to be both the initiator and receptor of its own signals. Moreover, Dennett points out, among creatures with large, complicated brains, this vocalized self-stimulation might even be an efficient way of communicating information from one part of its brain to another. "All that would have to be the case for this practice to have this utility is for the preexisting access-relations within the brain of an individual to be less than optimal" (ibid.). If our brains consist of an indeterminate number of specialized responsive systems, as has been suggested above, in some instances information garnered from one specialized system could be helpful to another system. When there is no "hardwired" route for sharing that information across the brain, then vocal self-stimulation could serve instead.

Over the centuries, the consciousness meme has been transmitted routinely from human to human with great efficiency, gaining refinements along the way. Dennett asks us to suppose for a "minute that there is a more or less well designed (debugged) version of this stream-of-consciousness virtual machine in the memosphere." It can be transmitted via imitation, reinforcement and training or, more likely, a combination of all three. "Think, for instance, of the sorts of habits that would be entrained by frequently saying, to a novice, 'Tell me what you are doing,' and 'Tell me why you are doing that.' Now think of the novice getting in the habit of addressing these same requests to himself" (ibid., 220). As Dennett sees it, the heart of the virtual single-channel machine that we call "consciousness" is the process of talking to oneself, stimulating oneself by asking questions that force a response. Our interactions with children around language don't just transmit the rudiments of grammatical and auditory patterns, but also teach the art of the internal monologue, which is the real source of thinking as we normally understand it.

Dennett's speculative reconstruction of the development of vocalization patterns in social animals might explain how consciousness arises, but it does not explain why it survives or what its benefits are. After all, a virtual serial processor (consciousness) will always be slower than a parallel processing brain that responds directly to the world's stimulation. Dennett argues, however, that constant self-stimulation offers distinct advantages in the areas of long-term planning and abstraction. Without this added "software," each hard-wired subsystem has only a limited ability to project into the future and anticipate changes. On Dennett's view self-consciousness begins as a form of "self-exhortation" and "self-reminding," which ultimately makes possible "long-term bouts of self-control without which agriculture, building projects, and other civilized and civilizing activities could not be organized" (ibid., 222). Viewed this way, consciousness is a tool designed for "sorting through" options and holding steady certain kinds of information and objectives while the rest of the brain proceeds apace with its various operations. This makes it clear that the hard-wired subprocesses and those that take place via the software we call "consciousness" *both* are designed to contribute to the overarching task of *constructing a future*. Viewed this way, Dennett's description of the rise of consciousness creates no separation of knowledge from action. The internal monologue, the self-exhortation, is not the free play of transcendent ideas before a mind's eye. There is no internal witness waiting to see how things turn out. It is, rather, a more complicated version of what all animals engage in as they deliberate over which among a variety of options will lead toward a desired goal (e.g., safety, food). Talking to oneself turns out to be a particularly powerful kind of action. It is a way of becoming who you are in response to the challenges that the world provides.

QUALITIES AND VALUES

At this point, I would like to return to the role that quality and value play in Dennett's epistemology. On a number of occasions, I have pointed out how Dennett's commitments to mechanistic materialism make it difficult for him to take seriously the objective reality of qualitative experience. In fact, throughout *Consciousness Explained*, Dennett sounds as if he is in league with those who seek to eliminate *all* talk of qualitative experience. For example, he points out how science seems to have "removed color from the physical world, replacing it with colorless electromagnetic radiation of various wavelengths" (ibid., 370). He also says that talk of qualitative experience is like a snarled kite string that should be abandoned rather than straightened out (ibid., 369).

> "[R]aw feels," "sensa," "phenomenal qualities," "intrinsic properties of conscious experiences," "the qualitative content of mental states," and, of course, "qualia," the term I will use. There are subtle differences in how these terms have been defined, but I'm going to ride roughshod over them. In the previous chapter I seemed to be denying that there are any such properties, and for once what seems so is so. I am denying that there are *any* such properties. But (here comes that theme again) I agree wholeheartedly that there seem to be qualia. (Ibid., 370)

Claims such as these seem to put Dennett in direct opposition to Taylor, who, as we have seen, defends the claim that qualitative and valuative experience should be understood as both real and objective rather than unreal and purely subjective. Moreover, Dennett seems to be contradicting a central premise shared by Whitehead, Dewey, and Wang Yangming. For all three quality and value have ontological status. Things are what they are by virtue of the qualitative and valuative patterns they embody. Without quality and value, there would be nothing, literally.

Contrary to Dennett's claim, however, things are not always as they seem. Though Dennett seems opposed to Taylor, Whitehead, Dewey, and Wang, I do not think he needs to be. A careful reading of chapter 12 ("Qualia Disqualified") shows that Dennett's real opponents are actually their opponents as well. Dennett's main argument is with those who follow Locke's distinction between primary and secondary qualities and the notion that our mind is filled with qualitative "ideas" that are awakened in us by sense data. Readers should recall that this "punctual" view of the self is precisely what Taylor complained about in *Sources of the Self*. Moreover, as we will see in chapters 5 and 6, both Dewey and Whitehead work hard at contradicting this version of the spectator theory of knowledge. Though Dennett's rhetoric makes it sound as if he is hoping to root out all qualitative talk from the philosophers' lexicon, he is actually working to find a way to avoid Cartesian/Lockian "ghost-in-the-machine" language as he describes *how* humans discriminate among the various qualities that we encounter in the world. In other words, as I read him (contra his own claims), Dennett's main goal is not to eliminate talk about qualities but to refine it.

Part of what leads people to the Lockian language of private ideas is the sense we have that despite the fact that we are taking in roughly similar sensory data, there is something unique about the way each of us experiences the world. Dennett argues, however, that the uniqueness of our point of view is not grounds for positing a purely private internalized immaterial self. He concedes the point that no two people "see" the world in precisely the same way, though he explains this fact by pointing to differences that contribute to the particularity of our lives rather than to some vague notion about the privacy of our innermost feelings. As Dennett points out, the human brain is capable of an almost indeterminate number of refinements. Each nervous system has its own unique history that shapes how it discriminates among various qualities and which it prefers. For example, people who like beer have refined their taste buds and nervous system in a very specific manner. To the beer drinker, beer tastes good and is sought out, while a nonbeer drinker simply does not like the taste and cannot understand why someone would. In either case, there is nothing behind the brain and taste buds, and habits (or software) that have been overlaid upon them. There is no need to presume the existence of an internal preexperiential self who likes or dislikes the way beer tastes! (ibid., 395–96). Moreover, if a nonbeer drinker wanted to know what beer tastes like to a beer drinker, he wouldn't need to cross an ontological divide and experience her world from the "inside." Rather, he would have to train his brain and taste buds to appreciate the world as she does. Of course, while it may be possible to cultivate a similar appreciation for the advantages offered by a good cool beer on a hot summer day, he could never duplicate her experience in precise detail. Therefore, there will always be something ineffable about an attempt to appreciate her point of view. But this has to do with the indeterminate complexities of life lived in a real world, rather than the ontological isolation of solipsistic selves.

To understand why Dennett sounds at first as if he is opposed to all talk about quality and value, we have to return to his ambivalent use of mechanistic metaphors. Readers will recall my complaint that Dennett waffles when he discusses the earliest organisms (he calls them "replicators"). On the one hand, he describes their actions as simple mechanisms. On the other hand, he uses them to account for the advent of purpose and value into what was previously a purely causal, non-teleological world. If one were to emphasize Dennett's mechanistic language and couple it with his critique of traditional talk about qualities and values, then he sounds like a reductionist for whom the scientific descriptions of qualitative experience (e.g., color is really radiation) are final and complete.

It is possible, however, to push Dennett in another direction. Were Dennett to play down his commitment to mechanistic materialism and adopt instead a metaphysical point of view that allows him to highlight the organic side of his story, he would stop sounding so reductionistic. What if, for example, Dennett were to give up the language of simple mechanisms when discussing early organisms and lean more heavily upon his point that replicators are centers of purposeful activity. All organisms are engaged in qualitative and evaluative assessments relative to specific objectives. Granted, some are more rudimentary than others. But ultimately, every organism is nothing more than a set of processes with a particular set of evolving objectives that it is struggling to realize within the broader matrix of organisms that make up its environment. Such a point of view, which is much closer to the way Dewey, Whitehead, and Wang might describe things, could accommodate Dennett's antirepresentationalism. There is no need to posit ghosts in machines. At the same time, however, it could handle the pragmatic, process, and Neo-Confucian conviction that qualities and values are objective and real. The reductionistic language that flows so easily from Dennett's pen would be countered by a fuller description of the role that quality and value play in all organic activity.

In all honesty, I do not really know how Dennett would react to such a reading. In part, this book aims to make such a reading seem plausible. At this point, however, it is time to turn away from contemporary thinkers and look back to what Wang, Dewey, and Whitehead have to say on these issues. So, let me end the discussion of Dennett by summarizing what I think we have learned. I find Dennett's rejection of the Cartesian theater and his introduction of the multiple drafts theory of consciousness to be particularly helpful attempts to find a way around the sorts of assumptions that have locked us into representational approaches to the theory of knowledge. Moreover, as I read him, his evolutionary understanding of the rise of consciousness is compatible with positions outlined by pragmatists such as Dewey and Mead, as well as process thinkers such as Whitehead. Most important, Dennett's whole approach to this topic leads him into a position that supports my basic claim that knowledge and action are really one thing. For Dennett, consciousness has little to do with the static contemplation of purely mental entities. Instead, it is an activity designed to "create a future" for an organism that is struggling to adjust to a constantly changing environment. Throughout this chapter, I have found reason to criticize Dennett's lapses into representationalist language and his rejection of qualia (and concomitantly values). Instead, I've tried to show how by adopting alternative metaphysical assumptions Dennett could retain most of what he has accomplished while opening his position to advantages found in the pragmatic, process, and Neo-Confucian claim that knowledge and action are really one thing.

Part II

PRELIMINARY REMARKS

The quest for a nonrepresentational theory of knowledge has many fronts. We have seen Taylor's critique of the "punctual self," David-son/Rorty's rejection of "scheme-content" dualism, and Dennett's attempt to frame a description of consciousness without a Cartesian the-ater. In each instance, I have also tried to show how Wang Yang-ming, John Dewey, and Alfred North Whitehead have important contributions to make to these contemporary conversations. Specifically, I have been arguing that these three figures bring to the conversation alternative metaphysical visions that render plausible the nonrepresentational approach to epistemological questions. In part 2 we will look directly at these metaphysical claims and their relationship to epistemology.

Chapter 4 argues that Wang means us to take literally his slogan *chih hsing ho-i* (the unity of knowledge and action). Too often Western commentators have turned to psychological, pedagogical, or political explanations to make "sense" of Wang's slogan. I argue that when seen in the context of Neo-Confucian organismic metaphysics, the idea that knowledge is always a kind of action makes sense as a literal statement.

By leading off with Wang, I am retracing my own route into the questions dealt with in this book. As I mentioned in the preliminary remarks to part 1, Wang's slogan set the stage for my own rereading of Dewey and Whitehead. My hope is that the arguments in chapter 4 will lead readers to find parallel claims in Dewey and Whitehead that rein-force and extend Wang's conclusions (Frisina, 1986; 1987).

In chapter 5 I argue that according to Dewey, knowledge is best understood as active, aesthetic, and hypothetical. Dewey posits a dynamic universe whose fundamental entities are forms of relatedness rather than substances. Moreover, he argues that aesthetic feelings dominate the "experiential realm" and that an organism is a set of processes that is con-stantly projecting itself into an indeterminate future. For Dewey knowl-edge is *active* (since all organisms are engaged in transitional relations), *aesthetic* rather than representational (because qualitative feelings form the basis for organic activity), and *hypothetical* (because an organism is always projecting itself forward into an indeterminate future).

Chapter 6 draws directly from arguments in chapter 5 as I develop a pragmatic reading of epistemological implications in Whitehead's cosmology. Specifically, I argue that Whitehead's "theory of feelings" leads to conclusions that parallel Dewey's claim that knowledge is active, aesthetic, and hypothetical. This chapter aims at setting Whitehead's central epistemological conclusions within the more nearly common language of the pragmatic tradition.

In the end, this whole section forms the argumentative heart of the book. It aims to display for readers the specific contributions these three thinkers have to make to the overarching effort to frame a nonrepresentational theory of knowledge. My expectation is that as readers grow more familiar with the positions, it will become clearer why the criticisms developed by Taylor, Davidson, Rorty, and Dennett simply do not apply to these thinkers. Most important, when all is said and done, this section should provide readers with some insight into the metaphysical moves that are necessary to develop a nonrepresentational theory of knowledge. Moreover, it will amplify and in some cases provide a fuller defense of claims made in part 1 where I argued that Whitehead, Dewey, and Wang were relevant to contemporary philosophical efforts to construct a nonrepresentational theory of knowledge.

CHAPTER 4

Are Knowledge and Action
Really One Thing?
Wang Yang-ming's Doctrine of Mind

In the phrase *chih hsing ho-i* (the unity of knowledge and action), Wang Yang-ming focuses our attention on the fact that knowing something is equivalent to reconstructing our relationship with it. By reconstruction he meant more than a reformation of purely cognitive attitudes. For Wang, our relationships with things constitute the essence of our being. Knowledge and action are one because there is no purely mental/subjective realm to be set over against a purely physical/objective realm. In this chapter I examine what Wang meant by *chih hsing ho-i*, setting this slogan into the context of his own thought and that of his Neo-Confucian predecessors. My aim is to demonstrate that Wang intended his phrase literally. Knowledge and action are, in all their forms, *really one thing*. Wang developed the doctrine of *chih hsing ho-i* to render the epistemological presuppositions of his day consistent with the central metaphysical claims of the Confucian tradition as he understood them. In short, to understand *chih hsing ho-i*, we must begin with its metaphysical presuppositions.

THE INITIAL RESPONSE TO *CHIH HSING HO-I*

The unity of knowledge and action is not a self-evident assertion. In Wang's *Instructions for Practical Living* there are many descriptions of his students' confusion over the issue. They reacted as most of us would when confronted with the claim that knowledge and action are originally one thing. On the surface knowledge and action appear separate and sequentially related. First we know something and then we act on it. First our mind forms an image of what we should do and then it somehow commands the body to act accordingly. First we formulate principles and then we use them to guide our actions. These commonsense divisions of mental concepts and physical actions are at the heart of most mind/body dualisms. Articulating exactly how mentality engenders physical acts is the fundamental problem for all such dualistic positions.

It is important to keep in mind, however, that Wang did *not* develop the doctrine of *chih hsing ho-i* to resolve the Western ontological dualism between mind and body. That kind of dualism was simply not an option for him or his students. Instead, his goal was to remove an *epistemological* dualism that focused a student's attention on learning before action. For example, in the *Instructions*, one of Wang's students reveals his sense that knowledge and action are separate and sequentially related when he says: "There are people who know that parents should be served with filial piety and elder brothers with respect but cannot put these things into practice. This shows that knowledge and action are clearly two different things" (1963, 10). The tendency among Wang's students (and colleagues) to separate knowledge from action was a product of the way they interpreted the then orthodox teachings of Chu Hsi (1130–1220 BCE). In Wang's day, Chu's reinterpretation of the Confucian tradition had earned a kind of preeminence that made it very difficult to question. Though some twentieth-century scholars now debate whether Chu Hsi intended to posit such a radical split between knowing and acting, most sixteenth-century readers thought that he did. Wang was struggling to overcome what he took to be pernicious implications stemming from this "misreading" of Chu Hsi's philosophy. As Wang saw it, such a division violated the spirit of the Confucian metaphysical tradition. His slogan *chih hsing ho-i* was a counterbalance, designed to protect his students' efforts at spiritual cultivation by developing in them a deeper appreciation for the key insights of the Confucian tradition that the orthodox position seemed to be ignoring.

In the twentieth century, some interpreters of Wang's philosophy try to transform Wang's slogan into a form that is compatible with more familiar (e.g., Cartesian, Kantian) theories of the mind and self (Cua, 1982; 2001). To do this, however, they tend to limit the applicability of Wang's slogan to *practical* knowledge only. From this perspective *chih hsing ho-i* points to a moral ideal that is rarely achieved rather than an objective statement about the structure of knowledge in all its forms. Thus, for some, *chih hsing ho-i* is not a general claim about all forms of knowledge. It is rather a statement that cognitive knowledge alone is insufficient within the realm of practical discourse.

I will say more about such interpretations in a moment. For now it is important to understand that I take literally Wang's statement that knowledge and action are unified in their original substance. I find support for my reading in some contemporary commentators, such as Tu Wei-ming (1978, 93), as well as in Wang's own words: "This doctrine of knowledge first and action later is not a minor disease and it did not come about only yesterday. My present advocacy of the unity of knowledge and action is precisely the medicine for that disease. The doctrine is not my baseless imagination, for it is *the original substance of knowledge and action that they are one*" (1963, 11; italics added). Wang seems to be saying that those of us who fall short of sagehood fail to recognize the unity of knowledge and action. We feel as if the two are separate when they are not. Sages do not achieve a complete integration of knowledge and action, for that already exists. Knowledge is always a form of action. Sages clear away the selfish desires that prevent us from recognizing this underlying unity. These same selfish desires are also the obstacles that prevent us from responding truly to the world around us. In brief, for Wang so-called pure cognitive knowledge simply does not exist. To believe that it does is a fundamental epistemological mistake that can lead to erroneous pedagogical methods, as was evident to Wang from his own struggles and the difficulties of his colleagues and students.

There are at least two reasons why scholars might shy away from this more literal reading of Wang's position. First, Wang makes statements that seem to allow for the sequential reading. For example: "I have said that knowledge is the direction for action and action the effort of knowledge, and that knowledge is the beginning of action and action the completion of knowledge. If this is understood, then when only knowledge is mentioned, action is included, and when only action is mentioned, knowledge is included" (Chan, 1963, 669). In another place he says: "Knowledge is the beginning of action and action is the completion of knowledge. Learning to be a sage involves only one effort. Knowledge and action should not be separated" (Wang, 1963, 30). Statements such as these give the impression that knowledge and action are different elements within a complex unit of experience. They are bound together, but not interpenetrating.

A second reason for limiting the application of *chih hsing ho-i* to practical knowledge is that such an interpretation is more compatible with representational-spectator theories of knowledge. If the *chih* (knowledge) in *chih hsing ho-i* refers *only* to practical knowledge (knowledge that is expected to engender action), then Wang's doctrine need have no impact on so-called purely cognitive forms of knowledge. Pure mental activity would not be connected to action. When it is connected to action, it is called "practical knowledge." Adopting this stance is the path of least resistance for many Western commentators. It is a natural response to a somewhat unusual slogan. It does not require that we reconstruct our understanding of mind and what it means to think. Instead, Wang's doctrine seems limited to the largely mundane claim that within the realm of practical knowledge *real* practical knowledge will always have some effect on the way we act.

As I see it, however, it is hard to explain why Wang would spend so much effort expressing what every Confucian already believed. Genuine practical knowledge always produces moral action. No Confucian could doubt that. Wang, however, was dealing with a different problem. He was struggling to understand why so many good Confucian scholars led themselves into academic dead ends, away from true spiritual development. His answer was that they had made a fundamental epistemological mistake at the beginning of their studies. By assuming they could study questions first and then put their knowledge into action, they missed the essential point that they had to begin by renovating themselves. This involved not simply asking the right questions but also forming the resolve to begin a quest that would alter their behavior. The quest for sagehood could not begin with abstract knowledge because it required a new existential beginning. (Tu, 1976, 169) Scholars made the mistake of replacing abstract information with true knowledge because, as Wang pointed out, they were mistaken about the very structure of knowledge. Knowledge, according to Wang, is not just "in the head"; it is a way of being in relation to that which is real. Ultimately, we know that knowledge is action because the correction of knowledge entails the renovation of ourselves. This position is most evident in Wang's *Inquiry on the Great Learning,* where he spells out his claim that the investigation of things *(ko wu)* is actually a renovation of oneself in an effort to attain the sincerity of will that enables us to deal with the world truly (Wang, 1963, 279).

Before turning to a defense of this reading of Wang's slogan, I would like to highlight the work of one commentator who takes a position similar to the one against which I am arguing. In *The Unity of Knowledge and Action: A Study in Wang Yang-ming's Moral Psychology,* A. S. Cua presents an extraordinarily sophisticated explanation of the moral psychology implied in Wang's doctrine from the perspective of Cua's own notion of "prospective" and "retrospective" moral knowledge. Early in this work he says: "I suggest that the question underlying Wang's doctrine of the unity of moral knowledge and action pertains essentially to understanding the *actuating import* rather than the *cognitive content* of moral knowledge" (1982, 5; italics added). By focusing on the actuating import of moral knowledge rather than its cognitive content, Cua restricts Wang's doctrine to one very specific kind of knowledge, that which precedes and issues into action. By limiting Wang's slogan to practical knowledge, Cua opens up the possibility that Wang did not mean it to apply to so-called cognitive knowledge. Cua makes this explicit when he says, "Moral knowledge, however we describe or justify its content, is a form of practical knowledge in the sense of possessing an actuating import" (ibid.). He analyzes Wang's understanding of moral knowledge only from within this severely circumscribed description of what Wang meant by *chih* (knowledge) in *chih hsing ho-i.*

Prospective moral knowledge, being anterior to action, is an acknowledgment of the projective significance of moral requirements as a guide to one's life. It anticipates the character of moral experience. . . . When understanding is unobscured and followed by appropriate action, it will eventuate in retrospective moral knowledge. It is a personal moral experience, an experience derived from encounter and participation in human affairs. (Ibid., 15)

Equipped with this definition of moral knowledge Cua is able to explain Wang's anomalous statements such as "Knowledge is the beginning of action and action the completion of knowledge." For Cua, when knowledge is the beginning of action, it is prospective knowledge anticipating the moral dimensions of a situation. When action is viewed as the completion of knowledge, it engenders retrospective moral knowledge that is knowledge confirmed by actual experiences in the world (ibid., 69).

The bulk of Cua's book describes the complicated processes that constitute the shift from prospective to retrospective knowledge. While I am largely in agreement with Cua's insightful analysis of the process of moral decision making, I disagree with the claim that Wang did not intend his doctrine to apply to knowledge in all its forms. I am convinced instead that Wang was trying to bring the Confucian epistemology of his day into alignment with its metaphysical insights. He was pointing out that Confucian metaphysics *requires* that we think of mind and knowledge in ways different from those to which common sense would lead us.

The initial limitations Cua places on his definition of *chih* preclude him from taking into account the metaphysical considerations that I feel are so important to understanding Wang's position. Cua intended to present a description of Wang's moral psychology independent of the metaphysical controversies that are common in Wang commentaries. As I see it, however, the bracketing of metaphysical considerations obscures rather than clarifies things. Cua, of course, does not claim that metaphysical reflection played no role in Wang's thinking (ibid., 3; also 2001). Nevertheless, for the purpose of clarity he tries to separate *chih hsing ho-i* from other metaphysical concepts central to Wang's philosophy. But the keys to understanding *chih hsing ho-i* are located within the metaphysical presuppositions that render it meaningful and in the metaphysical concepts that follow from it. The former set the stage, while the latter, by completing the thought, render it a much more coherent doctrine. Wang wanted to say something very different about knowledge and action, and he could do so because he had the metaphysical arguments to back his epistemological claims. To fail to see this is to fail to take seriously the radicalness of Wang's doctrine.

In a subsequent article, Cua argues that Wang's focus on pragmatic rather than theoretical concerns supports Cua's own willingness to bracket metaphysical issues. Wang did regularly warn his students not to get lost in abstract discussions. His aim was always the pursuit of sagehood, which he argued must begin with an inner commitment *(t'ou-nao)*, not abstract ideas (Cua, 2001). While never ruling out the metaphysical implications of Wang's thought, Cua does not see in Wang an explicit concern with metaphysical issues. In describing some of the technical terms Wang uses, Cua says: "Viewed from the perspective of practical understanding, these terms have no explanatory value in theoretical discourse. In other words, the terms are best construed as indicative of the ways of practical understanding" (ibid.). We can see from the above statements that Cua treats metaphysics as purely theoretical discourse separate from the realm of practical discourse. In discussing Wang's understanding of *li,* Cua contrasts Chu Hsi's explicit interest in metaphysical issues with Wang's practical concerns. "Unlike Chu Hsi, Wang has no metaphysical interest in accounting for the existence of things. Thus, the explanatory and descriptive uses of *li* do not help us in interpreting his doctrine. Only the normative use of *li* is at issue" (ibid.). It seems to me, however, that it *is* possible to retain Wang's focus on spiritual cultivation as well as the claim that he is concerned with metaphysical issues. This can be accomplished by rethinking what we mean by metaphysics. If Wang is correct and knowledge and action are truly one thing, then *purely theoretical* discourse is simply impossible. This does not entail the abandonment of metaphysics, but rather the reinterpretation of what we are doing when we do metaphysics. Metaphysical thinking becomes a form of action. *Chih hsing ho-i* breaks down the boundaries between theoretical and practical discourse and opens us to a whole new understanding of thought and the human mind. Cua's interpretation of Wang, though informative within its own parameters, does not make room for consequences as radical as these.

My concern in the following pages is to preserve the radical implications of Wang's *chih hsing ho-i* by uncovering those metaphysical concerns that Cua thinks should be put aside for the sake of clarity. My strategy for supporting this literal reading of Wang's slogan will be to discuss five metaphysical presuppositions that are built into Wang's theory of knowledge. I will end this chapter by exploring the implications these claims have for Wang's assertion that knowledge and action are truly one thing.

DYNAMIC CHARACTER OF BEING

The first presupposition is ontological, having to do with the structure of Being. The dynamic character of Being is an ontological presupposition consistent throughout much of Chinese intellectual history. Most Chinese thinkers viewed the universe as a single creative matrix that contains all manner of processes (i.e., creatures). To be something is to be a part of that dynamic activity. In describing the ancient Chinese ontology, Tu Wei-ming said: "The organismic process [is] a spontaneously self-generating life process [that] exhibits three basic motifs: continuity, wholeness, and dynamism" (1985, 38). Joseph Needham, who saw in China an early precursor to Whiteheadian process philosophies, made similar statements (1956, 291–92). The adoption of this process attitude reaches all the way back to the *I Ching* and is found consistently in Confucian, Taoist, and Buddhist thought in all of their varying manifestations (Mote, 1971, 19, 28).

For our purposes, we need only note that the primary figures who preceded Wang within the Neo-Confucian tradition all adhered to one or another form of this process vision (de Bary, 1981). For example, Chou Tun-i (1017–1073) begins *An Explanation of the Diagram of the Great Ultimate* by saying:

> The Ultimate of Non-being and also the Great Ultimate *(T'ai-chi)!* The Great Ultimate through movement generates *yang.* When its activity reaches its limit, it becomes tranquil. Through tranquillity the Great Ultimate generates *yin.* When tranquillity reaches its limit, activity begins again. So movement and tranquillity alternate and become the root of each other, giving rise to the distinction of *yin* and *yang,* and the two modes are thus established. (Chan, 1963, 463)

According to Chou, the Great Ultimate contains all things and is a pattern of movements from tranquillity *(yin)* to activity *(yang)* and back again. Chang Tsai (1020–1077), a contemporary of Chou develops a very different line of thinking on many issues but is in agreement with Chou over this process ontology. He says:

> As the great Vacuity, material force *[ch'i]* is extensive and vague. Yet it ascends and descends and moves in all ways without ever ceasing. This is what is called in the Book of Changes "fusion and intermingling" and in the Chuang Tzu "fleeting forces moving in all directions while all living beings blow against one another with their breath." Here lies the subtle, incipient activation of reality and unreality, of motion and rest, and the beginning of *yin* and *yang,* as well as the elements of strength and weakness. (Ibid., 503)

These are just two examples of what could be shown many times over. Notice that by citing Chuang Tzu (between 399 and 295 BCE), Chang is willing to recognize this process ontology as an insight available to Taoists as well as Confucians. I do not want to say that all Chinese thinkers think alike on this issue. I only mean to point out that it is a common starting point for their deliberations. Each tradition, and each individual within the traditions, develops variations on this process theme.

Wang illustrates his own understanding of the dynamic character of existence in the following statement: "In the dynamic operation of the material force of the universe there is from the beginning not a moment of rest. But there is the master. Consequently the operation has its regular order and it goes on neither too fast nor too slowly. The master [that is, the wonderful functioning of creation] is always calm in spite of hundreds of changes and thousands of transformations. This process makes it possible for man to live" (Wang, 1963, 66). After this passage Wang goes on to relate this explicitly dynamic understanding of *ch'i* (material force) to his understanding of *hsin* (heart-mind). He continues: "If, while the master remains calm, the mind is ceaseless as heavenly movements are ceaseless, it will always be at ease in spite of countless changes in its dealings with things" (ibid., 67). This link between a dynamic universe and a dynamic *hsin* provides part of the metaphysical rationale for Wang's claim that knowledge and action are originally one thing. According to Wang the sage establishes an equilibrium within the constant movements that constitute the universe. In pursuing sagehood we seek to maximize our integration with the macrocosmic movements or order (the master). Thus *hsin's* movements are a subset of the overall dynamic activity that constitutes the universe. This underscores the ontological continuity between human existence and nature. The "knowledge" *hsin* produces must be understood from within this dynamic continuity. As such, knowledge is ultimately identified with the movements as they occur. It is not a product existing outside an objective reality that is known by the mind. For Wang, there are not two realms of being, one mental, the other physical. There is only one realm, and that realm is essentially dynamic (Ching, 1976).

The full justification for this description of the dynamic character of cognition does not finally emerge until Wang promulgates his later theory that our *liang-chih* (innate knowledge) is identified with *ch'i* (material force) itself. I will turn to this topic shortly.

YIN/YANG

The quotes cited above make clear that Chang Tsai, Chou Tun-i, and Wang are not referring to random change, but to *patterned* creative activity. This brings us to the second metaphysical presupposition underlying Wang's theory of knowledge, namely, that the things that make up the universe should be understood as the interaction of vibratory wave patterns of *yin* contraction and *yang* extension (Neville, 1982, 150). On this view, each entity is a rhythmic pattern of *yin/yang* alternations. Resonating with one another, such patterns form the unceasing movement of *T'ai Chi.*

If existence is predicated on participation within the dynamic activity of *T'ai Chi,* and that activity is structured according to patterned relationships of *yang* extension and *yin* contraction, then the boundaries that define entities are necessarily transparent and continuous. On this point Robert Neville has observed:

> The genius of Wang's tradition was that it saw true human integrity to consist in making one's personal organization more rather than less responsive to external changes. One's personal borders should be optimally diaphanous and responsive, not opaque and defensive, so that it makes sense to say that the ideal is 'being one body with the world,' one body in the sense of a shifting resonating sensitivity of oneself to all other things. (1985, 286)

Along the same lines Tu Wei-ming says

> To them [traditional Chinese thinkers] the appropriate metaphor for understanding the universe was biology rather than physics. At issue was not the eternal, static structure but the dynamic process of growth and transformation. To say that the cosmos is a continuum and that all of its components are internally connected is also to say that it is an organismic unity, holistically integrated at each level of complexity. (1985, 39)

The idea of a permanent substantialist entity standing independent of other entities is untenable within this ontological framework. Instead, each entity is what it is through the relations or harmonies its own patterns set up within a world that is nothing but patterned movement.

We can see these metaphysical principles operating in the way Wang links his understanding of *yin/yang* with his claim that we should work to "form one body with all things." In trying to explain to a student the difference between Ch'eng Hao's claim that the sage regards Heaven, Earth, and all things as one body and Mo Tzu's doctrine of universal love, Wang says:

> Humanity is the principle of unceasing production and reproduction. Although it is prevalent and extensive and there is no place where it does not exist, nevertheless there is an order in its operation and growth. That is why it is unceasing in production and reproduction. For example, at the winter solstice first *yang* grows. There must be growth of this first *yang* before all the six stages of *yang* gradually grow. If there were not the first *yang*, could there be all the six? It is the same with the *yin*. Because there is order, so there is a starting

point. Because there is a starting point, so there is growth. And because there is growth, it is unceasing. . . . The love between father and son and between elder and younger brothers is the starting point of the human mind's spirit of life, just like the sprout of the tree. From here it is extended to humaneness to all people and love to all things. It is just like the growth of the trunk, branches and leaves. (1963, 56–57)

In both of these statements, Wang's point is that there is an order (or pattern) to the way things proceed. We should not form our human relationships (for example) indiscriminately, as the Moists claim they do. Rather, we must seek to cultivate patterns of *yin/yang* alternation that pick up on and respond to the natural patterns in the movements of the things that surround us. Thus, *yin/yang* patterning is a common matrix presupposed by the sage who seeks to form one body with all things.

The sage can form one body with all things because his own existence is also a pattern of *yin/yang* alternations. The boundaries that divide the world into discrete entities are overcome by the sage who recognizes his continuity with all things and adjusts his own *yin/yang* patterns in ways that maximize their potential for harmonic integration. These patterns, therefore, are not preexisting or permanent. They are created within concrete situations. We all exist as *yin/yang* patterns, or as I will later call them, harmonies, which bring the elements of the world into a new perspective on the world (ibid., 56–57).

Along these lines, Wang has sometimes been accused of being a subjective idealist who reduces all things to some form of mentality. I think this goes too far and would rather note simply that Wang accepts the metaphysical premise that things are internally related to one another. Nothing exists independently. When Wang points out to a student that a flower required his *hsin* (heart-mind) to awaken its colors, he was not reducing the flower to a mental image; he was acknowledging the ontological interdependence of flowers and humans (or any color-sensitive organism) with respect to the existence of color (ibid.). This affirmation of ontological interdependence blocks any attempt to set up a dichotomy between subject and object. If the subject and object cannot be separated, then there is no "knower" standing apart from and observing all that is "known." Knowing is always a way of adjusting to patterned movements, rather than a grasping of the essence of an independent entity.

Once we establish that all entities are patterns of *yin/yang* interactions and that they are internally related to one another, the next point to note is that all patterns have a qualitative dimension as well. At a minimum, bare existence entails the simple alternation of *yin* and *yang*. It is possible, however, to go beyond this bare minimum and cultivate patterns that are more complicated than those necessary to establish mere existence. In fact, the cultivation of more complicated harmonic patterning is the ontological task undertaken by the Confucian sage. By rectifying the self, the sage creates new harmonies that enhance the quality of one's own being and contribute to the whole of things. Thus, the knowledge associated with Confucian sagehood is always a form of action, a creative response to the world's prompting. It is never a mere cognitive collection of sensory data within a separate "mental" faculty. To get a clearer sense of the Neo-Confucian understanding of the qualitative dimension of these patterns, we turn to *li* (principle or principle of nature), the next metaphysical premise underlying Wang's claim that knowledge and action are one thing.

LI

Li is described by Wing-tsit Chan in his *A Sourcebook in Chinese Philosophy*.

> As conceived and understood by the brothers [Ch'eng], principle is self-evident and self-sufficient, extending everywhere and governing all things. It cannot be augmented or diminished. It is many but it is essentially one, for all specific principles are but principle. It is possessed by all people and all things. Even a very small thing has principle. It is laid before our very eyes. Man and all things form one body because all of them share this principle. To be sincere is to be sincere to it, and to be serious is to be serious about it. In short, it is one and all. It is identical with the mind and it is identical with nature. All things exist because of it and can be understood through it. It is universal truth, universal order, universal law. *Most important of all, it is a universal process of creation and production. It is dynamic and vital.* (1963, 519; italics added)

Thus, the single concept *li* contains two somewhat contradictory notions. On the one hand, *Li* is self-sufficient, unified, and cannot be augmented. Viewed this way, *Li* is harmony-itself, the barest patterning that all other patterns presuppose, and the ultimate source of all patterning. From this perspective *Li* is the unchanging container and generator of all harmonic principles, a never-ending fountain of *li* (patterns), which arise in conjunction with the dynamic activity of *ch'i* in the constitution of new entities. On the other hand, *li* is also the specific pattern that defines each entity. For purposes of clarity I capitalize *li* when referring to it in its universal sense, and leave it in lowercase when referring to individual instances of *li*.[1]

As the universal source of all patterns *Li* leaves no room for the subject-object dichotomy on which the spectator theory of mind depends.

There is no individual *li* (pattern) that is not drawn from and completely dependent on the creative unity of all the other patterns. Each pattern is what it is in relation to the others. Since even the patterns themselves are interdependent, there can be no perspective from which a mind could apprehend a static, objective order. Chan's emphasis on the dynamic character of *Li* is crucial here. He said *Li* is "a universal process of creation and production. It is dynamic and vital." All that can be felt are patterns of movement, and the feeler must be moving within the movement as well, ultimately reinforcing Wang's claim that knowledge must always be action.

There are, of course, other interpretations of *Li* within the Confucian and Neo-Confucian traditions. I highlight Chan's interpretation of a dynamic *Li* because it is compatible with my own understanding of Wang's statements on *Li*. For example in the *Instructions*, Wang says: "The mean is nothing but the Principle of Nature; it is the Change. It changes according to the time. How can one hold it fast? One must act according to the circumstance. It is difficult to fix a pattern of action in advance. Later scholars insist on describing principles in their minute details, leaving out nothing and prescribing a rigid pattern for action. This is the exact meaning of holding on to one particular thing" (1963, 42). The importance of Wang's insistence on a dynamic understanding of *Li* will become more apparent when we turn to his discussions of the link between *Li* and *hsin* (mind). If knowledge and action are really one thing, and *hsin* is in some sense identified with *Li*, then *Li* must be essentially dynamic, or the movements of the human mind will ultimately be illusory.

ONE BODY WITH ALL THINGS

Wang's moral imperative that we should act so as to form "one body with all things" also exhibits the internal relatedness of all things and the potential for creating harmonies that go beyond the minimum required for bare existence. It is therefore the fourth metaphysical presupposition central to Wang's claim that knowledge and action are fully unified.

The formation of one body with all things is accomplished by extending *li* in ways not previously realized. As we have seen, mere existence implies minimal participation in the harmonic structures of *Li*. Nevertheless, to be something specific requires the enactment of harmonic principles (patterns) that go beyond this minimal level of mere existence. Such *li* are the outcome of new and thicker relations, which create more complex harmonies where simple ones prevailed before. Forming one body with all things means maximizing the harmonic possibilities within any given situation. "The man of humanity regards Heaven and Earth and all things as one body. If a single thing is deprived of its place, it means that my humanity is not yet demonstrated to the fullest extent" (ibid., 56). Wang does not mean, however, that we merely "experience" the world as a unity. He is claiming that at the fundamental ontological level, it already is a unity. This becomes fully clear in his later years when he elaborates his system to include what he calls *"liang-chih"* (innate knowledge).

> The innate knowledge of man is the same as that of plants and trees, tiles and stones. Without the innate knowledge inherent in man, there cannot be plants and trees, tiles and stones. This is not true of them only. Even Heaven and Earth cannot exist without the innate knowledge that is inherent in man. *For at bottom Heaven, Earth, the myriad things, and man form one body.* The point at which this unity is manifested in its most refined and excellent form is the clear intelligence of the human mind. Wind, rain, dew, thunder, sun and moon, stars, animals and plants, mountains and rivers, earth and stones are essentially of one body with man. It is for this reason that such things as the grains and animals can nourish man and that such things as medicine and minerals can heal diseases. Since they share the same material force, they enter into one another. (Ibid., 221–22; italics added)

Thus, we are both already one body and striving to become one body with all things. We are *already* one body because all things are patterned alternations of *yin* and *yang* within a single all-encompassing *Li,* the source for all patterning. We seek to *become* one body by striving to create new, more complex ways of linking ourselves to the things that constitute our world. The sage acts to make this ontological unity manifest by building upon the interdependence of all things.

The complete defense of this reading of Wang's injunction to become one body with all things depends on having all five of its metaphysical presuppositions on the table. When we recognize that *chih hsing ho-i* presupposes a dynamic process ontology, *yin-yang,* the doctrine of *Li,* the formation of one body with all things, and the doctrine of *ch'eng,* it becomes possible to see how Wang could argue that on the ontological level, we are already one body with all things, while on the ontic level (the level of human moral experience), that underlying unity is not fully manifest. Moreover, as we have just seen in the previous citation, this position is ultimately confirmed in his later understanding of *liang-chih*'s implications.

The doctrine of forming one body with all things highlights Wang's naturalism, a position that allows him to assert consistently that there is genuine continuity among all forms of existence when they are understood as patterns of *yin* and *yang* alternations. Metaphysically, this underlying unity is a fact that it is our task to make manifest. Describing an ideal community Wang says: "For the learning of their mind was pure and clear and had what was requisite to preserve the humanity that makes them and all things form one body. Consequently their spirit ran through and permeated all and their will prevailed and reached everywhere. There was no distinction between the self and the other, or between the self and things. It is like the body of a person" (ibid., 120–21). Wang's metaphor is particularly apt. A body is a highly complicated interactive physical system whose parts support one another. At the same time, all those parts act in concert with one another and with the broader environment that sustains them, making possible the emergence of the human self. This perspective is similar to Dewey's claim that selves emerge within a broad transactional continuum (Neville, 1985; Odin, 1996).[2]

Wang found that the Confucians of his day were fundamentally dualistic in their epistemology, even though they shared his own view of the universe as a vast transactional field. Scholars operated as if there were a knowing order, where one garnered a cognitive awareness of *Li* and a physical order where the knowledge of *Li* was put to use in transforming *ch'i* (material force). It is important to note that in rejecting epistemological dualism, Wang was appealing to his understanding that the traditional Confucian ontology would not admit dualisms in any form, including any attempt to view *Li* and *ch'i* as separate. We are all one body because we all participate in the same dynamic *ch'i* and the same universal *Li,* with both of those concepts understood as ways of describing the internally related movement of Tao.

CH'ENG AS COMMON CREATIVE CONTEXT

As I read it, *chih hsing ho-i* represents Wang's reaffirmation of the Confucian position that there exists a profound continuity between human creativity and that creativity that is the source of all things. From this perspective human creativity must be understood as a species of the same universal creativity described above.[3] This is made even clearer if we examine Wang's understanding of *ch'eng* (sincerity), the fifth and final metaphysical presupposition underlying his doctrine of *chih hsing ho-i.*

In Confucian terms *ch'eng* is not simply an emotion that accompanies action. It represents the ideal manner in which humans participate in the creative processes of the universe. When our actions fulfill *ch'eng* they maximize the possibilities inherent within the creative process. To act without *ch'eng* is to act destructively, without direction. Such actions may have some minimal value (because to be at all is to exhibit a minimal pattern of *yin/yang* vibration). They are, however, far inferior to what could be accomplished if one were acting with *ch'eng*. To act with *ch'eng* is to become a full partner with Heaven and Earth in the creative transformation of existence.

In this interpretation of *ch'eng* I follow Tu Wei-ming who demonstrates in the monograph *Centrality and Commonality: An Essay on Confucian Religiousness* that a metaphysical interpretation of *ch'eng* is already present in early Confucian documents such as the *Chung-yung*. "Indeed, it can be further suggested that in *Chung-yung* not only human beings but things *(wu)* in general are also thought to be enactments of *ch'eng*. And since the cosmos is conceived as the effortless self-unfolding of *ch'eng*, nothing can come into existence without it. Thus, 'sincerity is the beginning and end of things. Without sincerity there would be nothing'" (1989, 80). According to Tu, in the classical Confucian tradition, *ch'eng* undergirds the organismic process ontology I have been outlining. In a sense, *ch'eng* represents primordial creativity, aspects of which are later thematized in the Neo-Confucian concepts of *ch'i* and *li*.

Wang Yang-ming takes the *Chung-yung's* understanding of *ch'eng* as a starting point and uses it to express his own vision of humankind's role in the creative processes of the universe. (Ching, 1976, 139). In the *Instructions* Wang says: "As to the doctrine of the sincerity of the will, it is of course the first principle which the Confucian school teaches people so that they may know how to go about their task, but recent scholars have regarded it as of secondary importance. For this reason I have to some extent pointed out the importance of sincerity. It is not something I am propagating for my own purposes" (1963, 91).

In this next passage Wang draws a link between the metaphysical understanding of *ch'eng* as it is presented in the *Chung-yung,* the more programmatic outline of human responsibility in the *Great Learning,* and his own understanding of the priority of the will in the pursuit of sagehood: "The teaching in the *Doctrine of the Mean* that 'Without sincerity there would be nothing,' and the effort to manifest one's clear character described in the *Great Learning* mean nothing more than the effort to make the will sincere. And the work of making the will sincere is none other than the investigation of things" (ibid., 15).

Wang uses *Chung-yung* and its central notion *ch'eng* to demonstrate that Heaven, Earth, and Humankind are bound together in a single matrix of creative activity and that the way for humans to maximize the possibilities within this triad is through the perfection of the human will. He does not, however, mean a will located on a separate mental plane. Rather, he points to a will that is the first step in actualizing the harmonic relations constituting our very being. *Ch'eng* is, therefore, an

essential element of *ko wu* (the investigation of things). From this perspective, we can see that knowledge and action are unified because both
are rooted in the human will.

The locus of *ch'eng,* according to Wang, is in the formation of this
will. In other words, a sage is one who can will in such a way that he
always finds himself in harmony with the things of the universe. The activity of mind *(hsin),* which for Wang is truly heart-mind, is nothing but the
cultivation of a sincere will, one that is in accord with the creative processes of the universe. This is the primary task of *hsin.* There is no purely
cognitive element providing information to the will. Instead, mental activity is primordially the establishment of will.[4] When the *ch'eng* and the will
are viewed in this light, it helps to make sense of those puzzling passages
where Wang seems to argue for an extreme form of idealism. If, as I am
claiming, Wang is citing a continuity between *Chung-yung's* metaphysical
understanding of *ch'eng* as primordial creativity and the *ch'eng* of *hsin,*
then all things emanate from *hsin* because *hsin* is the locus of creativity
within the human spirit. He is not arguing that things are "purely cognitive constructs." Rather, he seems to be pointing in the opposite direction,
claiming that nothing exists outside of *hsin,* because a *hsin,* which is ultimately *ch'eng* will, is tied to and therefore part of all that is.

Some might reply, however, that according to Wang sincerity is
something attained rather than inherently present within the mind/will.
However, Wang seems to argue otherwise when he says: "Sincerity is
sometimes interpreted as a task rather than as a state of mind. Sincerity
is the original substance of the mind. To try to restore this original substance is the work of thinking how to be sincere" (ibid., 78). Ultimately,
Wang ties sincerity to principle and *liang-chih,* making explicit the
metaphysical implications of his understanding of the term, "Sincerity is
a true principle. It is innate knowledge. The true principle in its wonderful functioning and universal operation is spirit" (ibid., 225). In reply
to a student who wanted to preserve an instantaneous distinction
between the moment of thought and the moment of action, Wang says:

> Are you not self-contradictory? This is particularly clear and can eas-
> ily be seen in your theories that one knows the food before he eats, but
> your understanding is obscured by recent opinions and you do not
> realize that it is obscured. A man must have desire for food before he
> knows the food. This desire to eat is the will; it is already the beginning
> of action. Whether the taste of the food is good or bad cannot be
> known until the food enters the mouth. . . . [The] . . . desire to travel
> is the will; it is already the beginning of action. . . . You said also that
> the difference is of course a matter of an instant and that you do not
> mean to say that it is clearly comparable to one's knowing today and
> then acting tomorrow. This shows that you have not examined the

matter thoroughly. But even as you say, the fact that knowledge and action form a unity and proceed simultaneously is as a matter of course absolutely beyond any doubt. (Ibid., 93)

I quoted this passage at length to point out that for Wang establishing the will is the root of all *hsin* (heart-mind) activity. This quote also reiterates Wang's seriousness concerning the identification of knowledge and action. They proceed simultaneously. A sincere will emerges from the activity of *hsin,* but this is only another way of saying that *hsin* is the locus of human activity; there is no gap between knowing something and forming a relationship with it (i.e., acting on it). On this point Tu Wei-ming says of Wang's philosophy:

> The establishment of the will as an inner decision is itself both *knowing* and *acting.* Only in the unity of knowing and acting can the true nature of inner decision be found, because the root of self-realization is inherent in the very structure of man. Self-realization, however, is not a process of individuation; it is primarily a course of universal communion. The more one sinks into the depth of one's being, the more he transcends his anthropological restriction. Underlying this paradox is the Confucian belief that the true nature of man and the real creativity of the cosmos are both "grounded" in *sincerity.* (Tu, 1978, 98–99)

The primary activity of *hsin* is not developing a cognitive grasp of an objective order. *Hsin* is the creative center from which our primordial relations with all things are established. Its aim, therefore, is not cognitive knowledge but *ch'eng,* absolute sincerity, where that is understood as an unadulterated creative spontaneity welling forth from Heaven, Earth, and ourselves. In the end, *hsin* is the human specification of the dynamic creativity that is Tao.

THE UNITY OF KNOWLEDGE AND ACTION IN LIGHT OF ITS METAPHYSICAL CONTEXT: HSIN AND LIANG CHIH

We have seen how Wang's interpretation of key Neo-Confucian metaphysical claims such as a dynamic ontology, *Li, yin/yang,* the formation of one body with all things, and *ch'eng* all undermine the internal/external and subject/object dichotomies that are essential to representational theories of mind. Instead, the ontology Wang affirms is dynamic, lacking any tendency to dichotomize mental and physical substances and therefore unable to dichotomize knowledge and action. Knowledge for Wang is a specific kind of movement set within the larger movements of the Tao itself. With the metaphysical background uncovered, these examinations of Wang's own doctrines should make my literal reading of *chih hsing ho-i* fully plausible.

Hsin as a Subset of Ch'eng

We cannot overestimate the importance of *hsin* as the starting point for Wang's metaphysical and spiritual insights (Tu, 1978, 98–99). On this topic Julia Ching writes:

> Yang-ming speaks of *hsin*, the mind-and-heart, not merely as the source and center of man's thoughts, intentions, emotions, and decisions, but also as the source and center of his vital functions and movement, and of all his conscious activities, sensory, and supra-sensory. It is that which gives unity to multiplicity, which organizes all our multiple experiences into one meaningful experience to which we ourselves are identified. (1976, 137)

When the activity of *hsin* culminates in a purified will, our immediate response to things always maximizes the potential for good. To act without *ch'eng* is to act discordantly by failing to maximize the harmonic possibilities. Put another way, discordant behavior conflicts with the *li* (harmonic patterns) constituting the individual entities within one's actual world. Recalling that each instance of *li* is itself a specific pattern of *yin/yang* oscillations, *ch'eng* is maximized when the emerging patterns enhance one another. It is within *hsin* that our most basic responses to the world are initiated. The central question arising within this kind of ontological and epistemological framework is: From where does *hsin* derive its capacity to measure relative harmonic possibilities?

In Wang's time, scholars were taught to pursue sagehood through the investigation of things *(ko wu)*, a meditative/scholarly practice that entailed the apprehension of the *li* inherent in external entities. The aim was always to cultivate better, more harmonious relations with those things constituting the natural world, but the premise was that the principles themselves were outside of us and needed to be drawn into one's *hsin*. When one had gathered enough individual *li* into the mind-heart, scholars expected a "sudden release" or enlightenment after which one would act virtuously without reflection because one would have achieved a union with *Li*. This was the common understanding of the natural goodness attributed to sages who could act without deliberation and still be confident that their actions align with *Li*. This model represented the then current answer to the question: how does *hsin* measure harmonic possibilities? *Hsin* measures harmonic possibilities by quieting the self so that the self could apprehend and internalize the values in those things that are outside of it.

Wang rejected this resolution, denying that *hsin* needed to seek outside of itself to find *Li,* and instead argued that *hsin* must be understood as fully identified with *Li* from the beginning. To understand how he arrived at this position, it is important to mention two central biographical events. The first was Wang's attempt to put Chu Hsi's spiritual methods into practice and the utter failure that effort produced for himself and his closest friend. The two spiritual aspirants spent several days engaged in intense meditation, trying to locate and internalize the *li* inherent in bamboo. Eventually, they both collapsed of what would now be described as nervous exhaustion (Wang, 1963, 249; Tu, 1976; Ching, 1976). Wang's failure in the bamboo grove undermined his faith in the methodology of *ko wu*. Nevertheless, it was not until his enlightenment experience, attained some years later during his banishment, that he felt he had something with which to replace the inadequate spiritual model he had inherited. Summarizing Wang's experience, Tu Weiming says:

> One night, in the "outpost of advancing day," it suddenly occurred to him that the true meaning of *ko-wu*, a concept he had encountered almost twenty years previously, was to be found internally rather than externally. . . . For the first time Yang-ming came to the realization that "My own nature is, of course, sufficient for me to attain sagehood. And I have been mistaken in searching for *li* in external things and affairs *(shih-wu)*." (1976, 120)

The sufficiency of human nature for the attainment of sagehood depends on Wang's realization that *hsin* and *Li* are not separate. *Hsin* does not need to seek outside of itself to find the general principles of harmony because from conception *hsin* is already participating in the creative specification of *Li*. As such, *hsin* is already fully unified with *Li* in its generic sense as harmony itself. Each individual's *hsin* is a single instance of the overall creative activity operating throughout the universe. We have already seen this in our discussion of *ch'eng*. From this perspective, the internal/external distinction becomes purely arbitrary. There is no discontinuity between the *Li* within *hsin* and the *Li* operative throughout the universe. Creativity (Tao) is the emergence of new patterns, new *li*, and *hsin* is the term describing the human form of that creativity. Because *Li* as harmony itself is indeterminate with respect to specific harmonies, the identification of *hsin* with *Li* is *functional* rather than isomorphic.

In the *Instructions* Wang says: "The human mind and the Principle of Nature are undifferentiated" (1963, 26). Given the two perspectives on *Li* mentioned earlier (i.e., the generic and specific), it should be clear that in this quotation *hsin* can be identified with the generic sense of *Li* as harmony itself. In other words, *hsin* functioning as a harmonizing element within the universe, *is* harmony itself. This does not mean that *hsin* contains all of the specific harmonic principles ever created, but rather that it can take account of all forms of harmony.

> Principle is one and no more. In terms of its condensation and concentration in the individual it is called the nature. In terms of the master of this accumulation it is called mind. In terms of its emanation and operation under the master, it is called the will. In terms of the clear consciousness of the emanation and operation, it is called knowledge. And in terms of the stimuli and responses of this clear consciousness, it is called things. (Ibid., 161)

From this citation, it is easy to see that for Wang the Principle of Nature is central to the creative activity sustaining the universe of our experience. To say that *hsin* is undifferentiated from *Li* is to identify *hsin* with *Li's* creative function. Heart-mind represents more than a cognitive center, though it is at least that. It is the locus of creativity within the individual. *Hsin* is the place wherein we create who we are by determining what our relations with others will be. *Hsin's* creativity, like the creativity of *Li* is the creation of harmonic patterns. In *hsin*, they are the patterns linking us to the world at large. In *Li* they are the patterns which bind all things into an organismic whole.[5]

What is most significant within Wang's identification of *hsin* and *Li* is the explicit links it draws among his epistemological, moral, and metaphysical visions. Julia Ching recognizes this when she says:

> Initially this proposition [*hsin chi li*] represents Yang-ming's attempt to internalize the moral quest, by claiming for the mind-and-heart, the possession of all moral principles, and even by identifying *hsin* with virtue or the sum total of moral principles. But it contains also the more hidden, metaphysical depths of Yang-ming's discovery, which is the understanding of the dynamic, existing self, *hsin*, as that which is somehow identical to *li*, previously understood as the more static principle, but now given a new dynamism in Yang-ming's teaching. (1976, 57–58)

The metaphysical implications of Wang's claim appear in the way Wang's identification of *hsin* and *Li* exposes the fact that the then contemporary epistemological dualism illustrated in the practice of *ko wu* had no metaphysical grounds. As taught in Wang's day, *ko wu* implied that the individual needed to search outside of himself in an objective world for the principles of nature. As Ching points out, Wang contradicts that notion by locating the "highest good" for humankind within the "original substance of *hsin (hsin chih pen-t'i)*, also translatable as "*hsin* in itself" (ibid.). As she translates him, Wang says: "To seek *li* outside *hsin* would divide knowledge and action into two things. To seek *li* in *hsin* is the teaching of the Unity of Knowledge and Action given by the school of the sages" (ibid., 61, note 27). Thus, *chih hsing ho-i* ties directly to Wang's identification of *hsin* with principle, which I argue is dependent on the five general metaphysical principles outlined above.

Hsin is identified with *Li* functionally, since each individual is an instance of the universal creativity at the base of all things. *Hsin* is the source for new relational patterns, it is the locus of will. There is no objective world outside of the self. All things are internally related, within a single organismic universe. Each individual's *hsin* is an instance of the universal creativity at the base of all things.

> And so Yang-ming directs the seeker of the highest good to an inner quest of the fullest moral development of himself. This would not isolate him from reality, nor remove him from the world of active involvement. Rather, it represents the fusion of inner and outer concerns. The development of an ever-deepening mind-and-heart in the aspirant for sagehood brings about a union between the agent and the object of his intentions and actions, thus transcending the dualism between self and non-self, between *hsin* and *li*. (Ibid., 59–60)

Hsin in itself is ultimately not separable from this underlying unity that binds all things together. This, I believe, is what Wang means when he says the mind has no substance of its own. "The eye has no substance of its own. Its substance consists of the colors of all things. . . . The mind has no substance of its own. Its substance consists of the right or wrong of the influences and responses of Heaven, Earth, and all things" (1963, 223). *Hsin* by itself, separated from the relations that create humanity, is empty and without substance. In a world without light, would it be possible to identify the nature of an eye? *Hsin* is a creative response to the influences of Heaven, Earth, and all things. As such, it is already a form of action. This is why Wang's identification of knowledge and action is so important. If there could be knowledge which was not action, then *hsin* would have a substance independent of its relations, the distinction between subject and object would be valid, and ultimately one would have to search outside of oneself to find answers to ultimate questions.[6] But for Wang, knowledge and action are one because the rectification of knowledge always entails a rectification of the self. This is necessitated by the metaphysical and ontological presuppositions that reject all metaphysical, epistemological, and moral dichotomies. We should recall Tu Wei-ming's statement about Chinese ontology: "A linkage will always be found between any given pair of things in the universe" (1985, 58). All things are internally related within a single creative matrix.

Liang-chih *and* Chih hsing ho-i

I have been arguing that Wang was making a case for a linkage between the universe's dynamic activity and *hsin's* own dynamic activity. Establishing this ontological continuity is important because it provides a metaphysical rationale for Wang's claim that knowledge and action are really one thing. So far we have seen evidence for it in his discussion of *ch'eng* (sincerity) as a prerequisite to *ko wu*. We have also seen it in his identification of *hsin* with *Li*. It comes through most clearly, however, in his final major doctrine called *liang-chih* (innate knowledge). *Liang-chih* is crucial for understanding *chih hsing ho-i* because it provides the final plank in the metaphysical structure supporting *chih hsing ho-i*. In his doctrine of *liang-chih* Wang attempts to answer his critics by arguing that we must extend the Confucian organismic ontology, which they all hold in common, to our innermost being, the primordial activity of *hsin*. While introducing her discussion of *liang-chih*, Julia Ching says that "after having been tested by trials and tribulations himself, [Wang] presented the final synthesizing concept of extending *liang-chih* as an all-inclusive way of self-cultivation transcending all divisions between the inner and outer realms of life, between activity and tranquillity" (1976, 106). *Liang-chih* transcends all divisions between inner and outer because it does not allow for any separation between the activity constituting the universe at large and the activity constituting the individual (Cheng, 1991, 400–02). As a philosophical doctrine, it also denies any dichotomy between mental and physical processes. For Wang, there is only a single process exhibiting the common ontological premise that each thing is inherently related to all things.

By innate knowledge, Wang was not arguing that the mind is omniscient. Instead, he was pointing to a prereflective moment that he thought preceded and provided the foundation for all more complicated cognitive activity. In translating *liang-chih* Tu Wei-ming offers as an alternative "primordial awareness." He says:

> To Yang-ming consciousness as cognition and conscience as affection are not two separable functions of the mind. Rather, they are integral aspects of a dynamic process whereby man becomes aware of himself as a moral being. Indeed, the source of morality depends on their inseparability in a *pre-reflective faculty*. Borrowing a classical term from Mencius, Yang-ming defines this pre-reflective faculty as *liang-chih* (commonly translated as "innate knowledge" but here rendered as "primordial awareness") signifying an innermost state of human perception wherein knowledge and action form a unity. (1985, 332; italics added)

I italicized *pre-reflective faculty* because it points to an important commonality in the epistemological positions developed by Wang and those developed by Whitehead and Dewey. All three founded a significant part of their philosophic work on the claim that experience is far broader than cognition alone. Whitehead contrasted experience in the mode of presentational immediacy (sense data) with a more primordial mode of experience that he called "causal efficacy." The former he described as sharply focused sensory data containing little if any emotional content, while the latter included the vaguely held but powerful emotional feelings underlying our sense of continuity with the world. Sense data, or experience in the mode of presentational immediacy, is, according to Whitehead, a later reformulation of data originally transmitted through causal efficacy (1978, 168–83). Dewey made almost the same point in his distinction between primary and secondary experience (1958, 21–39). Primary experience is the immediate precognitive response of an organism, human or otherwise, to its environment. As such it contains what Dewey called the "affectional" and "volitional" dimensions of experience. To ignore primary experience in favor of cognitive (i.e., secondary) experience, as most philosophers are wont to do, is to mistakenly exclude the affectional from the "real world," making it a purely private subjective creation. Thus, all three, Dewey, Whitehead, and Wang, felt it was necessary to go beyond cognitive experience and point to a more fundamental level of experience where the unity of heart and mind could be recognized.

It is important to keep in mind, however, that Whitehead and Dewey come at this epistemological conclusion from a different direction than Wang. If I am correct in the analysis of Wang's position, he develops *liang-chih* as an attempt to make clear, once and for all, the epistemological consequences of a commonly held organismic ontology. Whitehead and Dewey, however, appeal to this primordial mode of experience as preliminary evidence that substance ontology, with its accompanying epistemological consequences, is inadequate. In short, for Dewey and Whitehead, this previously ignored mode of experience is used to expose the perniciousness of dichotomies resulting from faulty ontological premises, whereas Wang appealed to this noncognitive dimension of experience as a means of arguing against those who wanted to introduce an epistemological dichotomy (between knowledge and action) that contradicted his tradition's fundamental organismic presuppositions.

There is also a second distinction between Wang's focus and that of Dewey and Whitehead. For Wang, *liang-chih* is as much a moral doctrine as it is epistemological and metaphysical. Wang argues that in this prereflective response, our truly good human nature shines through. For Wang, our immediate response is always innately good, undistorted by selfish desires. "Cognitive" responses, by contrast, always run the risk of contamination by distortions of that innate human nature.

Whether Whitehead or Dewey would agree with Wang's assessment of the inherent goodness of human nature is a complicated question. In a sense, Whitehead's claim that the initial data of each entity contains a "subjective aim" derived from a direct prehension of God might lend some cosmological weight to Wang's elaboration of the traditional Mencian claim, by asserting that all entities at least begin with an ideal model governing their own self-constitution. Dewey, however, worked very hard in *Human Nature and Conduct* (1922) to argue that there was no such thing as an "inherent human nature," good or otherwise.

It should be clear, however, that despite their differences, all three do appeal to a mode of experience undervalued by modern Western philosophers. Once we admit the importance of causal efficacy, primary experience, or *liang-chih*, the center of gravity for epistemology shifts. The true ground of knowledge is the more primitive mode of experience, the mode that contains affectional content. Having recognized this fact, it is again possible to discern the connection between heart and mind. Epistemologists who deal solely with presentational immediacy, secondary experience, or what Wang might have called "mere knowledge," render this connection incomprehensible because they unjustifiably cut cognitive knowledge from its affectional roots. If your starting point is pure sense data, there can be no clear connection between cognition and action. If, however, sense data is constructed from more primitive emotional responses to things, as Whitehead and Dewey both argue explicitly, then the unity of knowledge and action is much clearer, since this primordial response is as much an action as it is a thought. Wang's doctrines of *chih hsing ho-i* and *liang-chih* make this very claim.

In order to support this reading of *liang-chih* as primordial awareness (or a prereflective mode of experience), I will examine some of Wang's statements about *liang-chih*. These statements will at the same time shed further light on *chih hsing ho-i*. At the beginning of this chapter, I pointed out that the typical initial reaction to *chih hsing ho-i* is incredulity. It is not uncommon to think that knowledge and action are sequentially related, operating within two different kinds of "substances," mental and physical. Given the arguments above, it is now possible to see that this response was due in part to our tendency to isolate so-called pure cognitive knowledge from the more primordial forms of experience. With Wang's recognition of *liang-chih, chih hsing ho-i* is no longer mysterious because primordial experience is the common source for so-called cognitive knowledge and our everyday actions.

Wang is quite explicit in defining the relationship between *liang-chih* and cognitive knowledge. In one of his letters he says: "Thought and *liang-chih* should be clearly distinguished one from the other. Thought arises out of a response to an object, and may be either good or bad. *Liang-chih* is that which can distinguish between the good and the bad in the thought. When one follows one's *liang-chih*, all that one does cannot be wrong" (Wang, 1972, 114). *Liang-chih* is the material out of which we construct good thought. It is not the encounter of a subject with an object, which implies a false dichotomy between self and world. Instead, *liang-chih* represents the primordial relationships that bind *all* things together in an underlying harmonious unity. To act in accord with it is to reaffirm and make manifest that underlying unity. Knowledge not guided by *liang-chih* always undermines or denies the *experience* of a primordial unity, which is always ultimately real.

According to Wang, *liang-chih* is something we all share, sages and commoners alike. The difference between the sage and a commoner is that the former is capable of extending his *liang-chih*, while the latter is not.

> For the fact that innate knowledge is inherent in the human mind is the same throughout all generations and the entire universe. It is the "knowledge possessed by men without deliberation" which "always operates with ease and thus knows where danger is." It is "the ability possessed by men without having been acquired by learning" which "always operates with simplicity and thus knows what obstructions are." It may precede Heaven and Heaven does not act in opposition to it. . . . If even Heaven does not oppose it, how much less will man and how much less will spiritual beings? (Wang, 1963, 156; see also 146)

The above is actually a string of quotations from Mencius and the *I Ching* put together by Wang to illustrate the universality of *liang-chih*. He goes on to argue that the *liang-chih* we have can never be lost: "No matter what man does, innate knowledge is in him and cannot be destroyed. Even a thief realizes in himself that he should not be a thief. If you call him a thief, he will still blush" (ibid., 194). If everyone has this primordial response, how is it that there are so many among us who betray our naturally good human nature? Without providing a full explanation for the "origins of evil," Wang says that our selfish desires are to blame. It is important to note that selfish desires are not a product of primary experience. They stem from secondary experience. According to Wang, we have the capacity to block out or obscure our original *liang-chih*. The way to extend *liang-chih* is quite simple. By halting evil acts and clearing away selfish desires, our innate humanity (which is inherently virtuous) will emerge spontaneously.

The above citations, while outlining some important aspects of *liang-chih*, do not discuss the metaphysical issues that have been a crucial element in my exposition of Wang's epistemology. To enter this discussion one must ask the question: How does *liang-chih* relate to *hsin*? On this topic Julia Ching says: "The word *hsin* refers to the principle of our conscious and moral activities, as well as to the metaphysical self or 'being.' The word *liang-chih* refers primarily to the capacity of *hsin* to know and do good. . . . [Wang] speaks interchangeably of *hsin* and *liang-chih*, of *hsin*—in-itself and of *liang-chih*-in-itself" (1976, 136).

Wang's willingness to speak interchangeably of *hsin* and *liang-chih* indicates that he sees *liang-chih* as the functional equivalent of *hsin*. Viewed this way, *liang-chih,* like *hsin,* can also be identified with *Li* (the Principle of Nature). From this perspective, *liang-chih* is undifferentiated from the underlying principles that produce all things. *Liang-chih* like *Li* and *hsin* binds all things together.

In a letter to a disciple Wang also identifies *liang-chih* with *t'ai-hsü* (the Great Void), a term taken from Chang Tsai.

> Only a scholar of real virtue can see the brilliance and conscious intelligence of his *liang-chih* in harmony and penetration with *t'ai-hsü* [Great Void]. *T'ai-hsü* embraces all things without letting anything become a hindrance to itself. For the substance of my *liang-chih* is naturally and originally "quick in apprehension, clear in discernment, of far-reaching intelligence and all embracing knowledge" as well as . . . "self-adjusted, grave, never swerving from the Mean," . . . "vast and all embracing, deep and active as a fountain, sending forth its virtues in due season." (1972, 110; brackets in original)

Earlier we saw that for Chang Tsai *t'ai-hsü* is linked to *T'ai-chi* (the Great Ultimate), whose movement underlies all things. This identification reinforces my claim that *liang-chih* is as much a metaphysical term as it is an epistemological one. Moreover, the adjectives Wang uses to extol the virtues of *liang-chih* are all taken from the *Chung-yung,* a document that highlights ontological partnerships among Heaven, Earth, and Humankind. As we have seen, those partnerships center on the metaphysical concept *ch'eng* (ibid., 45). In the *Instructions for Practical Living,* Wang was asked about absolute *ch'eng,* and he responded: "Sincerity is true principle. It is only innate knowledge. The true principle in its wonderful functioning and universal operation is spirit. The point at which it emerges and begins to act is incipient activating force. The sage is the one who is in the state of sincerity, spirit and incipient activating force" (1963, 225).[7] It is not possible to explore here all of the metaphysical implications of Wang's willingness to link *liang-chih* with *hsin, Li, t'ai-hsü,* and *ch'eng* (Cheng, 1991, 401). For now I want only to make the point that Wang considers the creativity operating within the human spirit to be one aspect of the dynamic creativity that constitutes the universe at large. Since Wang agrees with the basic structure of the Confucian organismic ontology, his understanding takes this ontology as its starting point. Viewed from this perspective, Wang's claim that knowledge and action are unified is seen to have a metaphysical foundation, one that does not allow for the epistemological *dualisms* that seemed to dominate the work of scholars during his lifetime. According to Wang one cannot know first and then act because to do so would imply a false dichotomy between the self and other, knower and object. For that reason, the doctrine of mind that emerges from this model simply cannot be assimilated to Western models that view the mind as an information processor. It requires a different description of mentality, one that begins with the premise that the mind/body problem is a metaphysical impossibility.

I have suggested that Whitehead and Dewey are Western philosophers whose doctrine of mind seems compatible with that of Wang. My main point, however, is to use this reading of Wang as a tool for forcing us to rethink our own presuppositions about mentality. In short, what I have provided is a metaphysical and epistemological account of Wang's philosophy that allows for a literal reading of his claim that knowledge and action are really one thing. Metaphysically we have uncovered the process ontology that governs much of Chinese thought. We have found that this process ontology, in its Neo-Confucian form, is regulated through the creative activity of *Li*, the Principle of Nature, where everything is constituted by harmonies within the rhythmic movements of *yin* and *yang*. This ontology supports the claim that there exists a profound continuity among all creatures. This continuity was also represented in the Neo-Confucian doctrine of forming "one body with all things," a doctrine that Wang thematizes throughout his philosophy.

Given these metaphysical presuppositions, we were able to discuss Wang's fundamental epistemological claims. We have seen how mental activity must be considered from within the framework of the general creative energy of the universe. This was shown through Wang's interpretation of the Confucian doctrine of sincerity *(ch'eng)*, as well as his identification of *hsin* with *Li*. It was also supported by our discussion of *liang-chih*, which uncovered its role as a metaphysical concept. All of these conclusions work to undermine epistemological dualisms such as subject/object, self/other, knower/known, and support an epistemology that recognizes the interdependence of all things. From this perspective knowledge is action because there is no dichotomy between the kinds of movements that constitute knowledge and those that constitute action. In a sense, knowledge is action, just as each individual *hsin* is an aspect of the universal creativity that is Tao.

By understanding the mind as the place where the will is formulated rather than as a cognitive center for information gathering, we saw how so-called mental operations are the most fundamental form of human action, in no way separate or different from "physical activity." Through these processes, we establish the relations we have with the things in our universe and initiate the harmonic patterns that constitute who we are. This was demonstrated in my interpretation of *liang-chih* as a more fundamental mode of experience than cognitive or sensory experience. Moreover, exploring the metaphysical implications of *liang-chih* reaffirmed Wang's claim that the creativity operative within the individual is an aspect of and in no way separable from the creative matrix that is Tao. Finally, Wang's unique reading of *ko wu* as rectification of the self, rather than as a search for external principles, shows how he put his metaphysical and epistemological theories into concrete terms and practice.

CHAPTER 5

Knowledge as Active, Aesthetic, and Hypothetical: The Relationship between Dewey's Metaphysics and Epistemology

According to many commentators, John Dewey reclaimed the theory of knowledge from the epistemological cul de sacs of the early twentieth century (Smith, 1978; Alexander, 1987; Boisvert, 1988; Sleeper, 1986; Rosenthal, 1986). In his later works, he redefined knowledge as active, aesthetic, and hypothetical. This epistemological position was grounded in and dependent on the metaphysical claims outlined in *Experience and Nature*.

Some might find it perverse to link Dewey's name with epistemology, a mode of philosophic inquiry that he explicitly rejects. I am using the term as a shorter way of saying "a theory of knowledge." This usage is supported by dictionaries and within some philosophic circles. Dewey certainly had a theory of knowledge, though he just as certainly rejected epistemologies that began by searching the mind for internal "ideas" needing to be connected to an external world.

The linkage between Dewey's metaphysics and epistemology can be summed up in the following three sentences. *Existence* is inherently dynamic because entities are patterns of interactions rather than independent substances. *Experience* is a specific kind of interactional pattern within the wider interactions constituting individual entities and the universe at large. *Knowledge* is a species of experience and therefore also a specific kind of interactional pattern. Thus, existence, experience, and knowledge are primarily modes of interaction. This is the common denominator or line of continuity that enables Dewey to avoid the dualisms that have haunted Western philosophy since the Greek period. In light of this, any attempt to understand Dewey's epistemology must begin with his description of experience and his understanding of the relationship between experience and nature.

EXPERIENCE AS ACTIVITY

In *Experience and Nature*, Dewey argues that the separation of experience and nature undermines any attempt to understand experience. "To many the associating of the two words [experience and nature] will seem like talking of a round square, so ingrained is the notion of the separation of man and experience from nature" (1958, 1a). Too often philosophers have treated experience like a veil that hides the world rather than reveals it. Instead, Dewey argues that experience is continuous with and revelatory of nature. To support his position he points to the natural sciences, where experience is the starting point for all knowledge about the world. "In the natural sciences there is a union of experience and nature which is not greeted as a monstrosity" (ibid., 2a). Science presumes experience can penetrate into the character of our world. In scientific inquiry "experience presents itself as the method, and the only method, for getting at nature, penetrating its secrets, and wherein nature empirically disclosed (by use of the empirical method in natural science) deepens, enriches and directs the further development of experience" (ibid.). Science begins and ends with experience. The question is not whether experience is revelatory of nature but rather how best to organize experience to enhance our understanding of nature.

According to Dewey, the scientific method's success shows that experience is "*of* as well as *in* nature." Experience is *of* nature in the sense that it deals directly with natural objects. "It is not experience which is experienced, but nature—stones, plants, animals, diseases, health, temperature, electricity, and so on." Experience is *in* nature because we can point to specific kinds of natural interactions and recognize them as experience. Experience does not appear outside nature; it is one of nature's products. "Things interacting in certain ways are experience" (ibid., 4a).

Experience emerges in the shift from inorganic to organic patterns of interaction. Inorganic entities exhibit physico-chemical properties. Organic entities exhibit these same properties but in a different configuration: "The difference between animate and inanimate objects lies not in the fact that the latter has something in addition to physico-chemical properties, but rather in the way in which those energies are interconnected and operate, evoking different consequences" (ibid., 254).

As many have noted, Dewey's philosophy presumes the principle of continuity (Alexander, 1987, 105–18). He consistently works to undermine philosophical dualisms. Instead of separating organic and inorganic entities, Dewey locates what they have in common and then describes how they are distinguished. He points out that both inorganic and organic entities are processes in equilibrium. For example, in *Expe-*

rience and Nature, Dewey says: "Iron as a genuine constituent of an organized body acts so as to tend to maintain the type of activity of the organism to which it belongs" (1958, 254). In this statement Dewey deliberately stretches the term *organism* to include any organized body in order to point out that all entities are best understood as ordered processes. It is interesting to see him stretch the metaphor this far, because doing so places him much closer to the Whiteheadian position that all entities are "drops of experience." In other places, Dewey is very clear in his conviction that experience (and therefore organisms) is not everywhere. He tends to reserve the term *experience* for something that happens only at higher levels of organization. I discuss the relationship between Dewey and Whitehead on this issue in more detail in chapter 6.

Putting aside for the moment Dewey's relationship to Whiteheadian metaphysics, the main point I want to lift up is Dewey's conviction that *all* entities have an equilibrium, which they tend to maintain. Thus, using Dewey's language, a rock is a specific pattern of physico-chemical processes set within a wider environment over time. That pattern, the rock's equilibrium, is part of the wider pattern of interactions (its environment), which set a context for its continuity over time.

The difference between inorganic situations and organic situations is that the former lacks the capacity to restore equilibrium when it is disturbed. Organisms are living precisely because they manifest the capacity for recovery in the face of changes that might threaten their equilibrium. Put another way, living things have needs and are active in satisfying those needs; inorganic things have needs, but can do nothing about satisfying them. Dewey's definition of *need* is different from common usage.

> By need is meant a condition of tensional distribution of energies such that the body is in a condition of uneasy or unstable equilibrium. By demand or effort is meant the fact that this state is manifested in movements which modify environing bodies in ways that react upon the body, so that its characteristic pattern of equilibrium is restored. By satisfaction is meant this recovery of equilibrium pattern, consequent upon changes of environment due to interactions with the active demands of the organism. (Ibid., 253)

Experience *is* this tension (produced by transformations in the overall situation) and the reorganization necessary to restore equilibrium. In its broadest sense, experience is a tensional situation seeking equilibrium. Thus, for an amoeba, experience is the rhythm of its processes as it moves into a state of tension, searches its environment for food, and restores the organic equilibrium by ingesting that food.

> Indeed, living may be regarded as a continual rhythm of disequilibrations and recoveries of equilibrium. The "higher" the organism, the

more serious become the disturbances and the more energetic (and often more prolonged) are the efforts necessary for its reestablishment. The state of disturbed equilibrium constitutes need. The movement toward its restoration is search and exploration. The recovery is fulfillment or satisfaction. (Dewey, 1938, 27)

After making this statement Dewey goes on to discuss hunger as a prime example of this kind of rhythmic movement from equilibrium to tension and back to equilibrium.

The danger with the amoeba example is that we tend to separate an amoeba from its environment and locate experience solely within the amoeba. Dewey rejects this tendency and argues instead that the *situation* produces experience. The amoeba is ontologically continuous with its environment before philosophers or biologists impose a separation. The claim that experience is not a private possession is perhaps the most radical feature of Dewey's description of experience. If the *interactions* within nature produce experience, then experience is not the "possession" of any one entity. It is the product of the mutual activities constituting the whole situation. As Thomas Alexander puts it, "Situations are *ousiai* for Dewey; they stand for the primary realities, the basic ontic individuals from which philosophic understanding proceeds" (1987, 104).

Traditionally, philosophers have divided experience into the components *subject* and *object* and described experience as something that happens to the subject when it encounters the object. According to Dewey, this separation is at the heart of the bifurcation of experience from nature. When experience becomes a private internal affair, its connection to what is public and external becomes problematic. Experience becomes the "observation of nature" rather than a way of participating in nature. As an alternative, Dewey describes experience as a unit. Experience is not something possessed. It is a quality that emerges when entities within nature interact in a specific manner. From this perspective subjects do not have experience; they participate in experience, as do objects. Experience is a natural process that we later divide analytically into subjects and objects.

Above all, Dewey's position leads to the conclusion that experience is best understood as an activity rather than as a state or purely mental condition. John Stuhr articulates this when he says that

it cannot be over-emphasized at the outset that Dewey is not using the word, "experience," in its conventional empiricist sense. According to Dewey experience is not to be understood as the experiencing actions of a subject, or as the interaction of a subject and object mutually independent and existentially self-sufficient in that independence—i.e., two separate items which exist prior to their interaction. To "understand"

> Dewey in this way—with writers who find his metaphysics idealistic and subjectivistic, or incomplete—is to fail to grasp the very foundation of his position. By explicitly interpreting experience as activity, these difficulties are avoided. (1976, 117)

Stuhr has two main points. First, experience is a unified process, where subject, object, and the ends produced cannot be understood apart from the whole. Second, experience is the activity of these components.

> The notion of activity is that of a unity: product and end are not external to but internal and one with process and means in activity; activity is not a series of sporadic achievements but a unified, continuous, unfailing achieving and actualizing; subject, action, and object are inherently one actualizing and actualized existent in this activity. The notion of experience is, for Dewey, this notion of activity. Experience is existentially inclusive, continuous, and unified; it is the interaction of subject and object, of agent and environment which constitutes and unifies that subject and object, agent and environment; subject and object, agent and environment, then, are merely partial features of this on-going integrated function—features intrinsically interrelated and unified in the experience-activity. (Ibid., 118)

To say that entities participate in experience is not a strong enough statement of their role within an experiential event. In his later works Dewey uses the term *transaction* instead of *experience* because it captures the requirement that all constituents be present before the action can take place. Experience is a transactional moment. Subject and object constitute each other *within* the activity of experience.

From this perspective, the tensional situation (with all of its components) gives rise to experience. Experience is not the apprehension of nature from some otherworldly transcendental perspective. Instead, "Feeling is in general a name for the newly actualized quality acquired by events previously occurring upon a physical level, when these events come into more extensive and delicate relationships of interaction" (Dewey, 1958, 267). This means, however, that experience begins on a level far below cognition. According to Dewey the amoeba has experience but not cognition. Cognition cannot be the model for a description of experience because the activity constituting experience is not limited to a cognitive framework. Thus, by adopting a nondualistic position that understands experience to be continuous with nature, Dewey reconceives experience in a way that allows us to recognize it as an activity that is much broader than the cognitive activity that has been at the center of much Western philosophical reflection. In the late twentieth century, philosophers and cognitive scientists began to provide us with a much fuller picture of how our noncognitive activities set the stage for and give rise to cognition (Lakoff and Johnson, 1999).

NONCOGNITIVE EXPERIENCE:
EXPERIENCE IN ITS PRIMARY MODE

According to Dewey, those who limit their understanding of experience to mere cognitive experience suffer from the error of "intellectualism."

> By "intellectualism" as an indictment is meant the theory that all experiencing is a mode of knowing, and that all subject-matter, all nature is, in principle, to be reduced and transformed till it is defined in terms identical with the characteristics presented by refined objects of science as such. The assumption of "intellectualism" goes contrary to the facts of what is primarily experienced. For things are objects to be treated, used, acted upon and with, enjoyed and endured, even more than things to be known. They are things *had* before they are things cognized. (1958, 21)

Since philosophy is a cognitive activity that has been preoccupied with examining the very processes of cognition, it is easy for philosophers to miss the distinction Dewey draws between the secondary reflective structures of experience and experience in its primordial mode.

Primary experience consists of the immediate havings, enjoyings, and usings that are a part of all organic activity. The amoeba's situation is dependent on a continual intake of food. The equilibrium of processes becomes unstable and in tension when food is not present. The presence of that "tensional quality" is something the amoeba's situation has directly. It is what Dewey calls "primary experience." The same can be said of the satisfaction when the amoeba ingests food and restores the equilibrium. In both instances, the experience is rooted in immediate havings, enjoyings, and usings.

Some might object that this purely biological activity is not what philosophers have traditionally called "experience." Dewey responds, however, that an overly restricted definition of experience is responsible for many of the West's most difficult philosophic dilemmas (Dewey, 1938, 38; see also Lakoff and Johnson, 1999, 337ff). For instance, as Dewey reads them philosophers of a rationalistic bent replace the reality of primary experience with philosophically refined concepts such as 'being,' 'truth,' and 'goodness.' They argue we cannot get at reality until we find a way to get past experience and grasp the world in purely cognitive terms (Dewey, 1958, 19). Such a position overlooks the fact that primary experience already connects us directly to what is real in the world. We should be interpreting the primary biological interactions that we share with all organisms, not trying to overcome them. They are both *of* and *in* nature.

Even empiricists, such as Locke or Bacon, often fail to recognize the value of primary experience. They limited their definition of experience in a way that "reduced experience to 'sensations' as the constituents of all observation, and 'thought' to external associations among these elements, both sensations and associations being supposed to be merely mental or psychical" (Dewey, 1938, 38). Dewey rejects this form of empiricism because it makes "experience" a private purely mental condition and renders the connection between the experience and its object problematic. How do purely private mental states connect with physical objects? Dewey expands the term *experience* to include *all* biological activity and avoids this problem altogether.

To some, these claims might seem to situate Dewey quite close to materialists who reduce human experience to the movement of matter. But Dewey argues that materialism is plausible only within the context of the traditional division between the mental and the physical realms. Dewey rejects this division, arguing that though mentality emerges from and is dependent on physicality, it cannot be reduced to physicality. From this angle, Dewey's position is purely descriptive. "'Feeling' is in general a name for the newly actualized quality acquired by events previously occurring upon a physical level, when these events come into more extensive and delicate relationships of interaction" (Dewey, 1958, 267).

Dewey is not reducing experience to physicality; he is showing how experience emerges from and goes beyond physicality. "The primary postulate of a naturalistic theory of logic is continuity of the lower (less complex) and higher (more complex) activities and forms" (Dewey, 1938, 23). Moreover, his description of noncognitive experience provides the intermediate link between cognition and the physical world. Cognition is dependent on primary experience, which is a product of the physical processes constituting the organism and its environment.

When we cut cognitive experience off from noncognitive primary experience, we also sunder the links among thought, emotion, and value. The separation of mentality and physicality forces us to surrender the noncognitive passions that undergird all of our actions. Since these passions are not cognitive, they sometimes seem unreal, purely subjective creations that are not part of nature (Dewey, 1958, 26). "When real objects are identified, point for point, with knowledge-objects, all affectional and volitional objects are inevitably excluded from the 'real world,' and are compelled to find refuge in the privacy of an experiencing subject or mind" (ibid., 24).

The desires or urges, which are part of our fabric as living beings, are reduced to mere psychological phantoms rather than given their rightful place as products of genuine interactions with the things that constitute our world. Dewey's position blocks this loss of meaning. The emotional and valuational dimension of human experience is rooted in our larger biological struggle to maintain and enhance the equilibrium of processes that constitute our environment and us. It is not something superimposed onto nature. It is a part of nature. Dewey goes on to say: "The only way to avoid a sharp separation between the mind which is the centre of the processes of experiencing and the natural world which is experienced is to acknowledge that all modes of experiencing are ways in which some genuine traits of nature come to manifest realization" (ibid.). Dewey's understanding of primary experience avoids this sharp separation because he can ground his understanding of cognition in the biological matrix of experience (Dewey, 1938, 23–41).

EXPERIENCE AS INQUIRY

If primary experience is an immediate having, enjoying, and using of processes within a given situation, what is secondary (i.e., cognitive) experience? Where does it come from, and what is its connection to primary experience? Dewey begins the second chapter of his *Logic: The Theory of Inquiry*, with a disarmingly simple observation that goes a way toward answering these questions.

> It is obvious without argument that when men inquire they employ their eyes and ears, their hands and their brains. These organs, sensory, motor, or central, are biological. Hence, although biological operations and structures are not sufficient conditions of inquiry, they are necessary conditions. . . . The purpose of the following discussion is to show that biological functions and structures prepare the way for deliberate inquiry and how they foreshadow its pattern. (1938, 23)

There is no mind-body problem since inquiry emerges from the biological activities that are already a part of nature. Secondary experience emerges from and is dependent on experience in its primary mode. Dewey characterizes secondary experience as "inquiry" rather than as a state of consciousness or a condition of the mind. We can retain traditional terms for mental states, such as *belief* and *knowledge*, but he wants us to recognize the problems inherent in their usual definitions. Belief and knowledge are not something the mind possesses in abstraction from the process of inquiry. Instead, they are the consummatory experience that is the final product of inquiry. In this sense, they are reintegration or restoration of equilibrium (ibid., 8).

Inquiry is the basic pattern of all biological activity. When an organism's equilibrium is threatened, it acts to regain what was lost. Dewey likens this process to a circuit: "What exists in normal behavior-development is thus a circuit of which the earlier or 'open' phase is the tension of various elements of organic energy, while the final and 'closed' phase is the institution of integrated interaction of organism and environment" (ibid., 31). It is also possible to describe this pattern in four steps understood in aesthetic terms. The organism begins in the closed phase as a harmonic integration of processes (equilibrium). The "open" phase is uncomfortable as the conditions supporting the organism's equilibrium change and the situation exhibits the quality of tension. The organism then engages in activities likely to restore harmony (equilibrium). The final phase is closure, the satisfaction of regaining equilibrium. Of course, every closure is itself the first phase of the next cycle as the pattern repeats itself continually. All organic activity exhibits this pattern. Moreover, in higher organisms, "the close of the circuit is not identical with the state out of which disequilibriation and tension emerged. A certain modification of environment has also occurred" (ibid.). Organisms have the ability to restore equilibrium when it is disturbed. Higher organisms can modify the processes constituting their environment or their own behavior, creating new harmonic patterns when old ones will no longer do.

Dewey describes the modification of behavior as the beginning of habit and argues that habits are the basis for *all* organic learning (ibid.). We usually think of habits as something that stems from repetition. There is, however, more to creating habits than simply repeating an action: "In habit and learning the linkage is tightened up not by sheer repetition but by the institution of effective integrated interaction of organic-environing energies—the consummatory close of activities of exploration and search" (ibid., 32). In short, habits are cultivated and reinforced by the *satisfaction* of restoring equilibrium or establishing a new equilibrium. Thus in its most rudimentary form, learning (here understood as the acquisition of habits) is rooted in the quest to regain, sustain, or create an integrated relationship with the larger environment. This seems to be the starting point for Dewey's own form of nonreductionistic behavioral psychology. It is a position that resonates directly with that taken by his good friend and colleague George Herbert Mead (Mead, 1974).

This understanding of the organic roots of learning led Dewey to two specific conclusions. First, it is simply wrong to describe any of the elements of the more sophisticated forms of inquiry, such as doubt, belief, or ideas, as if they belonged to "an isolated organism (subject, self, mind)." If these things mean anything at all, they must describe the way an "organism and environment act together, or interact" (Dewey, 1938, 33). To do otherwise is to create an unnecessary separation between subjects and objects, minds and bodies that leads inevitably to an inability to explain the connection between "subjective" experience and the world, which is supposedly experienced (ibid.). Second, Dewey concludes that

> The structure and course of life-behavior has a definite pattern, spa-
> tial and temporal. This pattern foreshadows the general pattern of
> inquiry. For inquiry grows out of an earlier state of settled adjust-
> ment, which, because of disturbance, is indeterminate or problematic
> (corresponding to the first phase of tensional activity), and then passes
> into inquiry proper, (corresponding to the searching and exploring
> activities of an organism); when the search is successful, belief or
> assertion is the counterpart upon this level of redintegration upon the
> organic level. (Ibid., 34)

As Dewey understands it, inquiry is a mode of seeking reintegration
when equilibrium is threatened. Knowledge and belief are not states of
mind separate from the world. They are the respite (satisfaction) that
comes when successful inquiry ushers in a new equilibrium replacing
the old, no longer adequate patterns of interaction. From this perspective knowledge is not a mental "state." It is an activity, a way of being
in the world.

There is also a third conclusion that Dewey draws from the above
analysis. Inquiry produces patterns of behavior that maintain, regain, or
create equilibrium. Therefore, inquiry is a quest initiated by changes
within a situation, and it is a search for a way to take account of or deal
with those changes. Dewey points out, however, that the conditions regulating inquiry are always generated in the present with an eye toward
the future. This sets up the possibility of a discrepancy if there is a significant unanticipated change.

> The discrepancy exists because the means used, the organs and habits
> of biological behavior and the organs and conceptions employed in
> deliberate inquiry, must be present and actual, while consequences to
> be attained are future. Present actual means are the result of past con-
> ditions and past activities. They operate successfully, or "rightly," in
> (1) the degree in which existing environing conditions are very similar
> to those which contributed in the past to formation of the habits, and
> (2) in the degree in which habits retain enough flexibility to readapt
> themselves easily to new conditions. (Ibid., 39)

This leads directly to the conclusion that all modes of inquiry, all quests
for harmonic reintegration or equilibrium, are hypothetical. In other
words, all adaptive biological behaviors are hypothetical because they
are based on the assumption that present behavioral patterns will have
efficacy in the immediate future. All organic activity is a projection into
an uncertain future based on experience gathered from the past. Since
Dewey shows that human inquiry is rooted in these same biological
premises, human thought is also hypothetical. He writes that "the hypothetical nature of the conceptions and theories employed, is a relatively
late discovery. The meaning of the discovery has hardly penetrated yet

into inquiry about the subjects of the greatest practical importance to man, religion, politics and morals" (ibid., 40). Dewey could just as easily have included philosophy in the list of subjects of great practical importance that have yet to penetrate the meaning of the discovery that all modes of inquiry are hypothetical.

EXPERIENCE, CONSCIOUSNESS, AND LANGUAGE

Consciousness

I have not yet answered the question posed earlier: How does secondary experience (human inquiry) arise? What makes it possible for these more complicated forms of intellectual activity to take place? Where does Dewey think consciousness originates? To answer these questions we must first examine Dewey's understanding of consciousness and its relation to mind. Then we can turn to his understanding of language, culture, and communication to show how they make more complicated forms of intellectual activity possible. Before entering either of those discussions, however, we must confront again the question of reductionism. Specifically, we need to ask whether Dewey's doctrine of continuity leads him to reduce intellectual activity to organic activity.

The following statement displays Dewey's doctrine of continuity prominently as he discusses the organic roots of intellectual activity.

> To speak, to read, to exercise any art, industrial, fine or political, are instances of modifications wrought within the biological organism by the cultural environment. This modification of organic behavior in and by the cultural environment accounts for, or rather is, the transformation of purely organic behavior into behavior marked by intellectual properties. . . . Intellectual operations are foreshadowed in behavior of the biological kind, and the latter prepares the way for the former. (Ibid., 43)

For some, this statement will sound like Dewey is reducing intellectual activity to organic activity. This charge parallels the earlier concern that he was reducing organic activity (experience) to mere mechanical interactions. Dewey rejected that charge by arguing experience is a quality that comes from but goes beyond mere physicality. He made this point in a statement I cited earlier: "The difference between animate and inanimate objects lies not in the fact that the latter has something in addition to physico-chemical properties, but rather in the way in which those energies are interconnected and operate, evoking different consequences" (1958, 254). To clarify Dewey's distinction between organic and intellectual activities we can paraphrase this original statement in the following way: The difference between *organic* and *intellectual* activity lies not in the fact that the latter has something in addition to organic properties, but rather in the way in which those energies are interconnected and operate, evoking different consequences. The point here is that the shift from inorganic to organic activity is on a par with the shift from organic to intellectual activity. Dewey's evolutionary stance runs consistently from the simplest physical transactions to the most complex intellectual ones.

After stating that biological activities foreshadow intellectual activities, Dewey goes on to say:

> But to foreshadow is not to exemplify and to prepare is not to fulfil. Any theory that rests upon a naturalistic postulate must face the problem of the extraordinary differences that mark off the activities and achievements of human beings from those of other biological forms. The conception to be developed . . . is that the development of language (in its widest sense) out of prior biological activities is, in its connection with wider cultural forces, the key to this transformation. The problem so viewed is not the problem of the transition of organic behavior into something wholly discontinuous with it. . . . It is a special form of the general problem of continuity of change and the emergence of new modes of activity—the problem of development at any level. (1938, 303)

As Dewey sees it, we cannot charge an evolutionist like himself with wholesale reductionism. From his perspective, there is nothing unique about having to account for the emergence of higher intellectual activities from lower physical transactions. We need to provide the same kind of account we provide whenever a set of processes issues in something new or previously unprecedented. Naturalism, as Dewey practices it, is not reductionistic; it is rather continuous. The line of development from the simplest to the most complex forms of existence must be unbroken. The simplest is not more *real* than the complex, though the simplest may have a kind of priority as that which makes the more complex possible.

Having dealt with the problem of reductionism, we can turn back to an examination of Dewey's explanation of how intellectual feelings emerge. On this issue it helps to begin with a distinction he draws between *mind* and *consciousness*.

In *Experience and Nature* Dewey says: "Mind, denotes the whole system of meanings as they are embodied in the workings of organic life" (1958, 303). By "meanings" Dewey is pointing to the fact that all events (entities) have consequences. When an organism responds to the connection between an event *and* its consequences, that event has become meaningful (ibid., 324). We can see this point in an example cited in Dennett's *Consciousness Explained*. When we duck at the approach of an oncoming object, we are displaying sensitivity to meanings that are implicit in a specific situation (Dennett, 1991, 178) Thus, Dewey defines meaning as sensitivity to the consequences that flow from specific events. Rain clouds mean rain. To say that mind denotes a whole system of meanings is simply Dewey's way of describing an organism's ability to cultivate patterned responses to stable circumstances. For Dewey, *mind* is the system of meanings or consequences an organism anticipates and adapts to.

Meaning systems, of course, can be rudimentary or extraordinarily complex. Amoebas need, search for, and ingest food. This entails a high degree of sensitivity to the things that enhance or make this process possible. The meaning system constituting an amoeba's "mind" is relatively simple and not a foundation for any higher-level intellectual functions. In humans, however, complex meaning systems (mind) form the background necessary for higher intellectual activity (on this see also Lakoff and Johnson, 1999). Consciousness, as Dewey uses the term, is best seen as a higher level of sensitivity that emerges from and is dependent upon these less complex sensitivities and patterned responses. Dewey says that "consciousness in a being with language denotes awareness or perception of meaning; it is the perception of actual events, whether past, contemporary or future, *in* their meanings, the having of actual ideas" (1958, 303). In other words, consciousness is sensitivity to the fact that meaning is meaningful. Whereas mind indicates a capacity to react appropriately to the consequences (meanings) of an event, consciousness is the focus of mentality on a specific meaning as meaning. "The relation of mind to consciousness may be partially suggested by saying that while mind as a system of meanings is subject to disorganization, disequilibration, perturbation, there is no sense in referring to a particular state of awareness in its immediacy as either organized or disturbed" (ibid., 304). Viewed this way, consciousness is the focal center of mental activity. All the rest becomes the necessary background. Mind, as the system of meanings, is the ever-present structure underlying and making consciousness possible. Consciousness is an ephemeral activity focusing here and there on one idea after another. Ideas come and go, but the system to which they relate, the system that makes them meaningful, is a permanent (though always developing) substructure.

We cannot *know* immediate consciousness (i.e., pure awareness). "It is impossible to tell what immediate consciousness is—not because there is some mystery in or behind it, but for the same reason that we cannot tell just what sweet or red immediately is: it is something had, not communicated and known" (ibid., 307). Although pure awareness is simply outside the boundaries of knowledge, the ideas *had* in consciousness do not occur in isolation. We experience them as part of the wider meaning system and always in relation to that system. Viewed from this angle there are some things that we can say about consciousness: "These considerations enable us to give a formal definition of consciousness in relation to mind or meanings. Consciousness, an idea, is that phase of a system of meanings which at a given time is undergoing re-direction, transitive transformation" (ibid., 308). As Dewey describes it, consciousness is not a power or a state of mind; it is that focal point where we are in the *act* of determining what is still indeterminate (ibid.). No system of meaning is ever complete. Every situation is always changing, always calling for the discernment of new meanings in light of new events. Consciousness occurs in the *contrast* between the settled and the unsettled. Dewey reminds us: "The familiar does not consciously appear, save in an unexpected, novel situation, where the familiar presents itself in a new light and is therefore not wholly familiar" (ibid., 311). Consciousness is the focal point of human efforts to cultivate a harmonic equilibrium with the wider processes constituting its environment.

> If we consider the entire field from bright focus through the fore-conscious, the "fringe," to what is dim, sub-conscious "feeling," the focus corresponds to the point of imminent need, of urgency; the "fringe" corresponds to things that just have been reacted to or that will soon require to be looked after, while the remote outlying field corresponds to what does not have to be modified, and which may be dependably counted upon in dealing with imminent need. (Ibid.)

This description of consciousness leads directly to Dewey's claim that consciousness and inquiry only occur within *problematic situations*. Organisms instigate changes (in themselves or their environment) only when their equilibrium is threatened. Intellectual activity follows this same pattern. Consciousness focuses on those points in the meaning system that have a problematic or urgent character. "The *immediately* precarious, the point of greatest immediate need, defines the apex of consciousness, its intense or focal mode. And this is the point of *re*-direction, of *re*-adaptation, *re*-organization" (ibid., 312). We do not *think* about that which is already settled. Therefore: "A fixed idea is no idea at all, but a routine compulsion of overt action, perfunctorily and mechanically named idea" (ibid., 350). *Thought* is an active quest for that which might be but is not yet. Consciousness of an idea is already part of the action constituting that quest.

Consciousness is something attained but not necessarily sustained. It represents the peak of mental activity, not its starting point. We do not begin conscious and then fill the mind with information. Instead, mental activity begins below consciousness, below the cognitive. The mind, as a system of meanings, has noncognitive organic roots. The mind is the stable foundation that makes consciousness possible by setting up a contrast to what is new or imagined. Consciousness occurs only within such contrast. This leads to an apparently paradoxical fact about human beings. We seem to be among the very few organisms that have learned to cultivate the undoing of our meaning systems. Insofar as we seek to sustain, increase, or explore the satisfactions consciousness has to offer, we must actively undo the habits learned via experience over time. For most other philosophers the advent of consciousness seems like an unnatural break with the organic world. Dewey's naturalistic account of consciousness recognizes the way consciousness emerges from organic activity and manages to go beyond it. Consciousness, with its capacity to destabilize mind, is the apex of human intellectual activity. It teaches us how to appreciate instability itself. Instability within the system of meanings regulating our behavior can be empowering. Whenever consciousness illuminates another region of that system, we gain a measure of control that was not there before. Control comes directly through instability, since the opportunity to modify a meaning system depends upon our finding a way to challenge the habitual patterns already established. Dewey and the other early pragmatists realized how the scientific method thematizes the notion that the power to learn is dependent upon our ability to destabilize our meaning systems. By treating all claims as hypotheses to be tested, we render virtually our entire cognitive system problematic. Consequently, we gain access to new forms of control (including self-control) that were not possible without this systematic tool for destabilizing our meaning system. Dewey was enamored of science and the scientific method because, of all the modes of human inquiry, it seems to recognize most clearly what it is that makes knowledge possible.

Language

Given Dewey's definition of consciousness, it should be clear that consciousness could not spring forth full born in an individual human alone in the jungle. It grew out of language, culture, and communication. On this point, Dewey is very close to positions we have seen in Dennett's *Consciousness Explained*. Dennett speculated that the rise of consciousness could have developed out of early vocalization patterns and the internalization of the process of asking for and offering help (Dennett, 1991, 195). Along the same lines, G. H. Mead characterizes the rise of consciousness as an exchange of symbolic gestures with oneself (Mead, 1974). All of this resonates quite nicely with Dewey's claim that consciousness emerges when some aspect of a meaning system is rendered unstable and in need of reorganization. For what else are the vocalizers doing other than calling for help in the resolution of problematic situations?

To make Dewey's position clear on this point, we need to examine how language makes symbolic thought and abstract thought possible. As with all other things, Dewey understands language as yet another form of organic adaptation (Dewey, 1958, 175). Nevertheless, language is different from other organic adaptations in that it forces the users outside of their own perspective.

> The importance of language as the necessary, and, in the end, sufficient condition of the existence and transmission of non-purely organic activities and their consequences lies in the fact that, on the one side, it is a strictly biological mode of behavior, emerging in natural continuity from earlier organic activities, while on the other hand, it compels one individual to take the standpoint of other individuals and to see and inquire from a standpoint that is not strictly personal but is common to them as participants or "parties in a conjoint undertaking. (Dewey, 1938, 46)

The capacity to experience a situation from a perspective broader than one's own is perhaps the greatest human accomplishment. It lifts the single organism out of the singularity of its own perspective by creating a community with its language partners. This community, its interests, its aims, and the processes that constitute it become a new perspective from which a situation can be taken in and transformed. It liberates us from the tyranny of our own expectations by providing the necessary resources to lift our expectations into consciousness.

Dewey links the creation of this community with the definition and development of symbol. In this context, he claims that all language is symbolic, and all words are symbols. However, he extends his definition of language well beyond the use of words. All expressions of culture are instances of language and representative of symbolic thought for the purpose of communication. This is easier to understand when we take into account Dewey's claim that symbols are not mere representations of an event or entity. As Dewey sees them, symbols *are a means of directing behavior (or action) toward a common purpose*. Put another way words are enunciations of a whole system of shared activity. The shared activity creates the community, and language is the tool we have to accomplish this task. "The heart of language is not "expression" of something antecedent, much less expression of antecedent thought. It is communication; the establishment of cooperation in an activity in which there are partners, and in which the activity of each is modified and regulated by partnership" (1958, 181). For example, an object's meaning depends on its context. An arrowhead means one thing to an anthropologist and another to the individual who made it. The word *paper* can indicate a locus for artistic, political, or academic activity, depending on the context and aims of those who use the word. The meanings of words are always embedded in a context of conjoint activity. In *Logic: The Theory of Inquiry,* Dewey describes an anthropologist who wanted to ask several aboriginal boys the word for table. He tapped his finger on the table and asked: What is the word for this? He got back answers that included the word for tapping, wood, hardness, and table. Dewey concludes: "The word sought for was involved in conjoint activities looking to a common end. The act of tapping in the illustration was isolated from any such situation. It was, in consequence, wholly indeterminate in reference; it was no part of communication, by which alone acts get significance and accompanying words acquire meaning" (1938, 54). Words or symbols mean nothing when lifted from the community of shared activity.

Beyond liberating the individual from the tyranny of his or her own perspective, the acquisition of language liberates us from concrete existence. Dewey draws a distinction between natural signs and symbols. Actual smoke and real clouds are natural signs of fire and rain, respectively. When either occur, an organism can infer the consequences that follow. Actual occurrences regulate the meaning system. Clouds actually precede rain, and smoke actually indicates fire.

Dewey calls the words *smoke* and *cloud* "artificial" signs or symbols because there is no direct connection between them and any specific physical occurrence.

> [E]xistent things [i.e., smoke, clouds], as signs, are evidence of the existence of something else, this something being at the time inferred rather than observed. But words or symbols provide no evidence of any existence. Yet what they lack in this capacity they make up for in creation of another dimension. They make possible ordered discourse or reasoning. For this may be carried on without any of the existences to which symbols apply being actually present: without indeed assurance that objects to which they apply anywhere actually exist, and as in the case of mathematical discourse, without direct reference to existence at all. (Ibid., 52–53)

Symbols introduce a new dimension to human experience. They allow us to consider things from multiple perspectives. We can associate meanings in different combinations, combinations that are not immediately present to experience. The consequences of acquiring the capacity for abstract symbolic thought are enormous.

> The greater capacity of symbols for manipulation is of practical importance. But it pales in comparison with the fact that symbols introduce

into inquiry a dimension different from that of existence. Clouds of certain shapes, size and color may signify to us the probability of rain; they portend rain. But the word cloud when it is brought into connection with other words of a symbol-constellation enable us to relate the meaning of being a cloud with such different matters as differences of temperature and pressures, the rotation of the earth, the laws of motion, and so on. (Ibid.)

Thus, symbols deal with specific aspects of a particular event. This is abstract thinking. The power to think abstractly adds a whole new set of contrasts within our existing meaning system (mind). These abstract meanings can be set over against the system of meanings constituting mind, lifting even more of it, via the contrast, into conscious control.

To sum up, Dewey claims the acquisition of language liberates humankind in two ways. First, it provides a plurality of perspectives by creating a community of conjoint activity. Second, language enables us to look away from what actually occurs and view things abstractly. Both set up contrasts with the system of meaning constituting our mind, bringing the transformation of that system into our own control via conscious activity.

KNOWLEDGE AS ACTIVE, AESTHETIC, AND HYPOTHETICAL

I began this chapter by claiming that for Dewey knowledge is active, aesthetic, and hypothetical. Dewey bases his theory of knowledge on his theory of experience. Since *experience* is active, hypothetical, and aesthetic, knowledge, as a specific mode of experience, is also active, hypothetical, and aesthetic. We will start by rehearsing why these three terms apply to experience.

Active

As we have seen, Dewey argues that *experience* is a product of things interacting. It is continuous with and emergent from physical existence. Experience occurs when an equilibrium of processes is disturbed and there exists within those processes a capacity to restore or create equilibrium. Thus, the transition from equilibrium to tension and back to equilibrium is what Dewey calls "experience."

Inquiry is a species of experience. Dewey argues that inquiry is an instance of the quest by an organism to restore harmonic integration (equilibrium) with its environment. Inquiry is what an organism does when it finds itself in a tensive situation.

Carrying things one step further, Dewey argues that *intellectual experience* is a specific form of inquiry. Therefore, it follows the same patterns set out in Dewey's descriptions of experience and inquiry. Intellectual experience occurs when a meaning system (or mind) proves inadequate to a new situation, and the organism is forced to make changes in itself and its environment in order to restore equilibrium. Understood in this way, intellectual experience leads directly to Dewey's description of knowledge.

Knowledge occurs when an organism uses intellectual experience to restore an equilibrium of processes. Viewed this way, we truly know something when we adjust ourselves and/or the world to attain more successful ongoing relationships. This description of knowledge should make it easier to understand why Dewey titled his book *Logic: A Theory of Inquiry* rather than "a theory of knowledge." In common usage, we *engage* in inquiry. This seems different from the way common usage describes us as *having* or *holding* knowledge in the mind. As Dewey defines it, thought is the *act of reconstructing the meaning system that regulates our interactions*. Thus, thought is always an activity, and "knowledge" is always a way of describing a successful ongoing relationship with the things that constitute our environment.

Aesthetic

In addition to being active, knowledge is also *aesthetic*. It is always accompanied by the restoration of an equilibrium between the organism and its environment. Viewed this way, the felt satisfaction that comes with the cultivation of knowledge removes the underlying problem that initiated the intellectual activity in the first place. The quest for this satisfaction is what motivates all organic and intellectual activity. Knowledge, therefore, is associated with the successful removal of the tensions or problems in a given situation. This is the ultimate basis for Dewey's pragmatic theory of truth. The motives prompting intellectual activity cannot be found in pure reason or symbolic logic or any form of representation. It lies instead in the *aesthetic* satisfaction deriving from the resolution of a tense situation. When this tension is removed, the motivation for inquiry ceases and thought stops.

Of course, what counts as a tensive situation changes as we move up the scale from the simplest to the most complex organic beings. As we have seen, in humans, equilibrium includes the very layers of tension that make consciousness possible. We achieve a harmonic order by *holding together* the contradictory impulses that make us human, not by reducing them to a mind-numbing sameness. Therefore, we cannot find the aesthetic character of knowledge in the felt experience of attaining an equilibrium alone. It also depends upon the level or quality of the equilibrium that is attained.

Hypothetical

As we have seen, for Dewey, all organic activity is a struggle to integrate oneself with changes that are projected into an uncertain future, using only information derived from the past. Dewey describes the mind as a system of meanings designed to anticipate the consequences of the events that are currently making up its environment. Thought is the deliberate struggle to find ways to restructure this meaning system when it is inadequate to changes in the environment. A child, for example, might reform his or her behavior in light of indications from a parent she will not tolerate misbehavior. If the child is successful at anticipating the parent's wishes, we say he or she "knows" what the parent wanted. The only test, however, is to allow the scene to play itself out. The child's knowledge is always a hypothetical assertion based on evidence from the past. This argument, however, need not be limited to such concrete examples. Any claim is only as good as the arguments supporting it. Those arguments are always subject to revision and rejection. The introduction of non-Euclidean geometries, for example, makes clear the hypothetical dimension of even our most abstract forms of knowledge.

If knowledge is active, hypothetical, and aesthetic, what do we gain when we come to "know" something? The knowing act sensitizes us to the complex relationships that bind us to everything else and to those places where ordered relatedness trails off into disorder. Dewey's argument is that experience becomes more meaningful when we set the immediate qualities of the things we experience within this larger relational context (ibid., 162). When this happens, immediate qualities become symbols for the fuller relationships linking one thing to another.

This view of knowledge highlights the sociality of existence. Dewey's understanding of experience presumes a pluralistic environment that is constituted by an indefinite number of transactional subprocesses. Experience literally *is* an organism's sensitivity to this sociality. Knowing is a specialized form of this social activity. It is a patterned way of interacting with things that flow with the movements of that which is "known."

With the invention of symbolic gestures (Mead, 1974) or language, this kind of knowledge becomes a vehicle for transcending the singularity of one's own point of view. It literally makes possible the felt contrast between alternative ways of interacting with the things that make up our world. Viewed this way language is the vehicle by which we coordinate action with others and create thereby community. Moreover, language opens us to the power of abstraction, giving us the tools we need to integrate a plurality of processes into a coherent and meaningful system.

Finally, when we view knowledge the way Dewey suggests, it is an agent of change. The mind is not something that holds information like a cabinet. It is an ever-changing set of habits directing behavior. Consciousness is the point at which we are redirecting the way we interact with the things in our world. Consciousness occurs when humans are engaged in the act of trying to restructure those relationships. We only become conscious when old relations no longer work or no longer provide the same level of satisfaction. When we are conscious about our knowledge we are in the act of considering whether the habits we have constructed are adequate to our current situation.

Having explored Wang's claim that knowledge and action are really one thing and Dewey's assertion that knowledge is active, aesthetic, and hypothetical, I turn in the next chapter to an examination of the epistemological implications of Whitehead's cosmological theories.

CHAPTER 6

A Pragmatic Interpretation of Whitehead's Cosmology

This chapter examines epistemological implications of Whitehead's cosmology. Specifically, I argue that Whitehead's cosmological account of experience entails a definition of inquiry and knowledge similar to positions developed by Dewey and consonant with Wang's slogan, *chih hsing ho-i.* This is not a historical argument uncovering Whitehead's "true" position on these issues. Instead, I will be arguing that Whitehead's understanding of experience points toward epistemological conclusions that resonate with Dewey's own understanding of knowledge. This reinforces the epistemological conclusions of each by showing how they can be supported from different directions. Whitehead rooted his reflections in the discoveries of science, symbolic logic, philosophical cosmology, and art. Dewey, by contrast, was more interested in the scientific method than the discoveries of science. He also paid little attention to symbolic logic and seemed uninterested in cosmology. What they did share, however, was an abiding interest in art (aesthetic experience) and the way it emerges from our biological situation.

In the preceding chapter I argued that for Dewey, knowledge is always understood as a form of action; that the heart of the "knowing-act" is aesthetic rather than representational; and finally that inquiry and knowledge are always hypothetical and inductive rather than *a priori* or deductive. In this chapter, I argue that Whitehead's cosmological description of cognitive activity is congruent with Dewey's on all three points. It is important to be clear that I am *not* arguing Whitehead accepted the metaphysical conclusions Dewey draws from his pragmatic epistemology. When pressed by Dewey to choose between the "genetic-functional" interpretation of first principles and the "mathematical-formal" interpretation, Whitehead demurred, preferring to leave the question unanswered. For the most part Whitehead agreed with Dewey's claim that the limitations inherent in human cognitive activity prevent any final description of metaphysical principles. Nevertheless, Whitehead always held open the possibility that "in some flash of human consciousness" recognition of such principles could be

attained. Thus, unlike Dewey, Whitehead chose not to let his epistemology rule his metaphysics. This chapter raises but does *not* answer
the question: Is Whitehead's refusal to choose between the genetic-
functional or mathematical-formal understanding of first principles
legitimate given his description of cognitive activity? In short: If Whitehead agrees with Dewey on the structure of experience and knowledge,
can he escape Dewey's pragmatic metaphysical conclusions? (Whitehead, 1948, 93–99). The full answer to this question would bring us
well beyond this book's concern for the unity of knowledge and action.
Still, I will go some ways toward answering it by arguing that the pragmatic theory of knowledge developed by Dewey is compatible with
Whitehead's cosmology.

I am not arguing that the philosophies of Dewey and Whitehead are
completely compatible or unified on some deeper level. My aim is to
press this *pragmatic* reading of Whitehead's epistemology as an alternative to the more typically rationalistic readings developed by Hartshorne
and others.[1] In addition to my desire to explore the relationship between
knowledge and action in Whitehead's thought, I can think of at least
two other reasons why this pragmatic reading of Whitehead's epistemology would be valuable. First, setting process epistemological claims
in the more nearly "common" language of the pragmatic tradition
might help those who find themselves alienated by process philosophy's
specialized language.[2] Second, it may also lend support to those who feel
that pragmatism would benefit from more explicit attention to cosmology and metaphysics. I suggest this despite Richard Rorty's attack on
Dewey's metaphysics and the very idea of a "theory of knowledge"
(1979, 1982). Fortunately, Deweyan metaphysics is being pursued by a
number of thinkers, including Thomas Alexander (1987); Raymond D.
Boisvert (1988); and R. W. Sleeper (1986).

KNOWLEDGE AND ACTION
IN WHITEHEAD'S PHILOSOPHY

In assimilating knowledge and action, Whitehead takes a route similar
to that of Dewey. Both reject sensationalist theories of knowledge and
their metaphysical presupposition that matter is a passive, inert substance that suffers the imposition of knowable secondary qualities.
Dewey replaces inert substances with a dynamic interactionist ontology.
For similar reasons, Whitehead relies on biological metaphors, describing ultimate metaphysical entities as subjective processes called "actual
entities." Each entity constitutes itself by appropriating data from the
past for use in the present. The appropriation process (Whitehead

prefers the terms *concrescence* and *prehension*) is described as an *act* of self-construction. There is *no* given self apart from the prehension and integration of previous actuality into a single coherent feeling. The feeling *is* the entity. Thus, though they describe the process differently, both Dewey and Whitehead agree that we should understand all things primarily as moments within a dynamic process.

As was the case with Dewey, for Whitehead it is also true that entities displaying cognitive powers must be understood within this dynamic ontological framework. Mind or mentality cannot be a separate Cartesianlike substance suffering the imposition of abstract patterns. Whatever else, it must be some sort of pattern of dynamic interaction within the wider processes that constitute the universe because according to Whitehead the final real things that make up the world are ultimately such patterned actions (actual entities). In sum then, just as we saw in Dewey and Wang, a process ontology opens the door for Whitehead to think of knowledge as a form of action rather than as a possession or purely mental condition.

To some, however, the above arguments may seem to contain a hidden sophism. Is it really the case that Whitehead and Dewey can link knowledge and action simply by claiming that the ultimate metaphysical entities are dynamic processes? If what they say is true, then why is it difficult to see this link between knowledge and action? Whitehead believes the difficulty stems from our unconscious acceptance of traditional sense data theories of knowledge. Such theories define knowledge as the cognitive apprehension of secondary characteristics by an independently existing mental substance. To see how Whitehead wants us to overcome the feeling of implausibility connected with the claim that knowledge is a species of action, we must examine his critique of sense data theory and describe the central features of his ontology of experience. This should demonstrate why those who accept the Whiteheadian model must at the same time accept the claim that knowledge is a species of action.

Whitehead's Critique of Sense Data Theories

According to Whitehead, philosophy aims to explain common experience. Nevertheless, philosophers sometimes develop doctrines that *appear* to accord with common sense but actually contradict the way we act. The sense data theory of knowledge is an example of such a contradictory philosophic position. Viewed through the lens of this theory, common sense seems to indicate that our minds contain images of the world. The sense data position argues that we construct these mental images from abstract universal properties reported to the mind by the senses. On this model, the mind is supposedly a receptor of sensory images. We don't experience things directly; we infer their presence when images are paraded before our "mind's eye." Whitehead claims, however, that this model clearly contradicts the way we behave in the world. He begins his response to this problem by reminding us that we almost never feel as if we have only secondary contact with things. Rather, when we are not thinking about philosophical problems, our common sense tells us we experience them directly. How is this possible? The heart of Whitehead's position is tied to his claim that though sensory *perception* may be limited to abstract secondary properties, *experience* does not begin with sense data. Like Dewey, Whitehead points us toward noncognitive levels of experience, which precede and are a basis for the abstractive activity of sensory perception. Recognizing this noncognitive basis for cognitive activity changes everything.

According to Whitehead, the sense data theory of knowledge had its roots in Greek language. He believes the Greeks took the subject/predicate structure of their language and generalized it into a metaphysical hypothesis that the world is constituted by a collection of individual primary substances that pick up or slough off secondary universal characteristics (Whitehead, 1978, 158). As an example, he points to the sentence "This stone is gray." This sentence implies there is a particular primary substance (the stone), to which secondary universal characteristics (grayness) can be attached. Within such an ontology, knowledge begins with sensory apprehension of secondary universal characteristics rather than direct contact with the stone.

The problem with this approach, according to Whitehead, is that it inappropriately limits the range of experience. It presumes sight is an analog for the most basic form of experience. Whitehead rejects this claim and instead argues that sense perception is a very specialized operation dependent on a more primitive form of experience: "The Greeks started from perception in its most elaborate and sophisticated form, namely, visual perception. In visual perception, crude perception is most completely made over by the originative phases in experience, phases which are especially prominent in human experience" (ibid., 117). Less complicated levels of experience operate below and make possible the sophisticated processing of sense data. Before entities can construct abstract visual images, they must apprehend the world directly. Sense data, according to Whitehead, are derivative from this direct, *noncognitive* apprehension of the world. Whitehead describes this noncognitive apprehension of the world as an activity. Since it is the foundation for cognitive experience, it should be clear that for Whitehead knowledge must also be a form of activity. To understand what Whitehead means by noncognitive experience, we have to look more closely at his theory of experience.

Whitehead's Metaphysics of Experience

Whitehead begins with the traditional understanding that experience is constituted by the interaction of subjects and objects.[3] His approach differs, however, by denying that the subject is a preexisting substance passively qualified by another substance (i.e., the object). Instead, he describes the *process* whereby a subject constitutes itself through its own active inclusion (prehension) of the object as a fundamental element of itself. "It is fundamental to the metaphysical doctrine of the philosophy of organism, that the notion of an actual entity as the unchanging subject of change is completely abandoned" (Whitehead, 1978, 29). He also says, "The process of experiencing is constituted by the reception of entities, whose being is antecedent to that process, into the complex fact which is the process itself" (ibid., 178).

In the first citation, Whitehead signals his rejection of the substance metaphysics presumed by sensationalist epistemologies. There are no permanent substances suffering the imposition and removal of secondary characteristics, such as color, shape, and so on. In the second statement, he claims that the subject constitutes itself in the present and does so through its prehension of data from *antecedent* entities. In traditional subject/object ontologies, both subject and object are together in the present. For Whitehead, this is true only in the secondary sense that *the subject* grasps antecedent entities and includes them within its own concrescent process. Objects are settled matters of fact, appropriated for use in the present by yet unfinished entities. Subjects are "not-yet-actual entities" (concresing entities) in the process of determining how they will make use of the past. In Whitehead's model, the past is the locus for the permanent data out of which the indeterminate present constitutes itself.

At first, Whitehead's cosmology may sound like it is out of synch with Dewey's transactional metaphors. Elizabeth Kraus has argued, however, that the traditional interpretation of Whitehead's cosmology, which locates all subjective activity in the concresing entity, may be a misreading of Whitehead's intent. She claims there is a sense in which an entity remains "active" after it is complete. Her analysis focuses on the role of the objective past, raising the question of how the past acts as a permanent factor in the self-constitution of a new entity. Her aim was to show that a Deweyan transactional model could be applied to Whitehead's cosmology when it is interpreted in this way (Kraus, 1985, 349–66). Hers is just one way to draw lines of connection between Whitehead's unique attempt to subvert the dichotomy between subjects and objects.

The ontology outlined above entails two important changes in the definition of perception used by sense data theorists. First, Whitehead generalizes perception making it *coextensive* with experience. "Thus it belongs to the essence of each occasion of experience that it is concerned with an otherness transcending itself" (Whitehead, 1967, 180). An experiential entity does not merely perceive the "image" of a previous occasion of experience; it incorporates the previous entity as an element of its own self-constitution. To prevent confusion, Whitehead uses the term *prehension* to represent this broader understanding of perception. Second, within this broader understanding of perception, the passive reception of sense data is replaced by an active grasping of what occurred in the past for use within the present. Prehension is a fundamental metaphysical concept describing the way an entity *apprehends* the past as an essential step toward creating itself. It also represents the underlying physical link that binds the universe into a continuous flow of feeling. A concresing entity prehends the real accomplishments of the past and creates itself by responding to them.

Perception, in the limited sense of what we do with our senses, is one species of this prehensive activity. Perception of this sort only occurs in complicated organisms. By contrast, *all* entities are constituted by their *prehensions* of previous actuality, and all are moments of experience. *Most* entities are limited so that their prehension of the past fully determines their final character. Such entities are only capable of experience in what Whitehead calls the mode of "causal efficacy," which is not the same as perception. *Some* entities, however, have more creative potentiality and prehend in a way that makes them specifically *perceptive* moments of experience. These entities supplement the primitive mode of experience (causal efficacy) with experience in the mode of "presentational immediacy." Presentational immediacy is the kind of experience we normally refer to when discussing sense data.

At this point, some might be asking: Why did Whitehead feel compelled to posit these two separate modes of experience? Keep in mind that Whitehead's principle complaint against the sense data theory is that it limited experience to sense data and what can be derived from sense data. If sense data is our only source of information, as Whitehead claims, then there is no explanation for how we feel directly connected to the world and the values accomplished therein. Experience in the mode of presentational immediacy refers to the sharply defined information we receive through our senses. Taken alone, presentational immediacy provides very limited information.

> Gaze at a patch of red. In itself as an object, and apart from other factors of concern, this patch of red, as the mere object of that present act of perception, is silent as to the past or the future. How it originates, how it will vanish, whether indeed there was a past, and whether there will be a future, are not disclosed by its own nature. No material for

the interpretation of sensa is provided by the sensa themselves, as they stand starkly, barely, present and immediate. We do interpret them; but no thanks for the feat is due to them. (Ibid.)

Hume made this same point. Sense data contain no information about the connections that bind our world together. We cannot find things such as causality, value, and purpose, within bare sensa.

In contrast to experience in the mode of presentational immediacy, Whitehead argues that there is evidence that we do feel directly the connections that bind our world together. He called such feelings "experience in the mode of causal efficacy." Our feeling of the immediate past is one example of such direct perception.

In human experience the most compelling example of non-sensuous perception is our knowledge of our own immediate past. I am not referring to our memories of a day past, or of an hour past, or of a minute past. . . . Roughly speaking, it is that portion of our past lying between a tenth of a second and half a second ago. It is gone, and yet it is here. It is our indubitable self, the foundation of our present existence. . . . The present moment is constituted by the influx of the *other* into that self-identity which is the continued life of the immediate past within the immediacy of the present. (Ibid., 181)

Whitehead is pointing to feelings that are so pervasive that we cannot maintain consciousness of them. None of us would doubt that who we are at any moment derives directly from who we were a moment before. Yet where does such a conviction originate? It cannot result from sense data, as Hume has shown. Hume suggested it comes from inference through memory and habit. But Whitehead asks: Why are the experiences of memory and habit given special status? If our knowledge of the world begins with sense data, what kind of sensum provides an experience of memory or habit?

By contrast, Whitehead begins by assuming entities are constituted by the *relations they create* with previous entities. Experience, in any form, does not begin with sensa, but with a direct *prehension* of what has already been achieved (causal efficacy). To be related to what went before is to prehend the value that has been realized. "The crude aboriginal character of direct perception is inheritance. What is inherited is feeling-tone with evidence of its origin: in other words, vector feeling-tone. In the higher grades of perception vague feeling-tone differentiates itself into various types of sensa—those of touch, sight, smell etc.—each transmuted into a definite prehension of tonal contemporary nexus by the final percipient" (ibid., 182). From this perspective, the inheritance is not mediated through secondary universal qualities, as it is for sense data theorists. Rather the reverse is true. Universal qualities are abstracted from what is inherited. Abstract sensory data could not communicate the visceral feelings carried from moment to moment. "In practice we never doubt the fact of the conformation of the present to the immediate past. It belongs to the ultimate texture of experience, with the same evidence as does presentational immediacy" (ibid.). Given the pervasiveness of such feelings, Whitehead claims that it makes more sense to build an epistemology and ontology that takes them into account, rather than constructing philosophic systems denying their plausibility.

Taken together, causal efficacy and presentational immediacy are both modes of prehension. On both levels, the concresing entity's activity constitutes the data as data. In causal efficacy the entity prehends the past, incorporating it into its own self-actualization. Then, in presentational immediacy, it reworks the data, lifting up as important things such as color and shape. The data of presentational immediacy are constructed from the initial data acquired in causal efficacy. Thus, presentational immediacy is dependent on causal efficacy, and both are forms of self-constituting action undertaken by the concresing entity.

The failure of the sense data theory of knowledge is that it ignores experience in the mode of causal efficacy while trying to give an account of how we know objects in our world. It presumes a substance ontology that does not allow for genuine relatedness while trying to account for the relationship between knower and that which is known.

There are two important points to keep in mind when comparing Whitehead's presentational immediacy to traditional sense data theories. First, in presentational immediacy, the initial data are *not* sensa. The initial data are whatever has been previously actualized. Second, the *act* of constructing sense data is completed *by the concresing entity*. In its creative reaction to the initial data, the concresing entity lifts up certain qualities as more important than others. An entity engaged in a perceptual experience focuses on color and shape while downplaying other features. Concresing entities create sense data. External forces do not impose sense data. For there to be experience in the mode of presentational immediacy, the prehending entity must act in such a way as to make it possible.

So far, I have outlined Whitehead's alternative to sense data theories. In its place, we have seen his claim that sensory experiences are not the most primitive form of experience. They are preceded by experience in the mode of causal efficacy. Moreover, Whitehead replaces the picture of a mind as a separate mental substance passively bombarded by sensory images with a concresing entity engaged in the activity of prehending previous actuality. This should make it clear that Whiteheadians describe knowledge as a "knowing act" and not something that occurs separately from the rest of nature. All knowledge is created via higher integration of experience in both these modes. Since the modes are specific kinds of action, it is fair to say that knowledge is also a kind of action.

Whitehead's cosmological approach is different from Dewey's, so it would be wrong to claim they are in complete agreement on this issue. Nevertheless, they do agree on the dynamic character of existence, and that experience and the human mind must be understood as movements within that dynamism.

THE AESTHETIC FOUNDATION OF THE KNOWING ACT

According to Whitehead, all entities are no more than the relationships they form with previous actual entities. Entities are not permanent substances undergoing changes, each emerges for a moment by establishing its relationship to everything in its world. Whitehead argues that an aesthetic quest guides the formation of such relationships. An entity *enjoys* a moment of experience by determining how it feels about all that has gone before it. Most important, according to Whitehead, each entity aims at maximizing the intensity of its experience. Within the Whiteheadian system, the primary category regulating inorganic, organic, and cognitive activity is the "category of subjective intensity" (Whitehead, 1978, 27). Whitehead differentiates among inorganic, organic, and mental entities by the way each type of entity goes about maximizing the intensity of its experience. The difference is one of degree, not kind. All three share the same metaphysical structure. All three begin by conforming to initial data. An inorganic entity does little more than replicate its immediate predecessor. Organic and mental entities, by contrast, exhibit a significant degree of novel origination in establishing their relationship to their initial data. To categorize an entity as mental, in the common use of that term, there must be significant originality within the later reactive phases of the entity's self-actualization.

> It is a matter of pure convention as to which of our experiential activities we term mental and which physical. Personally, I prefer to restrict mentality to those experiential activities which include concepts in addition to percepts. But much of our perception is due to the enhanced subtlety arising from a concurrent conceptual analysis. Thus, in fact there is no proper line to be drawn between the physical and the mental constitution of experience. (Whitehead, 1959, 20)

It would take us too far afield to examine all of the metaphysical and cosmological arguments Whitehead marshals to defend this claim.

Nevertheless, from within this very simplified outline, it is possible to understand the structure of his position. All entities are drops of experience, aiming to maximize the intensity of that experience. Organic activity evolves from what we traditionally designate inorganic activity, and mental activity emerges from organic as entities pursue heightened intensity of experience. It is on this basis that we can begin to see how knowledge is ultimately rooted in aesthetic principles.

KNOWLEDGE AS AESTHETIC:
THE "HIGHER PHASES OF EXPERIENCE"

In part 3 of *Process and Reality,* Whitehead undertakes a cosmological description of the "higher" phases of experience, which he calls "intellectual feelings." In this discussion, he describes the "intuitive judgement" as the starting point for cognitive activity. To understand the aesthetic foundation of cognitive activity, it is necessary to examine the way Whitehead describes the structure of an intuitive judgment.

In an intuitive judgment a concresing entity integrates two different kinds of feelings about a single group (nexus) of past actual entities. The first is a "physical feeling," which is a direct prehension of the nexus. The second is a "conceptual feeling" of a pattern (e.g., color, shape), which may or may not be an accurate objectification of the prehended nexus. The integration of these two feelings constitutes an intuitive judgment.

The point to note here is that from the perspective of the concresing entity, it may not be important that the conceptual feeling be an accurate objectification of the prehended nexus. According to Whitehead's "category of subjective intensity," the key is not that the objectification be accurate but that its integration with the physical feeling provide an experience of significant intensity. This is the cosmological rationale for Whitehead's famous claim that it is more important that a proposition be interesting than true. To some extent, we see this in everyday experience. We often entertain systematic distortions about certain aspects of the world in order to simplify our experiences and render them more coherent, and therefore satisfactory. Usually accuracy plays an important role in rendering experience satisfactory. Nevertheless, Whitehead's metaphysical claim is that accuracy is not the primary goal of mental activity. It is only a secondary means to the overall end of intense experience. This underlying erotic drive is a crucial element in Whitehead's philosophy of organism. Without it Whitehead feels there is no genuine explanation for evolution or change (Whitehead, 1925, 111ff; also 1929).

Each entity envisions its own route toward maximizing the intensity of its experience. Whitehead calls this the entity's "subjective aim." The role that accuracy or truth plays within a specific entity depends significantly on the nature of its subjective aim. For some it might be crucial, but for others it is not. This means that from the perspective of his cosmology, Whitehead should agree with the basic pragmatic understanding of truth as defined by Peirce and elaborated by John Dewey. For Peirce and Dewey, "truth" becomes that point at which we stop seeking further explanation or greater accuracy because the experience satisfies the subjective purposes of the inquirer. Given the category of subjective intensity, the same can be said of Whitehead's position. There can never be an objective measure detailing when something has been most accurately settled. Therefore, any decision to stop is subjective and in service to the entity's own subjective aim.

It would be a mistake to attempt here a full-scale explanation and defense of the pragmatic understanding of truth and inquiry, though it should be clear that for Dewey, the pragmatic theory of truth depends in part on his claim that cognitive experience is rooted in aesthetic principles, as we saw in chapter 5. My present point is that for Whitehead, *all* entities operate within an aesthetic framework where enhancing the intensity of subjective experience is their primary goal. This includes the entities constituting human experience and the human mind. Whitehead does not say questions of accuracy and logic are not important for us. Surely they are. He does say, however, that these issues will always play a secondary role to the pursuit of aesthetic satisfaction through greater intensity of experience. In Whiteheadian terms we pursue intellectual activity because it enhances the primal satisfactions of organic experience by providing a means to integrate simple disconnected experiences into more complex and therefore more powerful feelings. By understanding mental activity in continuity with less complex forms of organic activity, Whitehead enables us to see that intellectual experience is primordially aesthetic and only secondarily regulated by the principles of accuracy and logic.

KNOWLEDGE AS HYPOTHESIS

I turn now to examine what I call the "hypothetical character of knowledge" in Whitehead's cosmology. Readers will recall that Dewey described knowledge as a patterned response to some aspect of the environment that results in the achievement of an aim or goal. Inquiry occurs when an organism's equilibrium is disturbed (through either some change in itself or in its environment). Inquiry restores or creates some new equilibrium so that the organism's movements fit with all the other movements of its environment. From this angle, it is possible to see an organism's movements as equivalent to expectations. Organisms move in ways that anticipate the movements of the things that surround them. An amoeba for example "expects" its environment to provide food when it launches its search. The scare quotes are meant to remind readers not to take the term *expect* mentalistically. Amoebas do not hold ideas about food. They simply act in a way that presumes its presence. Their processes are built to anticipate its existence. This suggests that according to Dewey, knowledge and inquiry operate within a three-step system of *expectation-problem-new expectation.* As we shall see, Whitehead believes the sophisticated actual entities constituting human consciousness are also subject to this same three-mode system.

Within Whitehead's ontology concresing entities reach back from the active present into the past for the material used in their own self-construction. A concresing entity prehends only what is already settled. Contemporary entities, entities together in the present, cannot prehend one another since they are not fully determinate and do not yet exist to be prehended. Whitehead literally defines *contemporaneity* as an inability of two or more entities to be objects for one another. This means that at the higher levels, the experience of the present is a construction based on our apprehension of the past. Entities capable of such experience project an image of the present constructed from what has immediately preceded it. Such is the essential structure of symbolic reference.

In *Symbolism: Its Meaning and Effect,* Whitehead gives the example of our perception of a chair to describe how causal efficacy and presentational immediacy are used to construct a third mode of experience, which he calls "symbolic reference" (Whitehead, 1958, 2–4). When we "see" a chair, Whitehead argues, we are projecting a particular contemporary spatio-temporal region and filling it with our image of a chair-like shape. The projection is based on our prehension of a spatio-temporal region of a fraction of a second ago. The feeling that the chair will be comfortable and that we would like to sit down right now is communicated through causal efficacy. As we have seen causal efficacy is a collection of feelings that include the direct apprehension of the entities constituting the chair, and us, just a fraction of a second ago. Presentational immediacy informs us about its shape, color, and other aspects. Experience in the modes of presentational immediacy and causal efficacy are taken together and used to construct the symbol of a chair.

A symbol, in Whitehead's sense of the term, is really a theory about the present, based on the *direct* experience of the past. Entertaining the concept of a chair involves projecting the possibility that there is a place of rest contemporaneous with me and located within a particular spatial region. We cannot experience the entities that are contemporaneous with ourselves. Therefore, we cannot know the contemporary chair directly. Nevertheless, we can experience directly entities in the immediate past, which we use to make a projection about the present. Knowledge, for Whitehead, is always an *indirect construction*; it is never the direct apprehension of a thing-in-itself. The direct apprehension of a thing is what he means by prehension. However, a prehension is *not* knowledge; it is one of the ingredients necessary for knowledge to be possible.

According to Whitehead, mentality in its higher forms is the *capacity to entertain theories about the world*. He also calls such mental ability the "entertainment of propositions." "But with the growth of intensity in the mental pole, evidenced by the flash of novelty in appetition, the appetition takes the form of a 'propositional prehension.'. . . They are the prehensions of 'theories.' It is evident, however, that the primary function of theories is as a lure for feeling, thereby providing immediacy of enjoyment and purpose" (1978, 184). Stated briefly, propositions are relevant possible ways of experiencing the entities constituting our actual world. Whitehead considers an entity "mental," as opposed to merely organic or inorganic, when it has the capacity to entertain such relevant alternate theories.

For example, the entities constituting a chair can only conform to their actual world. They are limited in their responses to the data and wind up replicating the experience of the entities immediately antecedent to themselves. Lacking conceptual origination, such entities are dominated by what occurs within their conformal phase. A more complicated entity with the capacity to "perceive" the chair (in the sense that we have discussed above), develops a symbolic representation by abstracting the qualities of shape, color, location, and so on, and applying them uniformly to its physical prehension of each individual entity within that region. Whitehead calls this the "transmutation of data." Transmutation is the ability to subsume vast quantities of concrete experience under a few abstract categories, thereby heightening the overall intensity of what is experienced. Thus, the individual entities that make up the chair are subsumed under an abstract feeling of a brownish shape. We then project this shape onto a contemporary spatio-temporal region, resulting in a symbolic representation of an old familiar easy chair. Whitehead calls this reconstruction of the data a "propositional feeling."

There are other ways to develop propositions, but the basic framework remains the same. "Intellectual feelings" are the active construction of such propositions coupled with the physical prehension of concrete matters of fact. Mentality, according to Whitehead, is not the simple impression of sense data on a passive mental substance as the sense data theorist would have us believe. Nor is mentality to be confused with Whitehead's term *prehension*. Mentality is a constructive activity generated by sophisticated entities seeking to maximize the intensity of experience.

This is a functional definition of mental activity, rather than one that proceeds by describing mental "capacities." Whitehead takes the same approach in defining *consciousness*. Rather than listing consciousness as a characteristic or capacity of human beings, Whitehead specifies the kind of mental activity that produces conscious experience. He argues that consciousness is a product of the "negative judgement" (ibid., 4, 262, 273). Consciousness is attained when a proposition that an entity felt to be true turns out to be false and a subsequent entity is sophisticated enough to coordinate the experienced disappointment with a review of the conditions that set up the disappointment (ibid., 15). From this perspective, consciousness is the subjective form of the feeling of contrast between appearance and reality. Thus, it is possible to experience consciousness of what something is only in the context of an experience of what it is not. Consciousness is the product of a very specific kind of subjective activity that produces vastly intensified experience by focusing a great deal of information through the prism of a very narrow question: Was it real or not? Consciousness is one method higher beings have for recovering a vast wealth of information from what otherwise would be the simple disappointment of expectations.

As we have already seen, this functional description of consciousness and mentality affects our definition of "truth." True knowledge does not simply re-present the objective world. It designates a successful projection leading to an anticipated satisfaction. This description of truthful experience highlights the hypothetical character of consciousness and of mentality in general. Only when confronted with an experience that confounds our expectations does the mind set to work in an attempt to reconstruct them. Consciousness and thought do not arise spontaneously. They stem from an attempt to resolve an experienced contrast between appearance and reality. Ultimately, all of the complex mental activities described by Whitehead can fit into this basic model: *expectation-problem-new expectation*. We think in order to restructure our expectations in light of new information. If our expectations (propositions) were completely accurate, consciousness could never arise.

Of course, new information can take many forms. It might simply be the entertainment of a "new proposition" that had not been included in the previous data. Thus, mentality is not inherently conservative. It does, however, seek coherence and stability in light of the information it has. Someone living within a social system containing systemic injustices might become conscious of those injustices by entertaining a proposition about a world where such injustices are rectified. That proposition could act as a revolutionary lure undermining the existing social structures in favor of others that promise greater intensity through fairness.

As is the case for Dewey's theory of knowledge, Whitehead claims that human mental activity is an attempt to grasp and transform the interconnective causal patterns that enable us to project satisfying expectations. Since this is a basic definition of *all* mental activity, it applies to all forms of theoretical activity from common daily decisions to esoteric studies in math, science, or metaphysics. Thinking occurs only within problematic situations, and therefore is never disconnected from the primordial organic task of restoring order as a means toward enhancing the intensity of experience. Of course, pure order may lack intensity relative to other alternatives.

The implications of this understanding of consciousness, thinking, and knowledge for our understanding of other realms of human inquiry are numerous. Metaphysics, for example, is a hypothetical inductive enterprise, rather than an *a priori* deductive one. Via the imagination and empirical observation, we generate first principles that may help us to better understand and relate to the things that make up our world. These principles are always hypothetical. Metaphysics is a process of creating and testing such hypotheses. Though some read Whitehead as a rationalist, he makes the point that metaphysical first principles are always hypotheses to be tested for coherence, logical consistency, applicability and adequacy (ibid., 3). When he spoke of rationalism at the beginning of *Process and Reality,* it was usually as a tool for testing the consistency of hypothetical claims and not as an *a priori* process for arriving at those first principles (ibid., 3–18). If this is an accurate reading of Whitehead's position, then he is not as far from Dewey as most would expect.

CONCLUSION

According to Whitehead intellectual experience is continuous with and emerges from less complex forms of experience. As one specialized kind of experience, it conforms to the basic metaphysical structure of experience. Thus, to "know" is a form of activity rather than a state or condition. Similarly, we have seen how the knowing experience is fundamentally aesthetic, as is the case for experience everywhere else in a Whiteheadian framework. It aims at maximizing intensity. Finally, conscious knowledge, according to Whitehead, is a unique form of experience because within it we entertain hypothetical propositions about the contemporary world. To "know" something in the sense of being conscious of it is to set our experience of it within a framework of possibilities made conscious by the experienced disjunction between appearance and reality. Knowledge is never the direct apprehension of an object or idea; it is always the juxtaposition of ultimately aesthetic feelings in a way that satisfies the subjective aims of the inquirer.

Exploring the consequences of this epistemological confluence between the philosophies of Whitehead and Dewey is beyond the range of this chapter. I would, however, like to end by citing some of the issues that might be addressed in light of the above conclusions.

First, the process tradition legitimizes a kind of metaphysical speculation that is viewed with suspicion and tentativeness within the pragmatic movement. Pragmatists need to confront the hard metaphysical and cosmological issues without fear of collapsing into old-fashioned foundationalist traps (Neville, 1982; 1989; 1991; Hall, 1982a; 1982b). Pierce, Dewey, and Whitehead have transformed the very word metaphysics. It is not an *a priori* deductive endeavor. Given the above epistemological conclusions, metaphysics is the continual process of hypothetical generalization that is essential to our self-understanding and our understanding of the world. This is as true for Whitehead's "categories" as it is for Dewey's "generic traits of existence." While Whitehead's format may have some of the trappings of a Spinozalike axiomatic system, his cosmology of experience *requires* that his system be understood as a hypothetical assertion rooted in the erotic desire for aesthetic satisfaction.

Process thinkers need to thematize this aspect of Whitehead's cosmology much more than they have to date. Despite his "rationalist leanings" Whitehead's cosmological arguments leave no room for such claims. The relationship between Whitehead's cosmology and his epistemology should be recognized and allowed to transform the language of process thinkers. Of course, Whitehead is partly responsible for the confusion because much of his language retains this rationalist "tinge." While I have not challenged his usage directly in this chapter, I have tried to show why I think such phrasings misrepresent the position he develops.

Of course, it is always possible that some process thinkers will choose to reject Whitehead's pragmatic epistemology. To do so, however, would entail a rejection of a significant section of his cosmology. The point I've been trying to make throughout this chapter is that if we take Whitehead's description of the higher phases of experience seriously, we find ourselves in a place that is not very far from Dewey's pragmatic theory of knowledge. I should end by saying again that though this chapter has pressed important similarities, there are, of course, significant disagreements between the two traditions. I am not interested in reducing process thought to pragmatism or pragmatism to process thought. The goal is to find a position that is stronger for having been informed by the thinking within both traditions.

Part III

PRELIMINARY REMARKS

In part 1 I argued that Wang, Dewey, and Whitehead can contribute to the effort to establish a nonrepresentational theory of knowledge by pointing out some of the ways their earlier work intersects with the work of influential contemporary philosophers. Taylor's critique of the "interiorization of the self," Davidson and Rorty's rejection of scheme/content dualism, and Dennett's efforts to eliminate the "Cartesian theater" are all compatible at key points with aspects of the Neo-Confucian, pragmatic, and process epistemologies. The difference, however, is that none of the contemporary thinkers provides the kind of metaphysical justification that is called for by their epistemological claims. There are a number of reasons for this. Perhaps the most important is the sense that many contemporary philosophers have that it was faulty metaphysics that led us down the garden path toward the very epistemologies that we are now struggling to overcome. Richard Rorty, for example, has argued that we should avoid metaphysics altogether or at best restrict it to a very limited area of highly abstract concepts. For Rorty its seems that metaphysics is always representational in some way and therefore to be avoided.

The point of part 2 was to present three metaphysical and epistemological positions that could not be described as representational. In sum, I argued that the Neo-Confucian, pragmatist, and process ontologies all take the "final real things" to be nodes of causal relatedness rather than fixed substances with secondary characteristics. For all three cognition is a specific kind of relational activity, rather than an ontologically distinct purely mental re-presentation of what is happening in the causal realm. These conclusions led directly to my assertion that for Dewey and Whitehead, knowledge is active, aesthetic, and hypothetical. Viewed from within this context, the products of metaphysical inquiry should also be understood as active, aesthetic, and hypothetical. In these cases, representational metaphors simply do not apply to knowledge generally, nor do they apply to metaphysical knowledge in particular.

The metaphysical visions outlined in part 2 have sometimes been described as organismic and/or panpsychist. At key points each of these thinkers substitutes organic metaphors for the mechanistic ones that typically rule Western descriptions of causality. Though I have argued that Wang, Dewey, and Whitehead have something to contribute to contemporary efforts to establish a nonrepresentational theory of knowledge, it is also true that most philosophers today view organism and panpsychism with deep suspicion. After all, to many such talk sounds like a return to prescientific pseudo-explanations that natural science overturned in the seventeenth century when it used mechanistic metaphors to establish a truly "natural" science. Richard Rorty, though no fan of Enlightenment theories of knowledge, argues that the passing of panpsychism from the screen of American philosophy is a good thing, and he urges pragmatists in particular to purge any remnants of it that may be lingering at the borders of their consciousness. In chapter 7 I outline and respond to Rorty's critique of panpsychism. As I see things, we have entered an age where the benefits of the panpsychist position are more readily visible than ever before. With cognitive science urging us to see a continuum among minds, bodies, experience, and nature, the panpsychists are among the very few philosophers who do not begin with the handicap of asserting a strict separation between cognition and perception. It is not hard for panpsychists to imagine how mental events connect with physical events because they project only a single organic continuum, where Descartes and his followers assert a mental and physical dualism. In short, according to Wang, Dewey, and Whitehead, there is no ontological divide separating minds and bodies, and this is what makes it easy for them to see the unity of knowledge and action.

My rejection of Rorty's critique of panpsychism does not lead, however, to a rejection of everything Rorty has to say. Rorty's work has garnered a fair amount of criticism from traditional American pragmatists who see his appreciation of postmodernism as a willingness to surrender the intellectual and moral insight of the pragmatic tradition. In chapter 8, I argue that the critiques of Rorty by American pragmatists sometimes sound very similar to the way traditional Confucians criticized Taoists and Buddhists. I develop this analogy in an effort to separate those aspects of Rorty's thinking that I believe are useful to the larger project of developing a nonrepresentational theory of knowledge from those that seem less helpful. Specifically, I find his Taoistlike appreciation for spontaneity and playfulness helpful in the way it lifts up some of the radical dimensions of the American pragmatic tradition. Rorty's mistake, I argue, is that he focuses too heavily on higher-order cognitive functions and fails to situate humans within the broader context of their organic relatedness. This leads, I claim, to his celebrated assertion of a permanent dichotomy between the public and private realms, a dichotomy that I reject.

In the concluding chapter of this volume, I turn away from Rorty to examine two contemporary philosophers whose work reasserts the organic basis of human cognition. My goal in this chapter is to turn our attention to trailblazers whose efforts seem to be heading in precisely the direction this book suggests would be most valuable. The first is Mark Johnson, a philosopher whose analysis of the "bodily basis of meaning" supports directly this book's central claim that knowledge and action are really one thing. Johnson makes no direct appeals to the classical American pragmatists, process philosophers, or non-Western thinkers. He draws instead on analytic philosophy, cognitive science, and linguistics. Yet, as I read him, Johnson is actually filling in the details and extending the process, pragmatist, and Neo-Confucian assertion that mind emerges from the organic transactions that constitute the natural realm. Johnson argues that patterned bodily movements establish "image schematas," which in turn give shape and substance to our cognitive functions. Avoiding purely mentalistic descriptions of cognitive activity, he helps to render plausible the very notion of a nonrepresentational theory of knowledge by explaining *how* mental activity emerges from and is dependent upon bodily activity. To do this, he has to enter into a kind of analysis that many would find paradoxical. Johnson, like Wang, Dewey, and Whitehead, describes experience in much broader terms than philosophers typically use. He argues that our cognitive experience is based upon experience in a *nonpropositional* mode that is akin to Wang's *liang-chih,* Dewey's primary experience, and Whitehead's causal efficacy. As I read Johnson, he demonstrates how our epistemology and metaphysics open up once we are willing to concede the point that experience is broader than cognition.

Johnson's project is an insider's attempt to dismantle traditional approaches to epistemological questions. In contrast to Johnson, I look finally to Robert C. Neville, who is one of only a handful of thinkers who have wrestled with the same three traditions I have been highlighting throughout this text. Neville's three-volume *Axiology of Knowledge* is a comprehensive attempt to put insights from the pragmatist, process, and Neo-Confucian traditions to use in developing a description of knowledge that takes account of the role that value plays in cognition. Neville replaces representational definitions of truth with the claim that truth is the "carry-over of value" from one entity to another. In this one brilliant move Neville draws upon all three traditions to mark out a "high road" around modernist assumptions about knowledge, truth, and value. Not being bound by mechanistic metaphors that banish talk about value to the limited realm of human ethics, Neville argues that these three traditions allow us to award ontological status to value,

The point of this final chapter is to allow Neville and Johnson to mark out two very different paths in the ongoing quest for a nonrepresentational theory of knowledge. Viewed from the perspective of contemporary philosophy, Johnson is the philosophic insider trying to break out of the limitations imposed upon us by Descartes and his followers, while Neville is an outsider using nontraditional lines of inquiry to storm the gates. Taken together they present us with important resources for a new and very productive line of inquiry that appreciates the implications in the pragmatic, process, and Neo-Confucian insight that knowledge is active, aesthetic, and hypothetical.

CHAPTER 7

Minds, Bodies, Experience, Nature: Is Panpsychism Really Dead?

In a paper titled "Dewey between Hegel and Darwin" (1994), Richard Rorty argues that while it is appropriate to describe Dewey as a radical empiricist and panpsychist, it would be better if we allowed those aspects of his thought to atrophy and eventually disappear. He claims: "If one looks at the end of the twentieth century rather than at its beginning one finds pragmatism enjoying something of a renascence but no similar renascence of panpsychism. The philosophers of today . . . tend to speak about *sentences* a lot but to say very little about ideas or experiences, as opposed to such sentential attitudes as beliefs and desires" (ibid., 55). Rorty goes on to argue that the atrophying of panpsychism enables us to better see what was truly innovative and important in Dewey's thought and in the thought of the other classical pragmatists.

Rorty is surely correct in noting that the percentage of active philosophers who take panpsychism seriously is smaller than it was during the earlier parts of this century. Nevertheless, and despite Rorty's ethnocentric views on philosophical argumentation, we ought not to assess a theory's value simply by virtue of how many people happen to be using it at a given time. Rather, it remains our responsibility to ask whether a theory might help us (as Rorty sometimes says) *cope* with the contemporary philosophical situation as we see it. In this instance I believe a case can be made that panpsychism has an important role to play and ought to be promoted rather than excised from our vocabulary. Were we to interpret ourselves and our world using biological metaphors derived from a panpsychist position, we might be better able to accept, understand, and interpret recent research by physiologists and neuro-scientists who continue to blur the lines among minds, brains, and bodies. We would also have disposed of much that has been troublesome in traditional epistemology and have a more fruitful, that is to say, more pragmatic, understanding of the relationships among knowledge, value, and action.

Since Whitehead, Wang, and Dewey all build their theory of knowledge upon panpsychist assumptions, it seems to me that we ought to be exceedingly careful about jettisoning them. In short, my argument contra Rorty is that we will lose the very rationale for the things Rorty likes best in Dewey if we simply jettison this aspect of Dewey's philosophy. We could say the same of both Whitehead and Wang.

RORTY'S CASE AGAINST PANPSYCHISM

Before beginning a defense of the usefulness of the panpsychist metaphor, I will outline Rorty's argument against it. Rorty concedes that panpsychism was important to Dewey, James, and Peirce. "A survey of the most interesting and original philosophers of the year 1900 would indeed show . . . that most of them wanted to close the epistemological gap between subject and object by some form of the panpsychist claim that the two were somehow continuous. For panpsychism seemed an obvious way to perform what Kloppenberg calls 'the marriage of Hegel and Darwin'" (ibid.). The image of Dewey as the thinker best prepared to "marry Darwin and Hegel" becomes a vehicle for Rorty to explain what he finds fruitful in Dewey's work and what has shown itself to be less than helpful. Though panpsychism was important to pragmatism's founders, Rorty argues that it has not turned out to be particularly relevant to thinking in the late twentieth century.

Pointing to the work of Donald Davidson, whose "distal theory of meaning . . . [and] . . . philosophy of language has no use for Locke and Hume's specifically psychic terrain, intermediate between physiology and linguistically formulated beliefs," Rorty says he would like to construct "a *hypothetical* Dewey who was a pragmatist without being a radical empiricist, and a naturalist without being a panpsychist. The point of constructing such a Dewey is to separate out what I think is living and what I think is dead in Dewey's thought and thereby to clarify the difference between the state of philosophical play around 1900 and at the present time" (55–56; italics added). In the past, Rorty has been chided by contemporary pragmatists for presenting a distorted picture of their philosophical heroes. I doubt that this "hypothetical" approach, which has the virtue of greater honesty, can ameliorate the anger Rorty evokes among those who prefer to remain faithful to Dewey's original intentions. To his further credit, however, Rorty goes out of his way at the end of the article to point out that his reading makes Dewey sound "more Nietzschean than most of his commentators take him to be" (ibid., 67). In the end, of course, Dewey himself would likely concede that the issue ought not to be who remains most loyal but rather whose vision of philosophy best contributes to resolving the problems that we face.

In developing this hypothetical reconstruction of Dewey, Rorty emphasizes Dewey's relationship with the historicist side of Hegel. Here he follows Manfred Frank, who describes Hegel as having removed the Archimedean point in historical consciousness leaving no "transhistorical frame of orientation beyond linguistic differentiality" (ibid., 56; Frank, 1989, 87). The roots of the linguistic turn are thus traced back to Hegel (and ultimately to Herder and Humboldt), who "made it possible for us . . . to think of 'transnational and transhistorical reason' as an 'image of the world' inscribed in a linguistic order" (Rorty, 1994, 56; Frank, 1989, 11).

In tracing the linguistic turn back to the historicist implications of Hegel's thinking, Rorty defines historicism as "the doctrine that there is no relation of 'closeness of fit' between language and the world: no image of the world projected by language is more or less representative of the way the world really is than any other." This definition of historicism is designed to contrast with scientism, by which he means "the doctrine that natural science is privileged above other areas of culture, that something about natural science puts it in closer touch with reality than any other human activity" (Rorty, 1994, 56).

Viewed in this context Dewey becomes for Rorty a "philosopher of the *via media*" between historicism and scientism. While many followers of the pragmatic tradition see Dewey as someone who brings together Hegel and Darwin "by finding a holistic, panpsychist way of describing the relations between experience and nature," Rorty argues that Dewey's real accomplishment was in finding a "historicist, relativist, way of describing Darwin's claim upon our attention. By a historicist and relativist way, I mean a way of seeing natural science in general, and Darwin in particular as simply one more description of the world to be placed alongside others, rather than as offering the *one* image that corresponds to reality" (ibid., 57).

Rorty goes on to point out that a true historicist is never in the position to complain that her opponent's views are out of joint with reality. She cannot resort to "notions of misleading abstraction" or "misplaced concreteness" since all descriptions must be viewed pragmatically as "more useful for the following purposes" (ibid.). By substituting such expediency for representational accuracy, Rorty believes that the true historicist is forced to opt for only *one* of the two famous formulations of the pragmatic theory of truth.

Citing William James, Rorty praises the formula that sees truth as "only the expedient in the way of our thinking, just as 'the right' is only the expedient in our way of behaving" (ibid., 57; James, 1978, 106). Rorty contrasts this with what he describes as James's unfortunate alternative formulation of the pragmatic theory of truth, namely, that "ideas (which themselves are but parts of our experience) become true just in so far as they help us get into satisfactory relation with other parts of our experience" (Rorty, 1994, 58). The former definition is compatible with Rorty's "historicist sense of truth as a property of linguistic entities," while the latter is not. He believes the latter necessarily points to a nonlinguistic realm of human activity that is ultimately the "germ of panpsychism." "'[G]etting into satisfactory relation with other parts of our experience' will be acceptable as an account of true beliefs only if both the distinction between the propositional and the nonpropositional, and the distinction between properties of the agent and properties of her environment, are blurred in the way in which Dewey blurred them in *Experience and Nature*" (ibid.).

For those who have taken the linguistic turn, there is no fruitful philosophical work in discussions of *nonpropositional experience*. Moreover, if one believes that philosophical reflection should be confined to discussions of what takes place within language, it is particularly important that we not confuse the language user with the objective world to which she refers when she speaks.

Put another way, Rorty simply has no use for the distinction Dewey draws between primary and secondary modes of experience and the principle of continuity that governs so much of Dewey's thinking (Alexander, 1987, 105ff.). Rorty makes this clear by discussing the relationship between Darwinism and pragmatism.

> Darwinism requires that we think of what we do and are as continuous with what the amoebae, the spiders, and the squirrels do and are. One way to expound this continuity is suggested by the second formula: we may think of these members of other species as sharing with us something called experience—something not the same as consciousness or thought, but something of which consciousness and thought are more complex and developed forms. This way of obtaining continuity is illustrated by Locke's attempt to tell a story about how we get from the baby's mind to the adult's—by adding in more simple ideas and then joining them up to produce complex ideas. This way of procuring continuity blurs the distinction that Peirce draws between cognitive and noncognitive mental states—between, for example, sensations and beliefs. As I have argued in my *Philosophy and the Mirror of Nature*, it also blurs the distinction between the question "What causes our beliefs?" and the question "What justifies our beliefs?"—a blurring that is essential for any representational theory of knowledge." (Rorty, 1994, 58)

I quoted this statement at length because it captures much of what Rorty finds objectionable in radical empiricism and panpsychism. Rorty cannot conceive of a reason to explore a link between cognitive and noncognitive mental states. Whether the latter exist simply cannot be established. In addition, even if they did exist, we would have no means of describing or knowing anything about them except propositionally. Therefore, they are irrelevant to philosophical reflection of the kind Rorty prefers.

Rorty's objections are rooted in his conviction that despite historicist leanings, Dewey remained under the influence of a "representational theory of knowledge." For Rorty, *any* talk of experience raises the specter of representationalism and all of the negative consequences that it entails. Ultimately, Rorty believes that panpsychism simply does not accomplish what it advertises. Instead of resolving long-held epistemological problems, it masks them by redefining the terms. He says that "when we invoke panpsychism in order to bridge the gap between experience and nature, we begin to feel that something has gone wrong. For notions such as 'experience,' 'consciousness,' and 'thought' were originally invoked to *contrast* something that varied independently of nature with nature itself" (ibid., 59).

According to Rorty, the problems motivating over twenty-five hundred years of epistemological reflection in the West have always been rooted in the distinction between appearance and reality. Though Dewey's objective was to dissolve such epistemological problems by redescribing truth in terms of warranted assertability, Rorty complains that by relying on the term *experience*, Dewey placed himself within the orbit of traditional epistemological problems. Dewey's attempt

> to get rid of . . . [the] appearance versus true reality distinction, and to replace it with a distinction of degree between less organized and directed and more organized and directed *empeiria* . . . was futile because his fellow philosophers insisted on language in which they could discuss the possibility of our being "out of touch with reality" or "lost in a realm of mere appearance." Dewey often rejoined by insisting that we replace the appearance-reality distinction by a distinction between beliefs useful for some purposes and beliefs useful for others. If he had stayed with that rejoinder, he would have been on firm ground. But unfortunately he also rejoined that his opponents had "misdescribed experience." This rejoinder was utterly ineffectual. (Ibid.)

Dewey's second response was ineffectual, according to Rorty, because by retaining the term *experience* he could not avoid giving implied consent to the possibility that experience might, in some contexts, be out of joint with reality. Thus, Dewey's theory of experience was viewed by his critics as dodging "hard epistemological questions by redefining the terms in which they had been raised" (ibid., 60) rather than by resolving them.

Rorty essentially agrees with Dewey's early critics. Unlike those critics, however, Rorty wants to press the historicist side of Dewey's thinking to its ultimate end, dropping forever the notion that mind mirrors world. Thus, he would have preferred it if Dewey had let go of epistemology completely and dropped the term *experience*. "He should have agreed with Peirce that a great gulf divides sensation and cognition, decided that cognition was possible only for language users, and then said that the only relevant break in continuity was between non-language users (amoebae, squirrels, babies) and language users" (ibid.). Throughout this discussion Rorty seems to be trying to nail down the implications of the linguistic turn for his reading of Dewey. Rorty sums up his arguments with the following statement:

> Dewey's and James' attempt to give a "more concrete," more holistic, and less dualism—ridden account of experience would have been unnecessary if they had not tried to make "true" a predicate of experience and had instead let it be a predicate of sentences. For then they would not have thought of "ideas (which are themselves but parts of experience)" becoming true or being made true. They would not have set themselves the bad question, Granted that truth is in some sense the agreement or correspondence of experiences with reality, what must experience and reality be such that they can stand in such relations?" (Ibid., 60–61)

As Rorty reads them, James and Dewey both tried to redefine *agreement* and *correspondence* so as to overcome the assumption that these terms entailed copying reality in thought. Insofar as their redefinitions were merely other ways of saying "truth is what works," Rorty finds them helpful for twentieth-century thinkers. Rorty observes, however, that "James and Dewey thought of them as more than that, and that is why they were led down the garden path of radical empiricism" (ibid.).

Rorty is objecting to what he takes to be a common assumption shared by James, Dewey, and a number of other late-nineteenth and early-twentieth-century thinkers that "an appropriate philosophical response to Darwin required a kind of vitalism—an attempt to coalesce the vocabulary of epistemology with that of evolutionary biology" (ibid., 62).

Instead of relying on panpsychism to legitimate a marriage of Hegel and Darwin, Rorty believes that *historicism* should be used to temper the excesses in each. Thus, Darwin's description of evolution as both *random* and mechanistic can be used to overcome Hegelian teleological tendencies that place humankind and Spirit at the center of a single unfolding drama whose end is ultimately predetermined. Those same evolutionary mechanisms are also sufficient for explaining both oral and written language and the meaning systems they imply. From a Darwinian perspective language is an adaptation, pure and simple. It occurs for the same reason birds build nests and sing songs. These spontaneous adaptations proved themselves useful over the centuries. According to Rorty, there is no need to posit a substratum called "experience," which all beings share and which gradually grows more complicated as we move up the evolutionary chain.

At the same time, a historicist understanding of science undoes the scientistic pretensions to ultimacy or finality that sometimes accompany the Darwinian scientific mentality. Randomness and mechanism are part of Darwin's elaborate metaphor *survival of the fittest*, which has been a helpful tool for understanding us and our relationships with nature. It is not, however, a final description of what is real about either nature or ourselves.

Rorty's hypothetical Dewey would, therefore, show us a way between the "reductionist use of Darwin and the rationalist use of Hegel." Dewey's contribution, as Rorty sees it, is to lead us to recognize the fruitfulness of replacing traditional questions about ultimate reality and human nature with Deweyan questions such as Which community's purposes shall I share? What sort of person would I prefer to be? Coupled with the increasing prominence of language as a topic for philosophic reflection, Rorty's Dewey helps us to "spend less and less time talking about the nature of ultimate reality" (ibid., 66) and more time exploring how our communities shape themselves.

In sum, Rorty begins by positing a hypothetical Dewey, one for whom a commitment to historicism outweighs a commitment to empiricism and panpsychism. According to Rorty, a historicist does not expect mental entities to map onto or represent the world. Concepts or ideas are components of a continually changing linguistic system whose properties we explore within the context of reflections on propositional attitudes (Rorty, 1979). Insofar as the real Dewey was interested in experience, especially in experience of a noncognitive sort, he showed himself to be still under the thrall of a representational theory of knowledge, one that requires some explanation for why it is that appearance so often varies from reality. Struggling with questions such as these led Dewey down the "garden path" toward radical empiricism and panpsychism. Rorty concludes that empiricism and panpsychism have proven to be unproductive. The linguistic turn outstripped earlier efforts to plumb the depths of nature and rendered talk of experience (in any but a linguistic context) obsolete. Rorty prefers to imagine a marriage between the historicist side of Hegel and the evolutionary vision of Darwin. Rorty's hypothetical Dewey, one who was a historicist rather than a panpsychist, would perform the honors by charting a *via media* that rejects Hegelian teleology and Darwinian scientism and in their place provides us with a vision of philosophic reflection that focuses our attention on resolving human problems.

PANPSYCHISM REDUX?

Rorty's arguments raise important questions for readers of this volume. I have argued throughout that Dewey, Whitehead, and Wang built their theories of knowledge upon organismic metaphysical assumptions that have panpsychist implications. I have also criticized Taylor, Davidson, Dennett, and Rorty for failing to recognize the metaphysical implications in their quest for a nonrepresentationalist theory of knowledge. Rorty, by contrast, is counseling us to simply "get over" the needs that prompt panpsychist thoughts. In what follows I want to suggest some reasons why we should take seriously Dewey's (along with Whitehead and Wang's) panpsychist and empiricist tendencies.

In "Dewey between Hegel and Darwin," Rorty portrays panpsychism as Dewey's response to the crises engendered by Darwin's evolutionary biology. It is also possible, however, to see panpsychism as a potential remedy for a number of other perennial philosophical problems (e.g., the problem of the one and the many, mind/body dualism, and, most important, the Enlightenment separation of facts from values and objectivity from subjectivity). Though Whitehead, for example, was certainly influenced by Darwin, his panpsychism is perhaps better described as an alternative accounting of causality inspired by implications in nineteenth- and early-twentieth-century physics. Once scientists began using energy as their basic metaphor for describing all things, including matter, the causal metaphors derived from Newton no longer functioned as smoothly as they had. Surely, Whitehead's organic metaphors are as much an attempt to deal with this problem as they are an effort to accommodate Darwin's discoveries. We can make similar claims about Dewey. Though he was not a scientist like Whitehead, he certainly kept up with the recent discoveries in physics and quantum mechanics.

In addition to the way he influenced Whitehead's thinking on causality, I suspect that Darwin's most significant influence over Whitehead can be seen in the way it led him to speculate about how the world might look if we were to make *biology* the "queen of the sciences." If we were to allow biological metaphors to perform the function that the metaphors of physics now perform, our understanding of ourselves and the natural world would be rather different.

Whitehead's panpsychism is thoroughgoing in the way that Rorty, and most critics of panpsychism, disparage. He argues that existence is inherently relational, that to be anything at all is to be a perspective on that which already is, that "being" is actually the process of coming to develop such a perspective, and most important, that the process of developing such a perspective is ultimately value-laden.[1]

Whitehead uses many metaphors for describing this process, but the one he shares with Dewey is *experience*. All of the "actual entities" constituting the universe are, according to Whitehead, "drops of experience." Each is a "perspective" on the whole of things, and there is nothing outside the plurality of perspectives that have been actualized or the potential perspectives still to be achieved.

There is one detail of Whitehead's cosmology that is important to note in the context of a discussion of Rorty's critique of panpsychism. For Rorty, any talk of experience, especially talk of what amounts to "precognitive" or "non-propositional experience," raises the problem of appearance versus reality and puts one on the wrong side of a line drawn in the sand by those who have taken the linguistic turn. I would like to suggest, however, that there is a way to see Whitehead's use of experience as more antirepresentational than would ever be possible for those who eschew metaphysical reflection.

Though Whitehead uses the metaphor of experience to describe the activity of actual entities, and says that each entity has both a "mental" and a "physical" pole, he is not attempting to smuggle in a representational theory of knowledge. Rather, his concern is to provide a metaphysical basis for *value*. Prehending entities do not "represent" mental images of previous entities; they incorporate previously actualized values directly into their own self-constitution. That which is prehended enters *causally* into the constitution of the concresing entity. Prehensions are not micro-mental pictures of the world. They are dynamic acts of energy transfer.

The term *experience* might lead one to assume a prehension is a "mental" representation, much like a photograph or a movie image. But this simply is not the case. At the microcosmological level mentality is valuative feelings of aversion and attraction. Since actual entities are evaluative responses to the whole of things, and since these responses (actual entities) are the "final real things," a prehending entity is not *representing* other perspectives so much as prioritizing and incorporating them. Thus, on my reading, Whitehead's panpsychism is not representational in any of the ways Rorty is concerned to avoid. On the microcosmological level there is no problem of "appearance versus reality." Instead, Whitehead has described a causal system that is nonreductive and physicalistic.

I choose the terms *nonreductive* and *physicalistic* to echo Rorty's call for a nonreductive physicalism that would erase long-held assumptions about an internal realm of the mind that is struggling to make contact with and come to know an external physical world (Rorty, 1991, 113–25). My suggestion is that Whitehead's microcosmology is physicalist in the sense that it is essentially a description of a causal system.

There is no "internal" mind separated from and trying to make contact with a world where physical causation holds sway. Moreover, Whitehead's panpsychism is nonrepresentational since an actual entity's mental pole is evaluative rather than representational.

Of course, saying that Whitehead's microcosmology is not representational does not absolve him from representationalism on all fronts. That was, however, the whole point of chapter 6's description of the epistemology Whitehead builds upon this panpsychist hypothesis. My main concern in this chapter is to point out how Rorty's assumptions about panpsychism do not apply to one of the most radically panpsychist positions available. Of course, to see that this is true one would have to take speculative metaphysical reflection seriously, something that Rorty, by his own admission, finds hard to continence (Rorty, 1963, 147).

What I have said about Whitehead's panpsychism should make it clear that I view his position as more radical than Dewey's. While there is no doubt that experience is central to Dewey's thought, he was unwilling to assert that experience is an ontological category, a feature of all forms of existence. In fact, in *Experience and Nature,* Dewey indicates that there is a clear delineation between situations that engender experience and those that do not. Dewey claims there is a level of physico-chemical interaction that is not organic (Dewey, 1958, 254). If, therefore, Dewey is not a panpsychist in the same way Whitehead is, then what kind of a panpsychist is he?

Rorty reads the entire panpsychist movement through the lens of Darwin's impact on nineteenth-century thought. As I see it, however, Dewey is like Whitehead in that his panpsychist leanings are of a piece with his metaphysical concerns. Though Dewey is not interested in either micro or macro cosmology, he is a process thinker (in a broad sense) who is eager to experiment with some of the hypotheses that a process orientation makes possible. Like many of his late-nineteenth and early-twentieth-century colleagues, Dewey flips the Newtonian metaphor and begins by presuming that individual existence is a cognitive construction and that ontological priority ought to be given to the *systems* that set the context for and thereby give rise to those things that we normally believe stand alone. This aspect of Dewey's process vision extends all the way down to the inorganic realm. He describes Newtonian atoms as patterns of movement within a larger system of movement. Though he didn't follow Whitehead in pressing the "organic metaphor" down to the microcosmological level, Dewey was clearly influenced by recent discoveries in physics and was responding to them in his own way.

The importance of Dewey's shift to this systemic-process paradigm ought to be considered in any discussion of his empiricism and panpsychism, though it is often ignored. Throughout his career, Dewey worked tirelessly to undo our habit of viewing organisms as isolated, self-contained individuals that only happen to be placed within an environment. While Rorty points out how "Darwinism requires that we think of what we do and are as continuous with what the amoebae, the spiders, and the squirrels do and are" (1994, 58), he doesn't acknowledge that part of what made this kind of Darwinism possible was a paradigm shift from thinking in terms of self-contained species (placed on earth by the divine hand) to thinking in terms of ecosystems and their impact on the development of species through evolutionary means. Whether this shift belongs solely to Darwin or is part of some larger nineteenth-century movement need not concern us. My main point is that Dewey's use of the term *experience* is of a piece with the Darwinian turn toward ecosystems. Dewey recognizes that to understand organic activity, we can no longer ask What is the nature of the organism under discussion? Rather, we ought to be looking to the broader environmental *situation* that makes possible and supports this particular form of organic activity. All of these assumptions lay behind the priority Dewey gives to what he calls the "situation." In fact, as Dewey uses the term, situation has a kind of priority over experience. Thus, to understand Dewey's panpsychist tendencies is to see them as an outcome of his situationalist approach to organic activity.

For Dewey organisms are systems of organized activity nested within larger systems. In fact, as we saw in chapter 5, he defines an organism as a pattern of movements with the capability of either maintaining or restoring its equilibrium when there are changes in its broader environment. This hierarchy of systems within systems is both compatible and incompatible with the linguistic turn as Rorty describes it. On the one hand, the linguistic turn allows us to see that any aspect of language is dependent on a broader linguistic system. Thus, Davidson's holistic approach to meaning and language, for example, seems like a natural outcome of both the linguistic turn *and* the turn toward systemic thinking in the late nineteenth and early twentieth centuries. On the other hand, Rorty seems to see in the linguistic turn a rationale for bracketing one organic system, that having to do with human language, from all other organic systems. This assumption, if it is true to the spirit of the linguistic turn, runs contrary to the spirit of the times and is, as far as I see it, completely out of line with Dewey's instincts.

Rorty is right to press the historicist implications of Dewey's thinking. Dewey is a far more radical thinker than he has been made out to be by either the scientist types who see in him the ultimate justification for a hegemony of the scientific method or the meliorists who read him as a lonely optimistic voice amidst the gloom that characterized the first half of the twentieth century. Nonetheless, Rorty is just wrong if he thinks he can create a recognizable image of Dewey (hypothetical though it may be!) who will allow human language to be the only organic system about which we cannot ask the question What makes this kind of organic activity possible?

Dewey's understanding of experience relates necessarily to his urge to describe organic activity as a set of practices that emerge from and are in continuity with their larger surroundings. Such an approach does not entail the representational implications that Rorty is so concerned to avoid. For Dewey, *experience* is a term describing the capacity of an organism to adjust to or cope with its environment. As Rorty himself points out, such adjustments (or coping) have little to do with mental mirroring of the world. Thus, Dewey would agree with Rorty's overarching effort to rid us of the specter of the ghost in the machine. Rorty's error, as I see it, is in assuming that *any* talk of experience necessarily entails such a ghost.

Perhaps some personal testimony will help drive home the point I am trying to make. When I first read Dewey's *Experience and Nature,* I was smitten by the overall process vision and by the way in which Dewey provided a completely naturalistic understanding of value and the role it plays in the constitution of organic activities. Dewey did all of this without appealing to God or eternal objects, Whiteheadian concepts that I found especially problematic. Nonetheless, I was confused by his use of the term *experience*. Written in the margins at a number of key points is my own impatient scrawled question "Whose experience?!!" What I came to understand upon successive readings is that in *Experience and Nature,* Dewey was working to undo any lingering Cartesian assumptions about what we mean by the term *experience*. Experience is not an essential characteristic of an independently existing subject. It is, rather, a *trait* exhibited within organic situations and in that sense is not owned by any individual. Since an individual does not own it, it is much harder to see in Dewey's use of the term the mental representationalism that Rorty fears. Organic systems are continually adjusting to changes within the broader environment. *Experience* is the term Dewey uses to describe those adjustments. Viewed this way, Dewey's use of the term remains compatible with Whitehead's, though Dewey does not have a parallel microcosmology to fill in the details.

CAUSAL EFFICACY AND PRIMORDIAL EXPERIENCE

Having described why I think neither Whitehead's nor Dewey's panpsychism can be viewed as representational, I would like to turn to a brief discussion of what Whitehead calls "causal efficacy" and Dewey calls "primary experience." Any analysis of their panpsychism ought to at least try to highlight why both felt compelled to include in their descriptions of human experience a level of human activity that, though well below the "cognitive" or "propositional," must still be described as experiential.

Rorty, of course, would prefer to rule consideration of such feelings out of philosophy altogether. His desire is motivated by what he perceives as an unbridgeable "gulf" between perception and conception. As I see it, however, ruling them out of philosophy *assumes* rather than *justifies* a dichotomy between feeling and cognition, minds and bodies, experience and nature. The Whiteheadian and Deweyan suggestion that we attend to such feelings serves as a reminder that we should not start from a position that predetermines our conclusions.

In chapter 6, for example, we examined Whitehead's response to the Humelike question: What justification do we have for claiming that who we are at this moment is continuous with who we were a moment ago? He answers that we *experience* a physical confirmation of that continuity over time. So long as we keep in mind that Whitehead understands experience as the continual adjustment of an organism to its environment, there is no reason to presume, as Rorty does, that talk of such "physical feelings" smuggles in a Cartesian ghost who "has" the feelings. Rather, because Whitehead's cosmology allows no division between the mental and the physical, he can argue that experience of this physical compulsion appears to be a characteristic of all organic activity. Moreover, Whitehead's description of causal efficacy as a response to Humean skepticism has an advantage over say Kant's *a priori* transcendental explanation by virtue of its not having to explain how a purely cognitive *a priori* compulsion (e.g., temporality, causality, etc.) relates to the body and an external physical world.

Most important, Whitehead's willingness to take seriously the notion of noncognitive physical feelings provides him with a way to understand those vague but powerful emotional overtones that color cognitive experience but have no explicit connection to cognition as we normally describe it. Understanding "feelings" such as rage, love, repulsion, or attraction, feelings that seem so clearly to blend the physical and cognitive, is much more difficult for those who take Rorty's version of the linguistic turn.

Dewey follows a route similar to Whitehead in urging that we attend to what he calls "primary experience" and the role it plays in relation to secondary experience. When he talks about primary experience, he is generally referring to the immediate "havings" and "doings" that constitute the vast majority of an organism's interactions with its environment. As Dewey describes them, organisms exhibit a rhythmic movement from equilibrium to stress and back to equilibrium. When stressed, perhaps in need of food, the situation calls forth from the organism a response that is rooted in its physicality. As is true of Whitehead, Dewey feels justified in calling such responses experience because they are the micro-adjustments the organism is making to its environment. Moreover, Dewey agrees with Whitehead in attributing to this level of experience the vague yet powerful emotional responses that form the background for our more sharply defined cognitive or secondary experience.

Since Rorty views the appearance of language as akin to genetic mutations, he feels justified in leaving it to the neurologist to describe the connections between our organic responses (e.g., brain states) and the higher-order cognitive activity, which language makes possible. No "explanation" is needed since language, like opposable thumbs, appeared spontaneously and has proven itself *de facto* to be a useful mutation. The problem with such a response, however, is that it ignores the ways in which this particular "mutation" is both dependent on and integrated with that which preceded it. Language *can* be viewed as a spontaneous mutation of human behavior. Moreover, Rorty is correct to describe language as a coping tool rather than a mapping device. Nonetheless, there is no reason for imagining that the differences between perception and cognition are so great that we cannot learn something from the way one (i.e., cognition) is dependent on the other (causal efficacy or primary experience). Moreover, there is no reason to allow an awareness of language's limitations to prevent us from recognizing that our organic responses are also efforts to cope with the world and in that way continuous with language as Rorty understands it.

Sometimes the way Rorty describes language gives readers the impression that he imagines us trapped within a fluid linguistic system with metaphor as our only escape and the world as an unknowable *ding an sich*. Actually, his position is subtler. He wants to undo the distinction we draw between world and language and replace it with an image of selves that are constituted only as a web of beliefs, which are continually weaving and unweaving so as to realize specific goals (Rorty, 1991, 93–110). Whitehead and Dewey would probably find much to agree with in Rorty's metaphor of the self as a web of beliefs. According to both, cognitive experience gains its precision by virtue of selecting particular perspectives from which to respond to things. An epistemology rooted in perspectivalism is less inclined to worry about getting things "right" and more inclined to worry about getting things done. In his early article on Whitehead, Rorty acknowledges appreciatively this aspect of Whitehead's theory of knowledge (Rorty, 1963, 153).

Ultimately, Dewey and Whitehead are both naturalists in a way that Rorty could never be. They see continuity among all of the ways we struggle to cope with the world where Rorty creates a divide between linguistic and nonlinguistic copings. In preserving this continuity, they do not reduce all copings to the same thing, a fear implied throughout Rorty's critique of panpsychism. Perceptions are different from conceptions, and neither Dewey nor Whitehead would deny the distinction. Nonetheless, they resist the impulse to insert unnatural dichotomies where they are not needed.

PANPSYCHISM'S NEW RELEVANCE

At the beginning of "Dewey between Hegel and Darwin," Rorty says he intends his paper to "clarify the difference between the state of philosophical play around 1900 and at the present time" (1994, 56). Rorty's ethnocentric approach to questions of truth and knowledge bars him from saying more than that panpsychism is out of fashion at the present time. Beyond that, the most he can do is retell philosophy's story over the last century in a way that highlights why he believes panpsychism is out of fashion and why it should remain so. By telling the story in the way he does, Rorty hopes to convince us that panpsychism is not responsive to problems in the current philosophical situation.

I will not fault Rorty for failing to tell Dewey's story in the way that I would. After all, Rorty signals his intentions right from the beginning by announcing that he is going to describe a "hypothetical" Dewey who better fits Rorty's own vision of the current philosophical situation. Though it is probably useless to protest that Rorty misreads Dewey, it is appropriate to complain that Rorty seems out of touch with the recent currents in Rorty's own cultural and philosophical world. Much of his critique of panpsychism hinges on what he takes to be the general acceptance of the linguistic turn and the gulf it creates between perception and conception. As a result Rorty unintentionally leaves open the possibility that panpsychism might be relevant at a time when such a gulf is not perceived to be as wide as he thinks it is. I would like to point to some general evidence and one particular study that indicates we are living in a time when we should be rereading Whitehead and Dewey, along with many of the other panpsychist thinkers from the late nineteenth and early twentieth centuries. Having thought long and hard about radical empiricism and panpsychism, they have much to teach those of us who are seeking new ways to understand the relationships among minds, bodies, and nature.

In light of recent philosophic movements in the late twentieth century, it seems clear to me that philosophers are now better positioned to take seriously the Deweyan and Whiteheadian call to attend to vague emotion-laden causal feelings than they were in the period between the mid 60s and the mid 80s. In recent years phenomenologists have published a broad range of material exploring the "bodily" background to higher-level cognitive knowledge. Though it would be wrong to assume that phenomenologists are necessarily panpsychists, it does seem fair to say that whereas Rorty (operating from within the assumptions of the linguistic turn) wants to draw a sharp line of demarcation between perception and conception, most phenomenologists are engaged in exploring the continuities that link them.

Feminist theorists represent another group of contemporary philosophers who have refused to allow the linguistic turn to circumscribe philosophic reflection. While most feminists readily acknowledge that we should attend to the way language structures experience, many also regularly appeal to modes of awareness that are not propositionally structured and that have not been taken seriously in the recent philosophic past. Again, I am not arguing that feminists are, or ought to be, panpsychists. Rather, I am claiming that panpsychism's emphasis on modes of experience that extend beyond the cognitive should make it a fruitful resource for feminist thinkers.

Sparked in part by both phenomenology and feminist theory, there has been a recent explosion of interest in the body among philosophers. This interest cuts across many fields including philosophy, anthropology, history, religion, Asian studies, etc. Rorty, of course, is aware of this work. What I find surprising is that he does not see in it a favorable context for naturalist philosophy and especially the panpsychist specification of naturalism. He might want to argue that all such work is unlikely to be productive if it does not take seriously the fact that thoughts are always embedded in linguistic systems. But that seems a tenuous stance for an ironist who refuses to allow that there is any value to philosophy other than its therapeutic resolution of philosophic problems. Phenomenologists, feminist theorists, and philosophers of the body all seem hard at work providing therapeutic responses to the excesses of positivism and an overly dogmatic understanding of the linguistic turn. I find it hard to believe that Rorty would want to rule these modes of philosophic reflection useless, yet his argument against panpsychism seems to turn on precisely such logic.

In the final chapter of this volume, I will present a detailed description of work by Mark Johnson, a contemporary philosopher of the body who draws upon both phenomenology and cognitive science to develop a more holistic description of the "embodied mind." The point of my analysis will be to suggest that in Johnson's work we can see a fruitful route for contemporary philosophical reflection that is not only compatible with, but would be enhanced by engagement with panpsychist philosophy from both the Western and Eastern traditions. Perhaps more than anything else, recent discoveries in cognitive science and cognitive psychology should be motivating us to take a second look at panpsychism. Johnson chronicles these discoveries with his sometime writing partner George Lakoff, in their recent *Philosophy in the Flesh: The Embodied Mind and its Challenge to Western Thought* (1999). This book, along with others by cognitive scientists like Francisco J. Varela, (1991; 1999) is causing us all to rethink the so-called boundaries between perception and cognition.

Throughout his career Richard Rorty has remained keenly attuned to the role that metaphor plays in both philosophical and everyday discourse. For Rorty there is a sense in which all language is metaphorical. Words, phrases and ideas are originally metaphors that lose their metaphoric glow when they become commonplace truths. Nevertheless, though the glow may be gone, it would be wrong to assume that a metaphor is ever anything but metaphorical. In addition, in that spirit, it is important to note that some metaphors can regain their "metaphorical glow" if they are cast again into a new context.

In his attack on panpsychism, Rorty is largely concerned about the term *experience*. He sees in it all of the bad old things he has fought so hard to overcome: essentialism and a world that knowledge mirrors; subjectivism and objectivity; appearance and hard core reality. In this chapter, I have tried to suggest some of the reasons Rorty's fears are misplaced. In sum, my argument is that Rorty has failed to appreciate the way panpsychists such as Whitehead and Dewey took an old term and put it to new metaphorical uses.

For a long time, I wondered what it was that rendered Rorty tone deaf to Deweyan naturalism. If "Dewey between Hegel and Darwin" is a true indicator of his position, it turns out, unsurprisingly, to be his early commitment to the linguistic turn and the gulf that turn creates between conception and perception. I say unsurprising because his early work in that area was a signal moment in American philosophy, and I guess one cannot begrudge him attachment to what was accomplished.

On the other hand, my own attachments are to ideas that, once unfashionable, have gained new currency in a world newly fascinated by the way bodies, minds, experience, and nature are all interwoven into a complex organic network. We live in a time when advances in brain research and artificial intelligence are calling for us to rethink what we mean by bodies, minds, experience, and nature. Rorty's response is to emphasize the gulf between perception and conception and argue that there is no interesting philosophic work to be done in discussing the way our bodies play a role in shaping our understanding. The other response, marked long ago by panpsychists such as Whitehead and Dewey, and now taken up by contemporary philosophers such as Mark Johnson, is to retrieve the metaphor *experience* and use it to describe the way all organisms struggle to cope with their environment. Viewed this way, panpsychism is likely to remain relevant in both the near and long terms.

CHAPTER 8

Heaven's Partners or Nietzschean Free Spirits?

Having rejected Rorty's criticisms of panpsychism in the previous chapter, I do not want to leave readers with the impression that I think Rorty's philosophy is completely out of synch with this volume's argument for the unity of knowledge and action. In fact, putting aside those things that I criticized above, I see much in Rorty's philosophy that is continuous with my own reading of Dewey, Whitehead, and Wang on this issue. To make this clear, and to draw upon what I think of as the best and most interesting aspects of Rorty's work, this chapter develops a comparison between the Neo-Confucian struggle with Taoism and the contemporary struggles between Deweyan pragmatists and postmodern pragmatists such as Richard Rorty. Specifically, I argue that Deweyan pragmatists can learn from Rorty just as Neo-Confucians like Wang Yang-ming learned from Taoists.

At the outset it is important to state that in developing this analogy between Neo-Confucianism and Deweyan pragmatism, I am not claiming Neo-Confucians and pragmatists say the same things, though there are important similarities, which I've been pointing to throughout this volume. Neither am I saying that Rorty's postmodernism is merely a contemporary form of Taoism, though again there are interesting parallels. I am arguing that the similarities between Neo-Confucianism and pragmatism on the one hand and Taoism and postmodernism on the other provide helpful information for contemporary pragmatists who are trying to react constructively to the postmodern movements. Were I to make a complete case for this claim I would have to demonstrate in detail how the overall situations are analogous and identify those things contemporary pragmatists ought to learn from Neo-Confucians. Such a task is beyond the scope of a single chapter or even a book of this length. It is an area for contemporary Confucians and pragmatists to explore cooperatively. My more limited purpose is to recover from Rorty's work those things that reinforce the point that knowledge and action are really one thing and that move us forward in the quest for a nonrepresentationalist theory of knowledge.

For the most part, I do not develop any detailed discussion of Whiteheadian process philosophy in this chapter. Partly this is due to historical reasons. As we have seen, Rorty left behind his early interest in Whitehead to pursue his reconstructed version of Dewey. Meanwhile, process philosophy continued on its own track, not always in contact with pragmatism and only rarely intersecting with Rorty. The pragmatic reading of Whitehead's theory of knowledge that I've been pressing throughout this volume may be seen by some as one route toward developing more frequent and detailed intersections among contemporary pragmatists, process philosophers, and postmodern pragmatists who follow Rorty's lead.[1]

Throughout history, Confucians have criticized Taoists for being too little concerned with moral and political issues, while Taoists have made fun of stuffy Confucians who get caught up in antiquated ritual practices. Nevertheless, the first Neo-Confucians, Chou Tun-i, Chang Tsai, Ch'eng Hao, and Ch'eng I, as well as later thinkers such as Wang Yang-ming, all had extensive training in the "heterodox traditions" of Buddhism and Taoism. Though they made use of the traditional Confucian language criticizing Taoism, they were not ashamed to draw from it when it seemed appropriate. In fact, most scholars now acknowledge that the early Neo-Confucians were deliberately syncretistic, appropriating many Taoist and Buddhist terms and meditation practices by adapting them to a traditional Confucian anthropology.[2]

In trying to understand how this process of assimilation took place, despite the anti-Taoist rhetoric, it helps to remind ourselves that Confucianism is not very far from Taoism on ontological issues. Recognizing this helps explain how Chou Tun-i was able to link *T'ai Chi* (the Confucian term for the Great Ultimate) with *wu chi* (the Taoist term for nonbeing). It also partially explains why later Neo-Confucians such as Chu Hsi and Wang Yang-ming allowed this identification to stand.

The real differences between Taoism and Confucianism are located in the philosophical anthropology each tradition adds to these largely common ontological premises. By identifying *T'ai Chi* with *wu chi,* the Neo-Confucians were acknowledging an ontological commonality with Taoism and using a Taoist concept to open up and transform a form of Confucianism (medieval Confucianism as practiced among the intelligentsia in the bureaucracy and in the courts), which had become overly rigid and sterile. In short, it was the shared ontological vision that made it possible for Neo-Confucians to use Taoist insights to remove some of the very things Taoists had been complaining about for centuries, without losing their identities as Confucians.

The story of the Confucian appropriation of *wu chi* contains a lesson for contemporary Deweyan pragmatists who are wrestling with how to respond to postmodernism and in particular Richard Rorty. American philosophers are currently struggling over the status of John Dewey's legacy. Some, like Rorty, see Dewey as a founding figure for America's version of the postmodern and deconstructionist movements. Rorty claims that by rejecting epistemological problems and arguing that we construct knowledge perspectivally, Dewey anticipates claims made by Jacques Derrida and others. As we have seen, to read Dewey this way, Rorty feels he also must jettison the "metaphysical" side of Dewey's thought, arguing that such reflections are really holdovers from a tradition Dewey was actually undermining. My argument, by contrast, depends on the premise that we cannot jettison Dewey's metaphysical reflections without losing the central insights of the pragmatic tradition. Like the Neo-Confucians who defended traditional Confucianism against the "excesses of Taoism," I have been arguing that Rorty's reading would transform pragmatism by emptying it of the ontological basis for its moral and political content. Put simply, for Dewey, every deconstruction, every dismantling of the cognitive structures regulating our appropriation of the world anticipates and serves a later reconstruction. That reconstruction is always guided by the pursuit of specific values that make little sense without the full complement of Dewey's metaphysical thinking. From this perspective, human creativity is not pure play or spontaneity, terms that have a prominent place in both traditional Taoism and contemporary postmodernism. Instead, human creativity is more like the Neo-Confucian struggle to create meaning without being tied to any single framework of meaningfulness.

Despite this clear difference with Rorty, I do believe that pragmatists have much to learn from him in much the same way that Neo-Confucians learned from Taoists. The Neo-Confucians accomplished the task by picking up and redeploying Taoist terms within a traditional Confucian meaning system. If it is carefully done, a similar redeployment of Rorty's concepts and terminology could have such a salutary effect on Deweyan pragmatic thought, helping us to shed for good some of the overly scientistic tendencies, which have sometimes made pragmatism seem less dynamic and useful for contemporary moral reflection than it really is.

NEO-CONFUCIANISM AND PRAGMATISM

Some might ask why I think the Neo-Confucian situation and the pragmatist's situations are roughly analogous. As we have seen, both Neo-Confucianism and pragmatism are rooted in somewhat similar biological, social, ethical, and political metaphors (Neville, 1981; 1985; Hall and Ames, 1987) They both support a modified process ontology, a naturalistic understanding of the human mind and its relationship to the world, a vision of the self as constituted by its relationships, an understanding of value as a developing ontological category, and an approach to politics as the quest for harmonic integration among disparate needs, rather than the imposition of some preexistent monolithic order.

Neo-Confucianism and pragmatism also both struggle against systems of thought which *seem* to undermine positive social theories, traditional ethical principles, and legitimate political claims. Neo-Confucianism struggled against Taoism and Buddhism, while contemporary pragmatism is struggling with a variety of "postmodernisms." I emphasize the word *seem*, because it is an open question whether Taoism, Buddhism, or postmodernism actually does undermine positive social theories, though there is no doubt that from the perspective of traditional Confucians and traditional pragmatists, that is what their opponents *seem* to do.

Confucians and contemporary pragmatists both criticize their respective opponents as morally vacuous because they lack an ontological basis for understanding or promoting familial, social, and political life. There is, however, something ironic in these charges since Confucianism shares a great deal with Taoist ontology, while pragmatists know that their openended, dynamic ontology is compatible with much of the indeterminacy postmodern thinkers find in language, the self, and our social structures.

In the contemporary pragmatists' conversation, everything seems to turn around what we mean by "ontological," a word that has fallen into serious and some might say permanent disrepute. Throughout this volume I have been presenting an interpretation of pragmatic metaphysical speculation that has little to do with the "onto-theological" quest for a transcendental permanent perspective—a quest that postmodern thinkers such as Derrida and Rorty have been urging us to surrender. Though Rorty may be right to warn American pragmatists to steer clear of scientistic tendencies, which have haunted pragmatism and which undercut Dewey's own approach to metaphysical questions, it would be a travesty to ignore the fact that pragmatic metaphysics is so much more than Rorty ever acknowledges.

One of the points I want to make about the Confucian/Taoist debates is that shared ontological and epistemological commitments smoothed the way for Neo-Confucians to appropriate significant elements of the Taoist tradition. Similarly, I believe that because pragmatists share important epistemological and ontological assumptions with many of their postmodern critics, they are in a good position to learn from postmodernism.

Neo-Confucians and pragmatists differ most from their opponents in the *philosophical anthropology* they build upon the ontological and epistemological positions that they hold in common. Neo-Confucians had a very different assessment of the role we play in the cosmos than that held by Taoists. For Neo-Confucians, humankind is a partner with Heaven and Earth. Our role is to cultivate new harmonics, new values. This resonates quite well with Dewey's description of humanity. Both Taoism and postmodernism challenge such assumptions about what it means to be human. Both lean toward a deep suspicion of human efforts to pursue the good, no matter how the good might be defined.

Apart from similarities listed above there is one significant difference that plays a large role in my reflections on Rorty's work. Neo-Confucians and Taoists both tried to be thoroughgoing naturalists. Both affirmed a line of continuity between the physical, organic, and human realms. The early pragmatists, especially John Dewey, were also naturalistic in this sense. As we have just seen, however (chapter 7), Rorty nods toward naturalism or what he sometimes calls "non-reductive materialism," but he is not naturalistic in the way the others are. His rejection of pragmatic metaphysical speculation, his emphasis on the distinction between conception and perception, and his almost exclusive focus on high-level cognitive activity make it impossible for him to develop a naturalistic theory of value and meaning. Were Dewey alive he would almost certainly accuse Rorty of succumbing to the fallacy of intellectualism (Dewey, 1958, 21ff). Rorty loses touch with the pragmatic heritage he wants to claim by failing to appreciate the linkages among Deweyan naturalism, metaphysics, and theory of knowledge. The Neo-Confucians by contrast were able to appropriate Taoist insights and preserve their Confucian heritage in part because they were largely in agreement with Taoist forms of naturalism. I think this is true despite the fact that I will argue Taoists are not as thoroughgoing in their naturalism as Neo-Confucians seem to be.

In the previous paragraphs, I have tried to outline the generic similarities between pragmatism and Confucianism. These can be rendered more specific by examining what Dewey and Wang each has to say about key issues such as the self, experience, social order, knowledge, and value.

While trying to overcome the Cartesian image of the self, an image based on the Newtonian metaphor of independent substance, Dewey adopted the "situation" as his basic ontological metaphor. As we have seen in previous chapters, for Dewey all things are patterned movements placed within an even wider set of patterned movements. Viewed this way, the universe is movement. Dewey coupled this process vision with a consistent naturalism that asserts a line of continuity from inorganic situations to self-conscious ones. All situations, insofar as they are identifiable, exhibit a patterned movement, which Dewey calls their "equilibrium." Inorganic situations exhibit an equilibrium that is supported or undermined by changes within the wider environment. Organic situations exhibit patterns that move from equilibrium to disequilibrium and back again. A situation is organic when it has the capacity to restore an equilibrium that has been disturbed by changes in its environment. Conscious situations occur when a situation becomes complicated enough to allow for a reflexive awareness of the patterning process.

The important point to note is that there are no independently existing entities on any level. A rock's identity is drawn from a pattern of interactions within a specific environment. Animals gain their status as organic entities only within the context of an environment that makes such processes possible. Similarly, human selves emerge from organic, social, and linguistic situations. We do not appear full-blown and then find our way into a situation. Rather, situations make us what we are: physical, organic, experiential, social, and self-conscious. Apart from the situation, there simply is no "self" as Dewey would want us to use the term.

The social and individual are both patterns of interaction set within a wider context of dynamic interactions. The situation we identify with selfhood contains patterns that are more tightly drawn than the looser patterns exhibited by the social. The important point, however, is that there is no dichotomy between sociality and selfhood, public and private. Dewey allows us to move from one context to the other without introducing ontological chasms or supernatural phenomena.[3]

For example, as Dewey sees it, experience is not something an individual possesses. It is the product of a given situation. For convenience, we might say, "Tom was afraid." However, the more accurate description, according to Dewey, is that the *whole situation* (a situation that contains the patterned movement we call "the subject, Tom" and the patterned movements we call "the objects of his experience") engendered fearful experience.

When we view experience this way, it becomes clear that it is always a kind of activity rather than the passive influx of data. Once the empiricist's passive observer is dissolved into Dewey's dynamic situation, we must rethink old cognitive models of thinking, knowledge, and the human mind. Experience becomes a specific kind of activity set within and dependent on a broader context of dynamic activity. The spectator theory of knowledge simply does not apply when knowledge is viewed from within such a dynamic process ontology. Knowledge, like experience, is always an activity in which "knowers" successfully integrate their processes with surrounding processes to achieve a specific end.

The resonance between Dewey's approach to these issues and the approach of a Neo-Confucian such as Wang Yang-ming is obvious to most people who know something about both traditions. For Wang, as for most Chinese thinkers, entities are patterns of dynamic movement (e.g., *yin/yang* alternations) set within ever-wider patterns of dynamic movement. As is true for Dewey, this process ontology is coupled with a naturalism that establishes a line of continuity between the various kinds of interactions that make up the cosmos.

Wang's slogan urging us to "form one body with all things" reveals the moral implications of his ontological vision. We are, in a sense, already one body with all things since we are constituted by our relationships. The sage, however, recognizes our ontological situation and builds on our interconnectedness by deepening and thickening the relationships that already link us to all things. According to Wang our task is to reform ourselves so that we generate actions from within a perspective that is broader than our own private needs and desires. In short, Wang expects us to cultivate solidarity with the cosmos that transforms us into a full creative partner with Heaven and Earth.

Beyond the continuities between Dewey's and Wang's understanding of selfhood and sociality, there is an important link in their description of knowledge. As chapters 4 and 5 point out in detail, for both, knowledge is a kind of action rather than the passive mental replication of the real. To know is to act wisely. Wang states this position most clearly in the slogan *"chih hsing ho-i"* (the unity of knowledge and action). Similarly, Dewey also viewed any attempt to separate knowledge from action as a violation of the principle of continuity that regulated so much of his thought (Alexander, 1987, 105ff).

In addition to the areas of commonality discussed above, it is important to note that Dewey and Wang took similar positions with respect to the nature and genesis of value. Dewey, of course, set his understanding of value in aesthetic terms. A careful reading of his *Art as Experience* will reveal that it contains his "moral philosophy." I say this not because Dewey reduces value theory to "mere" aestheticism, but rather because he elevates our understanding of the aesthetics to an ontological level (Alexander, 1987). In *Experience and Nature,* Dewey made it clear that all value emerges from an organism's need to integrate itself with the processes that surround it. On the biological level, this is expressed in the organism's need for a steady supply of food and protection from those things that might undermine its ongoing development. As organisms grow in sophistication, the sphere of integration becomes broader and more complicated. With the acquisition of language, it becomes the human quest for meaning.

Like all other organisms, humans are seeking to create a harmony of processes. They struggle to integrate their own needs, desires, and dreams with the realities of the contemporary and future situations. There are an indeterminate number of possibilities. But as Dewey describes it, all of them are measured within the overall quest for harmonic order.

Creating such an order does not entail the mere merging of all things into a single monolithic unity, according to Dewey. Rather, Dewey recognizes that aesthetic value requires the delicate balancing of a complicated collection of needs and satisfactions. To say that humans pursue the quest for meaning is to say that we are looking for a blend of struggle and satisfaction, which provides us with a sense of our own self-worth.

The resonance between Dewey's position and Wang Yang-ming's understanding of the sage's quest to maximize harmonic possibilities is striking. Both Dewey and Wang felt humankind was capable of recognizing value (at least from within a limited perspective). For Dewey, this conclusion stemmed from the biological roots of his understanding of value; for Wang, it was a component of the Confucian ontology and anthropology. Neither claimed that there existed a single transcendent set of values toward which all things aspire; and both assumed it was our *responsibility* or role to undertake the task of pursuing value even though it took on so many different forms.

CONFUCIAN SPONTANEITY

Having established why there is something analogous between the pragmatic and Neo-Confucian situations, I would like to turn next to a more detailed examination of the Neo-Confucian appropriation of the Taoist term *wu-chi*. How was it possible for Neo-Confucians to make use of such a central Taoist concept without losing their identity as Confucians? There are, of course, a great many sociological and historical factors that played a role. In the explanation that follows, I do not mean to underplay the importance of such factors. Nevertheless, I am interested in the intellectual moves because I think contemporary pragmatists have something to learn from them.

As I see it, classical Confucianism and Taoism are close on ontological issues (both reject the notion that the world is regulated by an unchanging set of transcendent principles) and far apart on anthropological ones (they disagree over our ability/responsibility to know and pursue what is valuable). This ontological convergence made it possible for Neo-Confucians to appropriate a Taoist ontological concept such as *wu-chi*. At the same time, however, Neo-Confucians had to struggle to keep the Taoist anthropological conclusions from infecting Confucian thought. In short, Neo-Confucian thinkers had to redeploy or reconstruct *wu-chi* not in terms of its central ontological meaning but rather in terms of anthropological associations that were far too negativistic about human activity and knowledge to be consistent with Confucianism.

In arguing that classical Confucianism does not presume a fixed ontology regulated by a transcendent order, I lean heavily on the book *Thinking through Confucius* (1987) by David Hall and Roger Ames. In that work, the authors demonstrate that the *Analects* presumes an open-ended ontology where spontaneity and flexibility are as important as the rituals handed down by one's ancestors. As it turns out, there is no analog in the *Analects* to the Western description of knowing as a purely intellectual mirroring of an external reality. Instead, knowledge is understood from the beginning in performative terms. Moreover, there is no analog to the platonic image of a fixed set of transcendent principles. Instead, the world is slowly (but always) changing, as are the rituals we use to guide ourselves through it.

The impression that Hall and Ames draw of classical Confucianism is also supported by another classical Confucian text, the *Chung-yung (Doctrine of the Mean;* Chan, 1963, 95–114). In the *Chung-yung* Heaven is described as the creative source of all harmonies (things). Humankind continues Heaven's creative activity by helping to bring about new harmonies that would not have emerged without human intervention. By creating new harmonies, the sage completes a trinity with *T'ien* (Heaven) and Earth. We are *T'ien's* highest product and an extension of its creativity. This creativity is not determined by a preexisting ontological or moral order. It is rooted in the same open-ended spontaneity that is the source of all things.

There is a resonance here between these classical Confucian texts and what we find in the classical Taoist understanding of *wu* (vacuity, emptiness). Both the *Lao Tzu* and the *Chuang Tzu* characterize the *Tao* as a nameless void (vacuity) that is at the same time the very heart of creativity. For example, chapter 25 of the *Lao Tzu* (tr. Lau, 1963) reads:

> There is a thing confusedly formed,
> Born before heaven and earth.
> Silent and void
> It stands alone and does not change,
>   Goes round and does not weary.
> It is capable of being the mother of the world.
> I know not its name So I style it 'the way.' (82)

Lao Tzu also uses the metaphor of a bellows to signify the *Tao's* productive emptiness.

> Is not the space between heaven and earth like a bellows?
> It is empty without being exhausted:
> The more it works the more comes out.
> Much speech leads inevitably to silence.
> Better to hold fast to the void. (61)

There is a sense in which this emptiness makes room for a creativity and openness that is the ultimate source of all things. In explaining the Taoist position Wu Kuang-ming posits a distinction between what he calls the "being-standpoint" (where most non-Taoists find themselves) and the "non-being standpoint" (which characterizes Chuang Tzu's position). The "being-standpoint," as Wu defines it, amounts to the unfounded elevation of a specific principle or set of principles for interpreting *experience to the exclusion of all others.* By fixing the principles used for interpreting experience, we fix the "things" in our world into inflexible categories. According to Wu, Taoists admit a tentative selection of principles is fair but reject exclusive adherence to a *single* set of principles as not ontologically warranted. He argues:

> In the final analysis, one must choose between two general kinds of regularity in the universe: either a regularity of a flexible sort or that of an inflexible sort. [By choosing the flexible sort one] . . . can vary one's explanation of the regularity of the universe from a mechanical one to a moral or a musical one; such variability allows one to manipulate the world, to submit oneself to it, and to enjoy oneself in it. (Wu, 1982, 71)

By opting for flexibility, the Taoist is not locked into contradictions that arise within the being standpoint. The universe is no longer a fixed block, understandable from a single perspective. It is an amorphous creative fluid divisible in many ways, some more fruitful than others. Quoting Wu again: "Nature is now seen and lived, in the vacuity of the standpoint of non-being, as a differentiated continuum (pace Northrop); it is many in one, one in many, on the move" (ibid., 72).

With the above characterizations of both the Confucian and Taoist ontologies before us, we can see that the stereotypical opposition between a rigid Confucian ontology regulated by a fixed set of ritual and cosmic principles, and an open-ended, spontaneous Taoist ontology, simply doesn't fit our current understanding of these traditions. Where Taoists and Confucians do differ is over the role humans play within this emerging order. Even though the *Chung-yung* and the

Analects acknowledge that there is no unchanging or transcendent order to appeal to when making judgments, they adhere to the basic Confucian intuition that all humans can tell better from worse *within a given situation* and that it is *our responsibility to pursue the better.* This is diametrically opposed to the Taoist intuition that a lack of a permanent moral order makes it difficult (if not impossible) to make positive claims about good or evil. The *Chuang Tzu* and the *Lao Tzu* both argue that given the human situation, our primary responsibility is to quiet our desires and integrate ourselves with nature because in most instances our desires are rooted in faulty self-serving assumptions about the self and the world. Putting this anthropological disagreement another way, we can say that while classical Taoists suspect that most human projects are out of joint with the *Tao,* the *Analects* and the *Chung-yung* see human creativity as an expression of the *Tao's* own spontaneous creativity. Confucians do not experience the same ontological estrangement from the *Tao* that Taoists describe and seek to overcome. When Confucians fail, they simply have not read a situation wisely and have made less than optimal choices. They failed to make full use of the possibilities created by Heaven and Earth. They are not, however, out of joint with the cosmos or a continually emerging cosmic order.⁴

This ontological commonality and anthropological disagreement goes a long way toward explaining how later Neo-Confucians were able to pick up central Taoist concepts such as *wu-chi* and still retain their identities as Confucians. As I see it, the Neo-Confucians were looking for a way to transform a tradition that had succumbed to its own internal conservative tendencies. The Confucian emphasis on rituals, coupled with its focus on moral responsibility, tended toward an overblown sense of the self's importance as well as a reverence for life's "forms" over its "contents." My description of the open-ended and spontaneous tendencies inherent in classical Confucian texts should not be confused with a description of Confucianism as it was practiced in the courts and in the bureaucracies over the many centuries that Confucians held power in China.

Throughout those many centuries of Confucian power, Taoism undercut this overblown sense of self-importance by poking fun at Confucian seriousness and formality. Moreover, by the end of the twelfth century, when the Neo-Confucians were first appearing on the philosophical scene, Buddhism and Taoism had already enjoyed considerable periods of power at the expense of traditional Confucian scholars. In this context, the Neo-Confucians were aware of the limitations of their own tradition, as well as the benefits that the "heterodox traditions" had to offer.

In seeking to break Confucianism free from the heritage of its own rigidity, they assimilated Confucianism to Taoism's ontological vocabulary while working assiduously to keep their distance from the Taoist anthropology. The paradoxical Taoist linking of vacuity and fullness in the term *wu-chi* was simply a powerful symbol that was better able to express tendencies toward openness and spontaneity inherent in the classical Confucian texts, but long forgotten by the Confucian culture. Like many reform movements, the Neo-Confucians felt they were going back to the roots of their tradition and recovering *T'ai chi's* original meaning when they associated it with the Taoist term *wu-chi.*

Despite its almost universal appeal among the principal Neo-Confucian thinkers, the appropriation of *wu-chi* was neither easy nor seamless. In fact, the transition was still not complete four centuries later when Wang Yang-ming's students continued to worry that the association of these two terms might undercut traditional Confucian values. Put simply, Wang's students were anxious to protect the Confucian understanding of our status as a full partner with Heaven and Earth from the negativistic anthropological images that are common to the Taoist and Buddhist traditions.

Evidence of this continuing struggle can be seen in the way Wang's students were repeatedly confused over his use of the term *tranquility.* Earlier I pointed out that in redeploying the Taoist concept *'wu-chi,'* Neo-Confucians were struggling to eliminate its negativistic anthropological associations. That, however, is only part of the picture. It is also true they were appropriating *some* of those negativistic terms for use within their own tradition. All concepts come in clusters, and the acquisition of *wu-chi* was accomplished by transforming a number of traditionally Taoist terms for Confucian use. Thus, tranquility, a term originally tied to *wu-chi* and associated with Taoist meditation, was given a positive character by Chou Tun-i, who tied it to the specifically Confucian understanding of *yin/yang* and the "five elements" as can be seen in this statement from *An Explanation of the Diagram of the Great Ultimate:*

> The Ultimate of Non-being and also the Great Ultimate *(T'ai-chi)!* The Great Ultimate through movement generates *yang.* When its activity reaches its limit it becomes tranquil. Through tranquility the Great Ultimate generates *yin.* When tranquility reaches its limit, activity begins again. So movement and tranquility alternate and become the root of each other, giving rise to the distinction of *yin* and *yang,* and the two modes are thus established. (Tr. Chan, 1963, 463)

When Wang's students expressed their concern that they might slip into Taoist or Buddhist forms of spirituality, which would leave them like "dry wood and dead ashes" (Wang, 1963, 135; 217), he responded by reiterating Chou's linkage of tranquility/activity with *yin/yang* and the five elements, adding his own claim that ultimately tranquility and activity are *both* included within the Principle of Nature.[5]

> The Teacher said, "Activity and tranquillity are one. If it is in accord with the Principle of Nature, the mind that is empty and tranquil at midnight will be the same mind that responds to events and deals with affairs now. If it is in accord with the Principle of Nature, the mind that responds to events and deals with affairs now is the same mind that is empty and tranquil at midnight. Therefore, activity and tranquillity are one and cannot be separated. If we know that activity and tranquillity form a unity, the fact that the Buddhist's infinitesimal mistake at the beginning leads to an infinite error in the end cannot be concealed. (Ibid., 203)

By joining tranquility to its polar opposite, activity, and locating both within the Principle of Nature, Wang successfully assimilates Taoist tranquility without surrendering Confucian responsibilities. Since Wang also argues that *hsin* (the heart/mind) is fully unified with *Li* (Principle of Nature), he can claim that the human *hsin* encompasses both tranquility and activity. In short, a sage can be fully *tranquil* while fully *active*. Viewed this way tranquility could never be confused with passivity (dry wood). At the same time, however, Wang gets to pick up all of the Taoist meditational and spiritual resonances that come with the term tranquility.

Wang was trying to point out to his students that tranquility could not be attained outside the movements of *yin* and *yang* (ibid., 138). Tranquility is not a goal unto itself, as it seems to be in Taoism. Tranquility/activity and *yin/yang* represent a *single* process viewed from different angles. The sage's task is to find tranquility *in* activity. They cannot be attained separately. This perspective legitimizes the quest for tranquility as an aspect of Confucian spirituality. This understanding of tranquility also makes it possible for Wang's students to return to the opening passages of the *Chung-yung* and see in its statements on equilibrium and harmony an early Confucian appreciation of tranquility.

Assimilating the Taoist understanding of tranquility with *yin* and *yang* has yet another benefit for Wang and his students. *Yin* and *yang* arise spontaneously, but not without some kind of order. The assertion that the world is constituted by expansion *(yang)* and contraction *(yin)* entails some minimal level of ordering. Both Taoists and Confucians cultivate an appreciation for spontaneous *orderings* that arise naturally. Confucians, however, add an awareness of the human potential to work with what occurs naturally in the creation of additional kinds of order.

This capacity makes us creative partners with heaven and earth. However, creating new orders is not, for Wang or most other Neo-Confucians, the simple imposition of the human will upon the world. Genuine creativity begins with a *sensitivity to and appreciation for* the already existing patterns. Tranquility occurs only when we are sensitized to the *yin/yang* patterns that constitute our world. In this, Wang agrees with Taoists, who press us to cultivate an appreciation for those things that emerge without human interference. But Wang and most other Neo-Confucians go beyond Taoists by insisting that mere appreciation is not sufficient. We have the ability to do more. We can take up our role as partners with heaven and earth and add constructively to the harmonic patterns in our world.

Wang's effort to integrate central Taoist ontological insights with a traditional Confucian anthropology helps illuminate the two doctrines that Western interpreters most often find confusing: *chih hsing ho-i* (the unity of knowledge and action) and *liang chih* (innate knowledge).

Earlier I mentioned how important it was for Wang to block any separation of knowledge from action. Given what we have seen of Wang's appropriation of Taoist insights, it is possible to argue that *chih hsing ho-i* parallels Taoist efforts to avoid the being standpoint.[6] With *chih hsing ho-i,* Wang joins Taoists in recognizing that the separation of knowledge from action always entails the existence of a cognitive self (knower) who is already separated from the *Tao.* The *Lao Tzu* puts it simply, saying: "The way that can be spoken of [named] is not the constant way" (tr. Lau, 1963, 57). In response, Taoists urge us to surrender our "knowledge" in favor of an aesthetic merging with nature itself. Taoist sages stop trying to gain control by "knowing" the world. Instead, they open themselves to experiencing a creative vacuity that is at the same time the very font of nature. In trying to overcome this same separation of self from world, Wang takes a completely different tack that is more radical. Instead of following the Taoists and calling for the erasure of the self as a cognitive entity, Wang presses for a complete redefinition of what knowledge is. By arguing that there is no such thing as a "pure knowing," which precedes action, Wang points out that we are never really separate from the world at all. The problem turns out to be an illusion rooted in a faulty understanding of what knowledge is. In this way Wang concurs with the Taoist criticism of knowledge as it was then understood, yet he retains his Confucian identity and avoids Taoism's tendencies toward quietism and passivity by restructuring our understanding of knowledge itself. For Wang, humans are not "knowers" apart from the world, we are the quest for new harmonies appropriate to our immediate situation. We find ourselves in a concrete world always already engaged in the struggle to constitute new meanings by responding to and taking a hand in directing changes in our world.

This delicate balance between Taoist openness and Confucian responsibility is also embodied in Wang's final major doctrine: *liang chih* (innate knowledge). As I explained in chapter 3, *liang chih* is not the assertion that humans hold *a priori* knowledge about a transcendent ontological or moral order.[7] Instead, *liang chih* is Wang's way of describing our participation in the open-ended, spontaneous creativity at the base of all things. In Confucian terms, as partners with Heaven and Earth, we find ourselves thrown into open-ended situations, and we respond by creating new values, new orders, new harmonies, new forms of determinateness, which are ultimately a genuine contribution to the whole of things.

Liang chih is *innate* because all human beings share in this indeterminate creativity. It is a kind of *knowledge* because the creative process always entails the act of choosing or valuing one thing over another. Thus, the translation "innate knowledge" makes sense only when seen in the context of Wang's insistence that knowledge is always a form of action and that human action is merely an instance of the open-ended creativity at the base of all things.

Viewed this way, Wang's culminating doctrine embodies much of what he learned from the Taoist tradition while preserving the central Confucian appreciation for our moral responsibilities and our cultural heritage. *Wu-chi* and associated terms such as *tranquility* helped open the door to a new understanding of the Confucian responsibilities. It helped counteract Confucianism's conservative and hierarchical tendencies by tying a Taoist's awareness that there is no single transcendent order to a Confucian's commitment to maximize the good in any situation. In the end, Wang's Neo-Confucian sages look very much like Taoist sages except that after quieting their desires, after appreciating the spontaneous appearance of new harmonic patterns, after joining in the cosmic dance and flowing with nature itself, Neo-Confucian sages strike out on their own, creating new steps that take account of the other movements and enhance the whole of things.

PRIVATE VERSUS PUBLIC: OVERCOMING THE RORTYAN SPLIT

By describing the Neo-Confucian sage as a dancer who takes account of others' movements while adding new steps of her own, I was portraying the very thing that Richard Rorty says most of us cannot have. In *Contingency, irony, and solidarity* (1989), Rorty says we should give up the hope of integrating private pleasures and public responsibilities. Instead, he argues that we must concede that there is no "comprehensive philosophical outlook [that would] let us hold self-creation and justice, private perfection and human solidarity, in a single vision" (xiv). Over the next few pages, I would like to use what we have seen of the pragmatic, Confucian, and Taoist traditions to demonstrate why Rorty is mistaken in this claim. In doing so, however, I am less interested in refuting Rorty than I am in identifying where I think he is right and how a pragmatist might be well served to accept much of what he has to say, even though I reject his final conclusions. My goal is much like that of those Neo-Confucians who looked to Taoism for tools to revitalize a tradition while taking care not to allow the transformation to become a complete surrender of their own tradition's best insights.

I am attracted to Rorty's thought because he has been the most successful at exposing the radical side of the early pragmatic thinkers, especially John Dewey. In his description of the self as a centerless web, his rejection of foundationalism in all of its forms, and his recognition that narrative and metaphor are the basis for theory rather than the other way around, Rorty takes basic pragmatic insights and extends them in very helpful ways. This is evident even in the description of his "liberal utopia." Though I disagree with the public/private dichotomy that lies behind it, there is much in Rorty's utopian vision that is true to pragmatism's most important discoveries.

> In my utopia human solidarity would be seen not as a fact to be recognized by clearing away 'prejudice' or burrowing down to the previously hidden depths, but rather, as a goal to be achieved. It is to be achieved not by inquiry but by imagination, the imaginative ability to see strange people as fellow sufferers. Solidarity is not discovered by reflection but created. It is created by increasing our sensitivity to the particular details of the pain and humiliation of other, unfamiliar sorts of people. . . . This is a task not for theory but for genres such as ethnography, the journalist's report, the comic book, the docudrama, and especially, the novel. . . . Such a turn would be emblematic of our having given up the attempt to hold all the sides of our life in a single vision, to describe them with a single vocabulary. (Ibid., xvi)

In this statement Rorty rejects all essentialisms, acknowledges the unity of knowledge and action, and recognizes the extent to which we are as responsible for the invention of the good as we are for its realization. In the call to develop solidarity with others, Rorty is echoing at least one aspect of a theme we saw in Wang Yang-ming's call to become "one body with all things," though Rorty would scoff at the idea that anything is related to "all things." Rorty's gloss on Dewey comes at the end where he elevates the importance of narrative. But even that could be read as a natural extension of insights gleaned from *Art as Experience* (Alexander, 1987).

The only notes of explicit discord with Deweyan pragmatism are Rorty's rejection of inquiry in favor of the imagination and his call to give up the attempt to hold all the sides of our life in a single vision. Rorty's antitheoretical bent clashes with Dewey's admiration for science and the scientific method. Nevertheless, I think the argument over inquiry will turn out to be less important once it becomes clear that despite Rorty's suspicions, neither Dewey nor his followers exhibit foundationalist or essentialist tendencies. In short, when Rorty complains about Dewey's metaphysics, I believe (with many others) that his criticisms fall wide of the mark because Rorty defines metaphysics too narrowly (Neville, 1982; 1992; Boisvert, 1988). In the pragmatists' hands metaphysics is no longer a search for absolute foundations.

I find the final claim in the description of Rorty's utopia the most troubling, that we should stop trying to hold all the sides of our life in a single vision. It contributes to Rorty's conclusion that we should posit a significant dichotomy between public responsibilities and private pleasures. Quite simply, Rorty does not feel we can hold those two perspectives together in a single vision. Instead, he argues we should simply accept the fact that we are constituted by a contingent collection of internal voices, with no reason to assume that they can be integrated into a single coherent unity. Ultimately the only way to answer Rorty's challenge is to hew closely to the pragmatic method and ask the question Are there advantages in seeing ourselves as he invites us? In the end, I think that the dichotomy Rorty creates is yet another false division that causes more harm than good. It feels like an intellectual failure of nerve, an unwillingness to accept the burden of trying to create conceptual orders that hold together both private pleasure and public responsibility, even though we know that any particular order will ultimately be less than it proposes. I do not doubt the truth of Rorty's diagnosis. We are collections of intractably contradictory narrative streams. I also do not doubt his prediction that no integrated sense of self is ever fully possible. Nevertheless, and despite the paradoxical implications, I believe that the quest to harmonize those voices is the task we face. In fact, I might even argue that one of the things that makes human life worthwhile is our unending struggle to find a way to turn our internal contradictions and conflicts into a productive harmonic tension.

Through a close reading of the first two chapters in *Contingency, irony, and solidarity,* I will argue that though Rorty is right about the contingency of language and the self, he is wrong about the impact that contingency should have upon how we view the relationship between our private and public responsibilities. In particular, I believe Rorty has lost touch with Dewey's understanding of the origin of language and the role it plays in the creation of community life. Put another way, I agree with many of Rorty's epistemological claims (though he might be horrified to hear them described as such) while disagreeing with many of his anthropological assertions about what it means to be human in an open, fully contingent world.

LANGUAGE IS CONTINGENT, BUT IS IT RANDOM?

Rorty's goal in the opening chapter of *Contingency, irony, and solidarity* is to redescribe language as something other than a "medium" standing between knowing subjects and an external world. Following Davidsonian themes we saw in chapter 3, Rorty sees in the traditional triune relationship (subject, language, and world) a basis for many of the foundationalist and essentialistic tendencies that have infected Western thought since Plato.

As has been the case since he wrote *Philosophy and the Mirror of Nature,* the first step in surrendering the idea that language is a medium is recognizing that there is no "truth" out there in the world waiting to be captured and re-presented in language. While Rorty acknowledges that "most things in space and time are the effects of causes that do not include human mental states," he presses the point that such a world cannot contain truth in itself. "Truth cannot be out there—cannot exist independently of the human mind—because sentences cannot so exist, or be out there." Truth is a character of sentences, and we have no reason to believe the world "splits itself up on its own initiative, into sentence-shaped chunks called facts" (Rorty, 1989, 4–5).

Rorty defends this claim by urging us to shift our attention from single words and declarative sentences to Wittgensteinian language games that contain their own internal criteria of rationality. At this level, it "becomes hard to think that [a] vocabulary is somehow already out there in the world, waiting for us to discover it." "The world can, once we have programmed ourselves with a language, cause us to hold beliefs. But it cannot propose a language for us to speak"(ibid., 6). We cannot say that our language accurately reflects the way things are. We can only point to whether it helps us to cope. If it does, we deem it successful and award the accolade *truth*.

Rorty's larger point, however, is that at the abstract level of language games, there are no criteria governing shifts from one game to another. "Cultural change of this magnitude does not result from applying criteria (or from 'arbitrary decision') any more than individuals become theists or atheists, or shift from one spouse or circle of friends to another, as a result either of applying criteria or of *actes gratuits*. We should not look within ourselves for criteria of decisions in such matters any more than we should look to the world" (ibid.). It is important to keep in mind that when Rorty uses the term *criteria* he seems always to mean universal ahistorical principles that transcend the particularities of any specific situation. He says that those who look for such criteria to govern shifts from one language game to another are succumbing to the "temptation to think of the world, or the human self, as possessing an intrinsic nature, an essence. [This is] a result of the temptation to privilege some one among the many languages in which we habitually describe the world or ourselves" (ibid., 6–7).

It is possible to hear in Rorty's refusal to "privilege" any one language a resonance with Wu Kuang-ming's description of the Taoist "non-being standpoint." By refusing to elevate any one set of principles over another, Taoists sought to prevent the fixing of all things into a single unchanging matrix. Like Rorty, they saw the link between a permanent set of interpretive principles (or languages) and the illusion that the world has a single character, which language can describe. Chuang-tzu's concern was to keep us open to the unending spontaneous creativity from which all things emerge. Similarly, Rorty is seeking to break the representational link between language and the world in order to free us up to enjoy the spontaneous eruption of new metaphors that create new ways of being in the world. In both cases, the key is to get back in touch with an underlying openness and fluidity that our habits of mind sometimes mask. The difference, however, is that Rorty is much closer to the Confucian interest in the human contribution to this unending spontaneous creativity. While Taoists generally counseled the quieting of the self in order to merge with nature's movements, Rorty and the Confucians both encourage us to think about the ways humans put a creative and positive new stamp on the flow of things. On the issues of anthropology that so divided the Taoists from the Confucians, Rorty is somewhere between them. He is near the Confucians in recognizing our role as creators, but closer to the Taoist sensitivity to the complete impermanent dynamism at the base of all things in his rejection of all criteria governing transitions in human language and in our understanding of the world. For these reasons, there is a genuine affinity between Rorty and the Neo-Confucians who were trying to strike a similar balance between Taoist spontaneity and Confucian responsibility.

Rorty goes on to argue that we can escape the search for ahistorical criteria if we become "reconciled to the idea that most of reality is indifferent to our descriptions of it, and that the human self is created by the use of a vocabulary rather than being adequately or inadequately expressed in a vocabulary." He points out that philosophers have typically imagined "the essential core of the self on one side of [a] network of beliefs and desires, and reality on the other side. In this picture, the network is the product of an interaction between the two, alternately expressing the one and representing the other" (ibid., 10). Rorty believes that by dropping the notion that the world has an essence represented in language, we are well on the way toward dropping the image of a self whose essence is to *possess* beliefs about the world, beliefs that are made possible because language mirrors that essence.

Much of this makes sense to a Deweyan such as me. The reformulating of the notion of truth in nonrepresentational terms, the shift to thinking in terms of language games rather than declarative statements, the rejection of substantialist descriptions of the world and the self are all consistent with Dewey's critique of the spectator theory of knowledge. The one important note of discord surfaces when Rorty says there can be *no* criteria governing the shift from one language game to another. If by rejecting all criteria Rorty merely means there is no atemporal set of principles governing all such transitions, then he is in line with the Taoist and Neo-Confucian insights mentioned above as well as with Dewey's own conclusions. Nevertheless, it would seem unnecessary to reject *all* criteria since we could define the term to include principles that are not atemporal or transcendental.

Dewey was adamant in arguing that all linguistic behaviors be understood *in continuity with and as an outgrowth of* other organic processes. He described organic behavior as a struggle to protect and enhance an organism's processes, and he argued that linguistic behavior could be understood as a special instance of such behavior. When Rorty says there are no criteria governing shifts in linguistic behavior, he makes it sound as if higher-order cognitive activity flows independently of all other levels of experience. Yet it seems hard to ignore the fact that when one language game takes precedence over another, it is because the newly adopted game offers greater satisfactions than the one left behind. Dewey leaves completely open how to define the term *satisfaction* since it will be defined differently in each situation. Nevertheless, it sounds foolish to stand on the sidelines and say that because there are no *universal* criteria governing such changes, they must happen willy nilly.

My concern in raising a challenge to Rorty's formulation is twofold. I want to preserve Dewey's fully naturalized understanding of mind and language from Rorty's "intellectualist" tendencies.[8] Nevertheless, I also want to join Rorty in emphasizing that there is no way to describe the criteria governing linguistic behavior in universal terms. As I see it Dewey and Rorty both agree with Wang Yang-ming's description of our human "core" (our *liang-chih*) as the indeterminate, dynamic process *whereby we establish criteria* and make the decisions that constitute who we are and how we relate to the whole of things. Unlike Rorty, however, Dewey and Wang are not afraid to describe that indeterminate center as our human "core," nor are they timid about venturing forth into hypothetical metaphysical speculations that allow them to see such human creativity as a special instance of the creativity at the base of all things.

Rorty's first step in convincing us that language is not a medium between self and world was to reject the notion that language could represent the "truth" about the world. His second step is to contrast the traditional image of languages as pieces of some universal "jigsaw puzzle" with the Davidson/Wittgenstein description of languages as "alternative tools." As we saw in chapter 3 the tool metaphor is apt because, unlike jigsaw puzzle pieces, tools need not fit together to accomplish a larger purpose. Each tool is designed to accomplish very specific and often disconnected ends. If there is no common human essence, and no common structure/truth about reality, then languages need not fit each other, nor can they represent aspects of some nonexistent totalized universality.

The limitation in the tool metaphor, Rorty points out, is that new languages necessarily arise without a clear sense of their goal because it is specific languages that make it possible to conceive of specific ends.

> The craftsman typically knows what job he needs to do before picking or inventing tools with which to do it. By contrast someone like Galileo, Yeats, or Hegel (a "poet" in my wide sense of the term—the sense of "one who makes things new") is typically unable to make clear exactly what it is that he wants to do before developing the language in which he succeeds in doing it. His new vocabulary makes possible, for the first time, a formulation of its own purpose. It is a tool for doing something which could not have been envisaged prior to the development of a particular set of descriptions, those which it itself helps to provide. (Ibid., 12–13)

In his sensitivity to the fact that languages make new goals possible, Rorty resonates with what we saw of the Neo-Confucian efforts to understand our creative partnership with Heaven and Earth. By letting go of the notion that "'our language' . . . is somehow a unity, a third thing standing in determinate relation with two other unities—the self and reality," we are forced to surrender the idea that there are nonlinguistic meanings which, it is language's job to express, and a nonlinguistic world, which it is language's job to re-present. Having let go of this representational understanding of language, we can see the truly creative role language plays by making possible new goals, or in Neo-Confucian terms, new harmonies (ibid., 13).

Continuing to follow Davidson's lead, Rorty argues that languages are more like "'passing theories' about a person's total behavior—a set of guesses about what she will do under what conditions." Viewed this way we cultivate languages pragmatically, as a means of coping with others. Just as we must cope with "mangoes or boa constrictors—we are trying not to be taken by surprise." In the end Rorty wants us to "[t]hink of the term 'mind' or 'language' not as the name of a medium between self and reality but simply as a flag which signals the desirability of using a certain vocabulary when trying to cope with certain kinds of organisms." This view "naturalizes mind and language by making all questions about the relation of either to the rest of the universe causal questions, as opposed to questions about adequacy of representation or expression" (ibid., 14).

The upshot of thinking about language as a tool for coping with the world, rather than as a representative medium that displays the world, is to drop the idea that language has any transcendental or universal purpose. As Rorty sees it, this leads us inevitably away from any sense that the history of language is guided or shaped by the progressive appreciation for the world's natural shapes. Rather, he argues that language develops like DNA mutations as one metaphor after another is fired off and tested for its usefulness. As Rorty sees us, we are continually in the process of redescribing ourselves, each other, and the world of which we are a part.

> Davidson lets us think of the history of language, and thus the history of culture, as Darwin taught us to think of the history of a coral reef. Old metaphors are constantly dying off into literalness, and then serving as a platform and foil for new metaphors. This analogy lets us think of our 'language'—that is, of the science and culture of twentieth-century Europe—as something that took shape as a result of a great number of sheer contingencies. Our language and our culture are as much a contingency, as much a result of thousands of small mutations finding niches (and millions of others finding no niches), as are the orchids and the anthropoids. (Ibid., 16)

Used this way metaphors are neither true nor false; they have no "meaning" in the literal sense of the term. They are either effective and therefore "savored" or ineffective and allowed to pass quickly from view. "Positivist history of culture sees language as gradually shaping itself around the contours of the physical world. Romantic history of culture sees language as gradually bringing Spirit to self-consciousness. Nietzschean history of culture, and Davidsonian philosophy of language see language as we now see evolution, as new forms of life killing off old forms—not to accomplish a higher purpose, but blindly" (ibid., 19). As I argued earlier, it is the final assertion in the above citation, the claim that metaphors are spewed forth blindly, that I find most difficult to accept. Because he is allergic to Dewey's broader metaphysical speculations, Rorty is unable to see that linguistic activity can be set within the context of organic activity without becoming essentialist or representational. While Rorty may be right that there is no determinate source for the metaphors that we invent, he is wrong not to consider the source of the *urge* to create new metaphors. Viewed as a species of other organic behavior, such urges are always part of a larger effort to protect and enhance the processes that constitute us. Such urges spring from some felt dissatisfaction with the way things are. The poet may not be able to articulate the problem, or describe beforehand what a new, more satisfying order might look like, but the felt need for something new, some other way to describe things, doesn't appear from the air. It is rooted in the poet's own situation. Thus, the rhythmic movement between need and satisfaction (disequilibrium and equilibrium), which is mirrored in all organic activities, is not a "blind" process. It is a response to specific problems within a specific situation. Even granting the Davidsonian claim that metaphors have no literal meaning, we can see that they would have no use if they did not provide some satisfaction, some way of resolving concrete problems that the poet faced. To describe this whole process as blind seems deliberately obtuse, and counter to Rorty's use of Davidson's other description of language as "passing theories" that help us to cope with our world. What else could he mean by cope than to find a way of getting around or removing felt dissatisfactions?

What Rorty does not seem to realize is that it is possible to go beyond merely labeling language a tool for coping without falling back into old fashioned essentialisms. We have seen in Dewey, Wang Yang-ming, and the early Taoists that it is possible to say something more specific about language, without losing sight of its spontaneous and indeterminate character.

Rorty goes wrong, I think, in elevating the creation of new metaphors over other aspects of language development and use. It may be true that each individual metaphor is like a mutation, springing from some indeterminate source. Wang Yang-ming, Chuang-tzu, and Dewey all could agree with that claim. But language is more than just the creation of new metaphors. By emphasizing the indeterminate side of things Rorty has lifted up one part of the process and abstracted it from all that goes with it. For all of Rorty's work in language theory, it turns out that Dewey has the more complicated vision of how languages arise and the multiple roles that they play. Dewey can see these complexities because unlike Rorty, who begins by focusing on high-order cognitive problems (e.g., appearance versus reality and the problem of truth), Dewey grounds his discussion of language in a broader understanding of the human as an organic entity interacting with other human beings and a much wider environment. In *Logic: The Theory of Inquiry* Dewey said:

> The importance of language . . . lies in the fact that, on the one side, it is a strictly biological mode of behavior, emerging in natural continuity from earlier organic activities, while on the other hand, *it compels one individual to take the standpoint of other individuals and to see and inquire from a standpoint that is not strictly personal but is common to them as participants or "parties in a conjoint undertaking."* (1938, 46; italics added)

Dewey would grant Rorty's point that there is something spontaneous about the invention of new metaphors. He might even grant (or at least I would argue that he should grant) Rorty's point that the history of language is the history of the invention of new metaphors. Nevertheless, Dewey recognized the communal side of language in a way that Rorty simply does not see. Rorty gives the impression that metaphors are created out of whole cloth in the smithy of a poetic soul and then dumped upon the world to be "savored" or "spit out." He feels secure from creeping romanticism because he has clearly rejected the idea that this poetic soul connects with some larger truth or being. But romanticism was overly committed to universal truths *and* overly enthralled with the *individual* poetic imagination. Rorty does not seem to notice that the latter commitment is as problematic as the former. Dewey's naturalistic approach makes it much clearer that language emerges from a *situation*. It is not the possession of any one individual (or strong poet!). Language is produced by situations that include human organisms as well as a much wider network of interactions. All parts of a situation play a role in making all aspects of language possible, including transitions from one language game to another.

The unnerving thing is that Rorty gives every indication of understanding all of these things at other places in his text. He surely knows that languages are created communally rather than the possession of individuals. He certainly has a pragmatist's sensitivity to the instrumental role that language plays. Yet when he turns to describe the creation of new metaphors, he seems to lapse into a neoromantic image of an independent soul, an image that runs counter to his other description of the self as a constantly changing network of beliefs.

THE SELF: CONTINGENT AND STILL INDEPENDENT?

The second chapter of *Contingency, irony, and solidarity* is called "The Contingency of Selfhood." It contains what seem to be two contradictory lines of thought. On the one hand, he presses the image of the self as a constantly changing network of beliefs, an image that resonates well with Dewey's descriptions and what we saw of the Neo-Confucian and Taoist traditions. On the other hand, he also struggles to preserve what I see as a neo- or postromantic description of the self as *individual* creator. In this latter mode Rorty points out that in his description of language as the history of new metaphors, he is trying to be true to the insights of "post-Nietzschean philosophers like Wittgenstein and Heidegger [who wrote] philosophy in order to exhibit the universality and necessity of the individual and contingent" (Rorty, 1989, 26). Rorty contrasts such thinkers with *all* other philosophers and critics who seem, according to Rorty, to be concerned only with continuities. Though I am usually ready to grant Rorty rhetorical leeway, this sweeping generalization seems patently false. It simply is not fair for Rorty to divide the world into poets who see life's discontinuities and philosopher-critics who are stuck with the fruitless task of uncovering nonexistent continuities!

To put this difficulty another way, it doesn't seem at all clear to me that we should simply assume that the argument over individual versus social descriptions of the self is linked in any particular way to conversations about contingency and necessity. After all, Deweyan pragmatists and Neo-Confucians both would reject Rorty's linkage of individuality with contingency and sociality with absolutism. Dewey wanted to eliminate all remnants of the idea of independent selfhood while at the same time preserving a clear sense for the open-ended, contingent dimensions to human life. Wang Yang-ming urged his followers to form one body with all things, while arguing that our *liang chih* is the indeterminate center of our own creativity.

Rorty's discussion of contingent selfhood helps me to clarify the analogy comparing the Neo-Confucian appropriation of Taoism with how I think Deweyan pragmatists should approach Rorty. Whereas the Neo-Confucians had to purge Taoist terms of negative anthropological images in order to integrate them into a truly Confucian discourse, Deweyan pragmatists need to purge Rorty's language of an unnecessary nostalgia for a self capable of rewriting itself in complete independence. At the very time when Rorty struggles to dedivinize everything, including the self, he seems to take a major step backward by allowing the strong poet's *independence* as *creator* a role in the construction of our "private life." Rorty's attraction to this now old fashioned image of the self as independent creator is yet another factor leading him to the unnecessary dichotomy between private and public discourse. He argues that in private discontinuities reign and everyone is a poet, whereas in public we act philosophical and cultivate those continuities that are necessary to allow us to have a private life. I am ready to accept Rorty's analysis of the pervasiveness of contingency. I want to appropriate his description of pragmatism as a system of thought capable of operating beyond the bounds of the traditional relativist and absolutist debates, but I believe we should not allow a Nietzschean image of independent creators to undermine Rorty's far more useful metaphor of the self as an ever-changing web of beliefs. The web metaphor entails an inherent relationality that simply does not connect with the idea of the self as an independent creator of its own private destiny.

Rorty uses the struggle between poetry and philosophy as a matrix on which to plot the history of modern and postmodern reflection. Beginning with Plato and ending with Kant, he argues that the entire philosophic tradition has foundered on repeated attempts to see the unchanging in divinity, nature, the self, or the conscience. Things finally change with Nietzsche, "who first explicitly suggested that we drop the whole idea of 'knowing the truth.'" Those who follow Nietzsche's lead recognize "that the important boundary to cross is not the one separating time from atemporal truth but rather the one which divides the old from the new" (ibid., 27–28).

Having dropped the idea that language fits the world, a Nietzschean philosopher "can see more clearly than the continuity-seeking historian, critic or philosopher, that her language is as contingent as her parents or her historical epoch. She can appreciate the force of the claim that 'truth is a mobile army of metaphors' because, by her own sheer strength, she has broken out of one perspective, one metaphoric, into another" (ibid., 29). This new "metaphoric" ties success to refusing to allow us to be defined by others or our situation and by taking charge in "recreating all 'it was' into a 'thus I willed it.'" In this Nietzschean view, the impulse to think, to inquire, to reweave oneself ever more thoroughly, is not wonder but terror. It is Bloom's 'horror of finding oneself to be only a copy or replica'" (ibid.). This is an "inverted Platonism" that replaces the quest for eternal verities with the quest to become something new and unprecedented. In a sense for Nietzsche and Bloom novelty becomes an inherent good, the only escape from having oneself determined by the structures of what precedes or surrounds you.

To his credit, Rorty recognizes that a Nietzschean-Bloomian "inverted Platonism" is almost as problematic as Platonism itself. To escape from both he turns instead to Freud, who "by breaking with both Kant's residual Platonism and Nietzsche's inverted Platonism, lets us see both Nietzsche's superman and Kant's common moral consciousness as exemplifying two out of many forms of adaptation, two out of many strategies for coping with the contingencies of one's upbringing, of coming to terms with a blind impress." As Rorty reads him, Freud "eschewed the very idea of a paradigm human being." Instead, he offered us a middle road between Kant and Nietzsche by exploring the "idiosyncratic contingencies of our individual pasts" and seeing in them the defining moments for each of us (ibid., 33–35). This avoids Kantian universalisms while at the same time not requiring us to become Nietzschean superhumans to acquire status as full-fledged human beings.

By tying our understanding of ourselves to a recounting of the details that make up our lives, Freud describes a self "which is a tissue of contingencies rather than an at least potentially well-ordered system of faculties." Moreover, he gives us "the equipment to construct our own private vocabulary of moral deliberation [enabling] us to sketch a narrative of our own development, our own idiosyncratic moral struggle, which is far more finely textured, far more custom-tailored to our individual case, than the moral vocabulary which the philosophical tradition offered us" (ibid., 32). Instead of exhibiting universal structures, our actions are taken to be, in Freudian terms, "alternative modes of adaptation" to our own situations. This makes it possible for us to "take seriously the possibility that there is no central faculty, no central self, called 'reason'—and thus to take Nietzschean pragmatism and perspectivalism seriously" (ibid., 33).

Some might call into question Rorty's reading of Freud, ignoring as it does the details of the overly mechanistic, hydraulic metaphors that permeate Freud's discussion of the individual. Putting that aside, however, I would use the contemporary literary critical term *strong misreading* in describing Rorty's analysis as one that lifts up important insights that have little to do with Freud's original intentions. Rorty is right to see Freud's attention to the contingent details that contribute to an individual's psyche as an important supplement to traditional pragmatic descriptions of the self as a web of relationships. Freud does help us to take "pragmatism and perspectivalism seriously." Where I think Rorty errs is in linking pragmatic perspectivalism to Nietzschean perspectivalism. Pragmatic perspectivalism recognizes that though each perspective is unique, it is always built upon and connected to an indeterminate number of other perspectives. Nietzschean perspectivalism, as Rorty describes it, is tied to transcending such relationships in an effort to "give birth to oneself."

Rorty says that he turned to Freud to avoid the most extreme implications of Nietzsche's inverted Platonism. Nevertheless, as we saw earlier, Rorty is captivated by the notion that metaphors appear spontaneously and have no literal connections to the world or even ourselves except those we imagine for them. Moreover, his reading of Freud makes it seem that we are makers of such metaphors (poetry making beings). Thus, though Rorty rejects the Nietzschean claim that we are not fully human unless we have recreated ourselves from scratch, he describes us in such a way that everyone is involved in the very task Nietzsche reserved only for the overman. If you tie Rorty's description of the spontaneous generation of new metaphors to his description of the self as poetry maker, it is hard to see how he avoided much in Nietzsche's description of what it means to be human except the obnoxious elitism. Ultimately, what is human in us is that we are the source of new metaphors that appear blindly, with neither rhyme nor reason.

Evidence supporting this interpretation of Rorty's analysis is in the regular references he makes to the random, accidental character of so much of what we do in constituting ourselves. Moreover, he extends the sense of randomness to how and whether our own so-called private languages have anything to do with others.

> The difference between genius and fantasy is not the difference between impresses which lock onto something universal, some antecedent reality out there in the world or deep within the self, and those which do not. Rather, it is the difference between idiosyncrasies which just happen to catch on with other people—happen because of the contingencies of some historical situation, some particular need which a given community happens to have at a given time. To sum up, poetic artistic, philosophical, scientific, or political progress results from the accidental coincidence of a private obsession with a public need. (Ibid., 37)

There is something overly contrived in Rorty's insistence that the difference between genius and fantasy is pure luck. I am sympathetic with most of what he has to say in describing the self as a poetic engine. I think such metaphors resonate well with Wang Yang-ming's understanding of *liang-chih* and Dewey's discussion of aesthetic creativity in *Art as Experience*. But I can see no benefit to insisting with Rorty that we must conceive of ourselves as containing a creative center that is so indeterminate it is devoid of any substantive relationship with anything else. With Wang and Dewey I would insist that whatever creativity we exhibit must be linked to a more naturalistic understanding of the relationship between this entity called the "self" and all of the entities that constitute what we call the self's "environment."

Wang, for example, insisted that his followers seek to form one body with all things. This means that before we can constitute new harmonies, we must come to grips with those harmonies that are already a part of our world. It does no good to strike up a new melody if that melody does not resonate with the surroundings. Similarly, Dewey describes the self as an organism struggling to maintain or improve upon an equilibrium of organic and cognitive processes that, taken together, constitute the current situation. To create new metaphors that have no connection to that situation would be to act blindly and without purpose. Dewey never claimed that we could appeal to universal criteria or that the self ever attains certainty about the world's true character. Wang did not understand *liang chih* to mean absolute certainty. Rather, both insisted that the pursuit of harmony is based on our imperfect efforts to hear the harmonies already all around us.

As was true in his discussion of language, Rorty mistakenly elevates one part of the process, the creation of new metaphors, over the whole process. It should be clear, however, that a great poet does more than merely come up with new metaphors. She *selects* them. It is easy to generate metaphors. The genius is in *identifying* metaphors that create new unanticipated satisfactions. This selection depends on the poet's assessment of her current situation using criteria that spring from within that situation. Similarly, as we construct the narrative that defines who we are, we seek symbols that resonate well with those that we find all around us. That we fail, that we often find ourselves lost in the cul de sacs of our own poetic self-deceptions, is only a measure of how difficult it is to be human. It is not a reason to stop listening.

Rorty is right in saying that language is not representational. There is no cognitively graspable atemporal truth. We should not ever expect to reach the one absolute. But surely there is a middle ground between absolutism and Rortyan contingency. Rorty recommends that we will appreciate "the power of language to make new and different things possible . . . when [our] aim becomes an expanding repertoire of alternative descriptions rather than The One Right Description" (ibid., 41). However, descriptions cannot be good in themselves without introducing yet another absolutism under the guise of genuine openness.

Though I've pressed this line of criticism as hard as I can, I should be clear that I do not think that it undermines what is most important in Rorty's thought. It seems to me that he could let go of the Nietzschean language of self-surpassing creativity and return to a Deweyan awareness of the way all things emerge from and remain connected with a network of other things. This may be too metaphysical for Rorty's taste, but it would keep him from drifting into the kind of intellectualist dead ends that Dewey struggled so hard to overcome. It would also undermine any need he might have to posit an unbridgeable gap between private fantasies and public responsibilities. Such a division only makes sense if you think there is something about us that is fully independent from everything else. While Rorty goes to great lengths to redescribe the self as a network of beliefs, it seems to me that his network surrounds a "hidden pearl" of purely independent, indeterminate creativity, which if not the whole self is the part that matters most in the crunch. When Rorty turns to a defense of liberal democracy in the third chapter of *Contingency, irony, and solidarity,* his position is based largely on the claim that liberal democracy is a system of government that seems to give this internal self-creative centerless center the greatest liberty to pursue its private pleasures.

I would like to conclude this discussion of Rorty by citing one of his descriptions of the self, which, when abstracted from the problematic Nietzschean tendencies I've criticized above, captures what is best in Rorty's radical revision of traditional pragmatic language: "The strategy is the same in all these cases: It is to substitute a tissue of contingent relations, a web which stretches backwards and forward through past and future time, for a formed, unified, present, self-contained substance, something capable of being seen steadily and whole" (ibid.). There is nothing in the above statement that conflicts with Dewey's understanding of the self as an indeterminate collection of processes all set within a larger and always changing environment. Rorty is right in that we cannot ever expect to see anything, much less the self, "steadily and whole." That does not mean, however, that we lurch forward blindly.

CONCLUSION

The arguments in this chapter are built upon an analogy. I have been arguing that contemporary Deweyan pragmatists can learn from a Neo-Confucian like Wang Yang-ming how to approach the thought of Richard Rorty. Though it will strike most as a comically roundabout way to approach something so close to home, I am struck by the fact that my difficulties with Rorty, like the Neo-Confucian difficulties with Taoism, turn largely around what I have been calling "anthropological" issues. Just as Neo-Confucians could not accept an image of a self disconnected from our role as creative partners with Heaven and Earth, I was unable to allow Rorty's Nietzschean tendencies to undermine my pragmatic sense that to be truly creative beings, we must see ourselves as *connected* and *responding* to the world. At the same time, like the Neo-Confucians who saw in Taoism a tool for opening Confucianism to a deeper understanding of its own radical insights, I remain convinced that Rorty's reinterpretation of the pragmatic tradition is and will continue to be an important tool in our effort to understand the radical implications of the American pragmatic tradition.

With respect to the larger issues addressed throughout this volume, we can see (with Rorty's help) that a new description of the self is beginning to emerge. Once we acknowledge that knowledge and action are really one thing and let go of the representational theory of knowledge, the ground for our understanding of the self necessarily shifts as well. When Rorty sticks closely to his metaphor of the self as a tissue of contingencies and a web of beliefs, he quite accurately characterizes a position that is supported directly by the metaphysical speculations of the pragmatic, process, and Neo-Confucian traditions. For historical reasons, Rorty necessarily finds it difficult to acknowledge the metaphysical implications in the position he has taken. Once we realize, however, that metaphysics is not necessarily absolutist, representationalist, or essentialist, then the door opens to a whole new way of thinking through these issues.

In the next chapter, I turn to a discussion of two contemporary philosophers whose work builds easily from the position I have been outlining. Neither would characterize himself in quite the way I will. Nevertheless, both are better than Rorty at recognizing the unity of knowledge and action while simultaneously avoiding Rortyan lapses into neoromantic characterizations of the self.

CHAPTER 9

Knowledge, Action, and the Organicist Turn

Throughout this book, I have been arguing that the path to a nonrepresentational theory of knowledge entails a complete rethinking of the fundamental assumptions that we make about minds, bodies, and the world at large. This epistemological quest has metaphysical and ontological implications. In this final chapter, I turn to Robert C. Neville and Mark Johnson, two philosophers who have not been afraid to face the fundamental questions that are implicit in our situation. Both embrace what I am calling the "organicist turn." Early pragmatists and process thinkers took this "turn." Unfortunately, those philosophers who thought that the later "linguistic turn" was going to provide a route out of the philosophical conundrums of the previous centuries have ignored it.

Neither Johnson nor Neville would label his work in the way that I have. They do not use the phrase *organic turn*, nor do they place as much emphasis on organicism as I will in this chapter. Nevertheless, I believe that by pointing to their organicist roots, we can see connections between two thinkers whom most would place in very different parts of the contemporary philosophic landscape. As I said in the preliminary remarks to part 3 of this volume, I view Johnson as a philosophical insider who is attempting to dismantle what he calls the "objectivist position" by exploiting conflicts and contradictions that are implicit in its dualistic tendencies. (Johnson, 1987, xxxvii).[1] Neville, by contrast, is something of an outsider, who appeals directly to the three traditions I have been highlighting. Building upon the Confucian, pragmatic, and process traditions, Neville marks out a wholly new way to talk about truth, calling it the "carry-over of value" from one entity to another.

Taken together, these two thinkers point us in a positive direction, where knowledge and action are really one thing and a nonrepresentational theory of knowledge is a genuine possibility. The moves suggested by Johnson and Neville seem to me to be the right way to build on what Dewey, Whitehead, and Wang have already accomplished.

LOCATING THE BODY IN THE MIND

In *The Body in the Mind: The Bodily Basis of Meaning, Imagination, and Reason* (1987), Johnson argues that the time has come for us to develop a fully embodied description of mind. Johnson is aware that his position is unorthodox when viewed from the perspective of contemporary analytic philosophy. Nevertheless, he describes it as a necessary response to problems raised within cognitive science, cognitive psychology, and analytic philosophy. His text makes no direct appeals to the classical American pragmatists or to anyone who might be associated with the American process tradition. Moreover, he makes no references to non-Western thinkers or any mention of panpsychism per se. In short, Johnson stands largely outside the traditions I have been promoting throughout this text. Johnson does, of course, call on contemporary figures that have been influenced by American pragmatism, including Rorty, Putnam, and Quine. My point, however, is that Johnson does not acknowledge the extent to which his positions are anticipated by the classical pragmatists and process philosophers. His critique of Rorty, for example, could be read as a challenge to Rorty's interpretation of Dewey, except that Johnson never actually mentions Dewey. I do not mean these observations to be a criticism of Johnson's scholarship. I suspect it is simply evidence that Johnson came to his conclusions by a route very different from the one I have been marking out in this book. I cite him here in part to help confirm my claim that the quest for a non-representational theory of knowledge is a point of intersection for many philosophic schools in the late twentieth century. Johnson's position is an illustration of what can happen when evidence in cognitive science and cognitive psychology moves someone trained in analytic philosophy to question the efficacy of the linguistic turn (ibid., xxxvii).

Taylor, Rorty, and Davidson all struggle within (and in some cases against) strictures imposed by the linguistic turn. Johnson, by contrast, has a completely different frame of reference. His objective is to describe how cognitive activities are embedded in and emergent from organic transactions. Dennett, of course, also develops an evolutionary description of cognitive activity that might be viewed by some as organicist. As we have seen, however, Dennett's commitments to mechanistic materialism render his description of mentality reductionistic. Dennett is more a mechanist than an organicist. While it would be a stretch to claim that Johnson is an organicist like Wang, Dewey, and Whitehead, his work lends support to and expands upon the organismic position that I have outlined in part 2.

In *The Body in the Mind* Johnson begins by chronicling the collapse of what he calls "objectivism." In essence, Johnson asks whether the

Cartesian separation of cognition from perception should be supplanted by a point of view that acknowledges the extent to which cognition is rooted in and dependent upon physical interactions. He says that for too long we have spoken as if ideas, concepts, and thoughts were disembodied spirits, floating somewhere in "mind space." As his title indicates, Johnson's aim is to develop a theory of *meaning* and *reason* that takes proper account of the way our body sets the stage for and contributes to human understanding. According to Johnson, objectivists are convinced that "The world consists of objects that have properties and stand in various relationships independent of human understanding. The world is as it is, no matter what any person happens to believe about it, and there is one correct "God's-Eye-View" about what the world is really like. In other words, there is a rational structure to reality, independent of beliefs of any particular people, and correct reason mirrors this rational structure" (ibid., x). According to Johnson, objectivists view *meaning* as an abstract relationship between conceptual symbols and objective reality. Concepts are disembodied representations of objects, properties, and relations. Apart from their reference to this "objective" world, such concepts are meaningless. Most important, on the objectivist's view, all concepts aim for literal rather than metaphorical assertions about how the world would appear were we to view it from a God's-eye point of view.

The objectivist theory of meaning also links with a concomitant theory of *reason*. As Johnson sees it, objectivists describe reason as the manipulation of symbols. Its core is a formal logic that must transcend bodily experience in order to achieve universality and render plausible the very notion of a God's-eye point of view (ibid., xxii–xxv).

The most problematic feature of the objectivist position, according to Johnson, is the way it assumes that rationality transcends the "structures of bodily experience." His whole project aims to demonstrate why the very notion of disembodied concepts is dangerous and misleading. Citing arguments from both Rorty and Hilary Putnam, as well as empirical studies that examine the way we deal with categorization, metaphor, and polysemy, Johnson argues that the objectivist position has been discredited, though it continues to define the "context in which our most popular theories of meaning and rationality are articulated" (ibid., xxix). Johnson views his book, and parallel efforts in linguistics and cognitive science, as the beginning of a new description of thought and understanding that will avoid objectivism's limitations.

It is ironic that Johnson cites Rorty's *Philosophy and the Mirror of Nature* as the text that best sums up the story of the development and decline of objectivism (ibid., 215). On the one hand, Rorty sees the problem as Johnson does. Both agree that philosophy has suffered under the tyranny of an inadequate metaphor for knowledge (vision), one that mistakenly describes thought as outside of time and truth as the equivalent of a cognitive mirror of objective reality. On the other hand, Rorty's insistence on the centrality of the linguistic turn (which I discussed in chapter 7) runs directly counter to Johnson's proposed remedy to the crisis engendered by objectivism's collapse. Where Rorty praises Davidson for arguing that there is no "psychic terrain, intermediate between physiology and linguistically formulated beliefs" (Rorty, 1994, 55), Johnson argues that "bodily experience and problem-solving" produces a vast network of "image-schematas which contribute directly to human imagination and understanding" (Johnson, 1987, xx). Johnson turns to an analysis of "the nonpropositional, experiential, and figurative dimensions of meaning and rationality" in order to lay out the extent to which bodily patterns set a context for and thereby make possible our higher-order cognitive structures (ibid., xxxvii). Rorty seems unable to imagine that there is any room for philosophic analysis in prelinguistic, organically based human actions. As a result, and despite the fact that he promulgated the now classic attack on objectivism, on this key issue, Rorty remains in the objectivist camp.

Johnson's argument for the existence of bodily generated image schematas rests on his ability to make sense of the very notion of *nonpropositional* experience. Like Dewey, Whitehead, and Wang, he calls on us to expand our definition of experience so that it includes a whole range of activities that philosophers often ignore. He approaches this task from two directions. First, he asks us to attend to aspects of our experience that can only be described as nonpropositional. "My present sense of being balanced upright in space at this moment is surely a nonpropositional awareness that I have, even though all my efforts to communicate its reality to you will involve propositional structure" (ibid., 5). Johnson's point is that this vague awareness of *being* balanced precedes and makes possible any cognitive awareness we may have of the concept of 'balance.' In short, our concept of balance stems from the physical feeling of being balanced.

Readers might recall at this point Whitehead's effort to render his discussion of causal efficacy plausible by appealing to our unshakable conviction that who we are *now* stems directly from who we were a moment ago. This felt continuity could hardly be the result of a propositional inference. We do not draw the conclusion that we are continuous. Rather, the experience of bodily continuity leads us to act on the assumption that this sense of continuity is valid. It is interesting to see both Johnson and Whitehead drawing our attention away from the clear and distinct ideas that typically served as the starting point for modernist epistemology and pointing us instead toward vague powerful feelings that they believe precede and underlie cognition.

Having made the point that experience is broader than cognition, Johnson goes on to describe in some detail how this nonpropositional physical experience shapes our imagination and the way we use metaphor to come to grips with the world we inhabit. For example, Johnson argues that our preconceptual sense of what it means to be balanced serves as the metaphorical basis for what we mean when we talk about balanced systems, a balanced argument, an unbalanced personality, a balanced judicial decision, balanced morals, and even mathematical equality (ibid., 80–96). In all of these ways, our imagination and our higher-order cognitive processes are shaped by what Johnson calls "image-schematas" that are derived directly from what it feels like to *be* balanced.

It is at this point that Johnson's position both resonates with and goes a step beyond Whitehead's causal efficacy, Dewey's primary experience, and Wang Yang-ming's *liang chih*. Like each of them, Johnson describes experience as emergent from the adjustments an organism makes in response to its environment. Moreover, he agrees that those adjustments serve as the background upon which humans cultivate higher-order cognitive activity. Johnson, however, goes beyond Whitehead, Dewey, and Wang by developing extended analyses of this background and its structures.

> In order for us to have meaningful connected experiences that we can comprehend and reason about there must be pattern and order to our actions, perceptions, and conceptions. *A schema is a recurrent pattern, shape, and regularity in, or of, these ongoing ordering activities.* These patterns emerge as meaningful structures for us chiefly at the level of our bodily movements through space, our manipulation of objects, and our perceptual interactions. (Ibid., 29)

Throughout *The Body in the Mind* Johnson explores some twenty-seven different image schematas that extend metaphorically to create the conceptual tools for grasping the world. He acknowledges that there is ultimately no end to the many bodily patterns structuring our interaction with the world. He says that "there is clearly nothing sacred about 253 patterns versus 53 or any other number of patterns, but it is certain that we experience our world by means of various image-schematic structures whose relations make up the fabric of our experience, that is, of our understanding" (ibid., 27).

In chapter 5 we saw how Dewey argues that "primary experience" consists of the immediate havings, enjoyings, and usings that are a part of all organic activity. In humans this primary experience precedes and is the basis for the higher cognitive functions that Dewey calls "secondary experience." Dewey claims that philosophers who ignore primary experience find it difficult to explain how ideas and concepts (secondary experience) connect with the so-called external world. This was the point behind Dewey's claim that experience is both *of* and *in* the world. He avoids modernist paradoxes by arguing that "mentality" stems from an organism's ability to respond to and anticipate changes in its environment or within itself. Unlike objectivists who tie meaning and mentality to conceptual representations of an external world, Dewey embeds his theory of meaning in an organism's active engagement with the world. Things have meaning for an organism in relation to the role they play in the satisfaction of its purposes and needs. When an amoeba encounters food, it experiences it as a potential release from the tensional energies that accompany hunger. The food "means" precisely that. The behaviors that the amoeba displays in an effort to satisfy those needs (e.g., pursuing food) are expressions of a rudimentary meaning (mental) system. Thus, in contrast to materialists such as Dennett, Dewey considers *all* organic behaviors, whether hardwired or learned, to be rudimentary forms of mentality. Taken together these behaviors constitute a system of meanings wherein things are associated with their ability to satisfy or frustrate particular needs or purposes. As we saw in chapter 5 Dewey calls such a meaning system "mind." Mind is the collection of settled associations and linkages that lay behind and direct the vast majority of our actions or behaviors. Animals and humans are capable of adding to the store of such associations and do so whenever they learn new things. The specific form of mental activity that we call "consciousness," according to Dewey, is only a limited subset of this meaning system. It is, in Dewey's view, the focal point within a meaning system that is constantly reconstructing itself in response to frustrated purposes.

All of this fits quite easily with Johnson's claim that nonpropositional experience generates image schematas that in turn form the basis for higher-order cognitive experience. Like Dewey, Johnson makes it clear that image schematas are patterns of action, not fixed cognitive structures.[2]

> The view I am proposing is this: in order for us to have meaningful connected experiences that we can comprehend and reason about, there must be pattern and order to our actions, perceptions, and conceptions. *A schema is a recurrent pattern, shape, and regularity in, or of, these ongoing ordering activities.* These patterns emerge as meaningful structures for us chiefly at the level of our bodily movements through space, our manipulation of objects, and our perceptual interactions. (Ibid., 21; italics added)

In short, for Johnson experience is action all the way down, just as it is for Dewey, Whitehead, and Wang. Moreover, the patterns shaping these actions are neither eternal nor unchanging. They are "structures *of an activity* by which we organize our experience" (ibid., 30; italics added), and they are capable of changing with changing circumstances. Johnson goes on to point out that all of this has important implications for our view of meaning and rationality. "Insofar as meanings involve schematic structures, they are relatively fluid patterns that get altered in various contexts. They are not eternally fixed objects, as Objectivism suggests, but they gain a certain relative stability by becoming conventionally located in our network of meaning. So there is a large part of our meaning structure that can be treated as 'fixed' most of the time" (ibid.). Johnson's "network of meaning" sounds extraordinarily close to Dewey's description of mind as "the whole system of meanings as they are embodied in the workings of organic life" (Dewey, 1958, 44). For both Johnson and Dewey, the vast majority of this "meaning system" or "mind" will be relatively fixed and operating below the levels of consciousness because the world it deals with is for the most part quite stable. In *Experience and Nature,* Dewey points out that since our world exhibits stability and dynamism it is not surprising that our meaning systems (minds) exhibit those same generic traits.

The need to see mind as a blending of stability and dynamism is also present in Wang's attempt to strike the right balance between Confucian stability and Taoist/Buddhist spontaneity. For Wang, the human mind shares in the creative spontaneity of Heaven but can do so productively only by building on the structures already in place. As I argued in chapter 4, *liang-chih* (innate knowledge) is not knowledge of the world's underlying rational structures, but rather the capacity to elicit new patterns, new harmonies that make their own contribution to the cosmic symphony.

To understand Johnson's point it is important to be clear about what he means by "meaning." Like Whitehead, Johnson is pointing to feelings that are so pervasive that cognitive experience typically overlooks them. He is not talking about meaning in the romantic sense of being profoundly moved. "[I]t is meaningful in a more mundane sense, namely, it involves an exceedingly complex interaction with your environment in which you experience significant patterns and employ structured processes that give rise to a coherent world of which you are able to make sense" (1987, 31). For example, Johnson outlines what he calls the schemata for "in-out orientation" by listing many of the ways we use the in-out schemata in the first few minutes of our day: "You wake *out* of a deep sleep and peer *out* from beneath the covers *into* your room. You gradually emerge *out* of your stupor, pull yourself *out* from under the covers, climb *into* your robe, stretch *out* your limbs, and walk *in* a daze *out* of the bedroom and *into* the bathroom" (ibid., 30). In sum, the in-out schemata are central to our ability to make sense of experience. Without these mundane meaning structures, there would be no way for us to experience the world as either orderly or coherent. This may sound vaguely Kantian, as image schematas seem to play a role similar to the categories that give structure to cognitive experience. However, unlike Kant, Johnson locates these structures in our preconscious physical interactions with the world rather than in a transcendental ego.

It is important to keep in mind that Johnson is not arguing that we are routinely conscious of these schematas. He is claiming, however, that consciousness is dependent on them. Without these physical patterns, there would be no consciousness. Moreover, on Johnson's view, linguistic meaning is a specific instance of meaningfulness as such. Thus, language is meaningful to the extent that it exhibits or makes use of schematas such as the in-out orientation, our sense of balance, and so on. This reverses the approach of those who have taken the linguistic turn and seek to understand meaning primarily through the lens of linguistic structures. As his subtitle indicates, for Johnson there is always a "bodily basis for meaning, imagination and reason."

To defend the claim that there is a bodily basis for meaning, imagination, and reason, Johnson must also explain what he means by the experience or *gestalt* of image schematas. As I noted earlier, this is difficult since he has to use propositional language to describe nonpropositional or prelinguistic experience. What can we really say about an experience that takes place outside of the organizing structures of language? A great deal, according to Johnson, who argues that a prelinguistic, or nonpropositional gestalt is "an organized, unified whole within our experience and understanding that manifests a repeatable pattern or structure. Some people use the term gestalt to mean a mere form or shape with no internal structure. In contrast to such a view, my entire project rests on showing that experiential gestalts have internal structure that connects up aspects of our experience and leads to inferences in our conceptual system" (ibid., 44). Image-schemata gestalts are not just amorphous unstructured and therefore indescribable feelings. Instead, they have identifiable parts and patterns that can be abstracted and described.

As an example, Johnson undertakes an extended description of the preconceptual gestalt for force.

> In order to survive as organisms, we must interact with our environment. All such causal interaction requires the exertion of force, either as we act upon other objects, or as we are acted upon by them. There-

fore, in our efforts at comprehending our experience, structures of force come to play a central role. Since our experience is held together by forceful activity, our web of meanings is connected by the structures of such activity. (Ibid., 42)

Johnson's main point is that organisms feel and respond to the forces that are active around them. They do not react willy nilly. There is structure to what happens to them, and their responses can be ascribed to both the multiple-orderings within the world around them and to the order that they seek to either accomplish or preserve. Johnson wants us to recognize that the *everyday experience* of the interplay of such forces is the ultimate source for our understanding of force itself. "Even though we do not tend to pay attention to the forces that are everywhere inside us and in our environment, it is clear that these forces manifest structures that are very much a part of our having coherent, meaningful experiences that we call into consciousness, understand, reason about, and communicate in language" (ibid., 42–43).

Philosophers raised within the confines of late modernist philosophic assumptions such as the linguistic turn will likely find it strange to hear Johnson talking about the "structure" of this prelinguistic experience of force. From an organicist's point of view, however, it all makes good sense because organic activity, at all levels, can be *meaningful*. As I said above, there is a prelinguistic "meaningfulness" to an amoeba's behavior. This was Dewey's point when he described mind as a system of meanings embedded in the workings of organic life. Those who refuse to follow Johnson down the organicist path, however, will find this whole discussion odd and implausible.

In sum, all organisms experience the impositions of forces and are themselves the initiators of force. Concepts such as 'interaction,' 'directionality,' 'origins,' 'power,' 'intensity,' and 'causality' all can be abstracted from and dependent on the physical experience of force (ibid., 41–42). According to Johnson, however, none of these abstract concepts makes any sense without the underlying experience of what it feels like to be forced and to exert one's forces on something or someone else.

Johnson's work draws out epistemological implications embedded in many of the metaphysical conclusions I outlined in my discussion of Dewey and Whitehead. Though Johnson never claims to be undertaking metaphysics as they do, his description of image schematas makes the most sense when it is viewed from the perspective of the organicist position I've attributed to Dewey, Whitehead, and Wang. Like Dewey and Whitehead, Johnson looks to the "generic traits of organic experience," although such traits lack clarity or distinctness. This approach is very different from what we have seen in Taylor, Davidson, Rorty, and Dennett. While each struggled to find a path toward a nonrepresentational theory of knowledge, metaphysical assumptions about the nature of minds, bodies, experience, and nature blocked the way. To remove these roadblocks required a more fundamental metaphysical reconstruction than they were inclined to undertake. Johnson does not seem to have this problem. For him it is patently clear from the beginning that knowledge is a kind of action, that experience is much broader than cognition, and that cognition must emerge from organic activity.

Up until this point, I have been emphasizing the link between Johnson's arguments and those of Whitehead and Dewey. What about Wang Yang-ming? Wang's Neo-Confucian metaphysics is organismic, so it is easy to see why Wang would be as good a conversation partner for Johnson as Dewey and Whitehead, with respect to the issues discussed above. However, there is one area where Wang seems to have a special set of insights that resonates with an important aspect of Johnson's position. Both Johnson and Wang emphasize the extent to which humans are creative contributors to the ongoing emergence of pattern in a world that is ultimately nothing but patterning. Readers will recall how Wang describes humans as "partners with heaven and earth." He says that it is our responsibility to *create* new patterns, new ways of being in the world by drawing on our *liang-chih* and applying it to new situations as they arise. Similarly, Johnson argues that our cognitive activity is a *creative* extension of our bodily experience. Through *metaphor* and *imagination* we move beyond routine responses and create new patterns, new ways of being in the world.

Wang, however, does not go very far in explaining the *how* of this creative process. He asserts that humans have *liang-chih* (innate knowledge or primordial awareness), which I interpreted as a preconceptual attunement to the qualitative dimension of a given situation. Drawing upon this "feel" for good, bad, better, and worse, we formulate "innate" responses to a world that we simultaneously react to and help to form. Johnson's situation, however, is somewhat different from Wang's situation. Whereas Wang was merely trying to convince his students that knowledge and action are one thing, Johnson has a more formidable task before him. He is struggling against the epistemological *and* metaphysical assumptions of objectivists who insist upon a sharp distinction between the cognitive and the physical realms. Wang shared with his opponents basic ontological and metaphysical assumptions that would not allow such a dichotomy. His students were making an epistemological mistake, one that could be corrected by an appeal to metaphysics. By appealing to commonly held metaphysical assumptions, Wang could easily justify his claim that knowledge and action are really one thing. Because Johnson does not share such assumptions with objectivists, he finds himself having to go much further to make plausible his argument for an embodied understanding of the mind.

In order to make sense of his claim that there is a bodily basis for meaning, Johnson has to explain how physical patterns map onto or give structure to cognitive patterns. In other words, he must answer the question *How* do the physical feelings give rise to concepts? To explain this process, Johnson redescribes *metaphor* and *imagination* in a way that avoids the paradoxes that objectivists generate when they posit an unbridgeable dichotomy between our physical and cognitive activities. Ultimately, Johnson claims, it is our capacity for *imagination* that makes it possible for us to move from mere organic to cognitive responsiveness. *Metaphor* is the specific form of imaginative activity whereby we translate physical patterning into image schematas that provide the basic structure for our understanding. I will look first at Johnson's description of metaphor and turn afterwards to his Kantian approach to imagination.

According to Johnson, objectivists typically think that we resort to metaphors when we do not have concepts that will provide us with a literal mapping of some aspect of the objective world. On this view, we fall back on metaphor when we do not have words to say what we mean directly. Johnson, however, moves metaphor from this late-auxiliary role in the cognitive process to the very starting point of our conceptual activity. We do not use metaphors merely to help us through the times when we do not have literal truth. Instead, on his view, metaphorical extension is the basis for *all* "higher" meanings and the ultimate grounding for what we think of as "literal truths."

According to Johnson, metaphors get short shrift in an objectivist context because they play off the ambiguities that we experience in the world and mix apparently distinct categories. Objectivism presumes that there is always some literal way to describe things and that if we work at it we can see how all metaphors are ultimately reducible to literal propositions (ibid., 67). In contrast to this approach to metaphor, Johnson sides with those philosophers (most typically romanticists) who appreciate the creative side of metaphor. He points out how Samuel Coleridge, I. A. Richards, and Max Black all recognized the extent to which our metaphors shape our experience of the world. Instead of merely illuminating preexisting correlations among objective realities, these philosophers argue that metaphors create relationships where before they simply did not exist. While Johnson agrees with this claim, he also complains that those who take this position often fail to explain *how* metaphors can be creative. "In order to give any real punch to [the claim that metaphors play a constitutive role in structuring our experience] one must treat metaphors as operating in a non-propositional, image-schematic dimension where structures emerge in our experience. That would constitute genuine creativity, in that metaphors would be taken as a mode of activity in the structuring of experience" (ibid., 70).

When metaphors are purely cognitive efforts to imitate literal relationships, their creative function is hard to see. By asserting the existence of nonpropositional, precognitive organic activity that mediates between the physical and cognitive patterns, Johnson can make the claim that metaphors are creative seem more plausible. Metaphors play a crucial role in structuring our experience by serving as the link between the noncognitive and the cognitive. Instead of merely mirroring aspects of the world, they become the very activity by which we come to *have* a world.

Though this nonpropositional, precognitive activity is necessarily murky, we can describe it. It is, Johnson claims, the natural elaboration of patterns rooted in the body's physical transactions with the world. The physical experience of balance and force (to cite two examples mentioned above) provides the raw material that shapes many aspects of our understanding. "The view of metaphor that emerges goes beyond the purview of traditional theories insofar as it treats metaphors as a matter of projections and mappings across different domains in the actual structuring of our experience (and not just in our reflection on already existing structures)" (ibid., 74). In sum then, for Johnson, metaphor is the human activity whereby we use physical patterns rooted in our interactions with the world to give structure and meaning to our understanding. "It is the projection of such structure that I am identifying as the 'creative' function of metaphor, for it is one of the chief ways we generate structure in our experience in a way we can comprehend" (ibid., 98).

This structuring process takes place in a realm of human activity that objectivist assumptions render largely invisible. By adopting a thin disembodied description of understanding, they lose touch with the ways in which our cognitive activities emerge from and are dependent on our physicality. I have been arguing throughout this text that to escape from this error, we must cultivate a much richer understanding of human understanding that recognizes the role of primary experience (Dewey), causal efficacy (Whitehead), *liang chih* (Wang), and in Johnson's case, image-schemata.

> A crucial point here is that understanding is not only a matter of reflection, using finitary propositions, on some preexistent, already determinate experience. Rather, *understanding is the way we "have a world," the way we experience our world as a comprehensible reality.* Such understanding, therefore, involves *our whole being*—our bodily capac-

ities and skills, our values, our moods and attitudes, our entire cultural tradition, the way in which we are bound up with a linguistic community, our aesthetic sensibilities, and so forth. In short, our understanding *is* our mode of "being in the world." It is the way we are meaningfully situated in our world through our bodily interactions, our cultural institutions, our linguistic tradition, and our historical context. Our more abstract reflective acts of understanding (which may involve grasping of finitary propositions) are simply an extension of our understanding in this more basic sense of having a world. (Ibid., 103)

A typical objection to Johnson's position would be to ask him to specify "where" these image schematas reside. Are they in the mind, or are they in the body? But this question masks the objectivist presuppositions that render it unanswerable. If understanding is limited to concepts, beliefs, and propositions, then there is no "place" for Johnson's image schematas because they lie between physical transactions and abstract cognitive structures. If we adopt Johnson's much fuller description of understanding and see understanding as a way of "having a world," then the gap between conception and perception disappears and the problem evaporates. "The obvious problem here is an unquestioned assumption of all Objectivist orientations, namely, that all meaning is representable entirely by means of finitary propositions. I am suggesting that we submit this foundational bias to criticism, on the hypothesis that propositions might be dependent on embodied, nonpropositional dimensions of meaning" (ibid., 103). Image schematas are then metaphorical extensions of physical patterns. The creative dimension of human understanding is located in our capacity to employ metaphorical extension as a tool for creating patterns that go beyond the organic transactions that make up our physical world. To put this in Wang Yang-ming's terms, we become partners with Heaven and Earth as we call on our *liang-chih* and contribute to the ongoing creation of patterns that go beyond but remain connected to those that make up the organic realm. Johnson's metaphorical extensions and Wang's *liang-chih* mark out similar territory as they highlight human creativity while maintaining that our understanding is grounded in an embodied sensibility.

Along these same lines, the final issue that I want to look at in Johnson's argument for an embodied description of our cognitive activity is his account of the imagination. It is crucial to consider the imagination because Johnson describes it as *the* capacity that makes possible the metaphorical extensions described above. Viewed this way, metaphor is a technique the imagination uses to create the image-schematas that structure our understanding.

Unfortunately, according to Johnson, we typically think of imagination in objectivist terms that tend to minimize or diminish its role in making meaningful experience possible. Platonists, for example, complain that our imagination is the source of passing fancies that distract us from the final real things. Aristotelians, by contrast, portray imagination as a tool for producing necessary but imperfect reminders (images) of the objective world that we are seeking to know (ibid.). Johnson rejects both these limiting descriptions and argues that we must

> revive and enrich our notion of imagination if we are to overcome certain undesirable effects of a deeply rooted set of dichotomies that have dominated Western philosophy (e.g. mind/body, reason/imagination, science/art, cognition/emotion, fact/value, and on and on) and that have come to influence our common understanding. . . . Only in this way can we understand how it is possible for us to "have a world" that we can make sense of and reason about (Ibid., 140)

The key, of course, is Johnson's interest in using the imagination to help explain how we come to "have a world." Objectivist philosophers typically view the physical patterns that organisms embody as mere mechanical adjustments to the environment. Johnson, however, wants us to see in these physical patterns the seeds of mentality. Since *all* organisms act purposively, their actions display rudimentary forms of "meaningfulness." Johnson's argument for the embodied mind depends on the assumption that there is a line of continuity between these rudimentary forms of mentality and the full-blooded subjectivity of human beings who enjoy self-consciousness. Ultimately, for Johnson, it is the capacity for imagination that distinguishes us from other organisms and explains how we come to "have a world." As was the case with metaphor, Johnson is repositioning imagination so that we can see the primordial role it plays in making knowledge possible. Imagination is not an ancillary activity, producing imperfect imitations of real knowledge. Without imagination, there would be no knowledge.

It is interesting that Johnson points to Immanual Kant as the philosopher who has provided the most comprehensive, though still flawed, description of the role imagination plays in structuring our understanding. It makes sense that Johnson turns to Kant at this point since Kant was the one who argued that to understand consciousness and knowledge we must look to the *activity* of the knowing subject rather than to the way the objective world imposes itself on a static mind. According to Johnson, Kant saw clearly that imagination is an essential ingredient in the process that culminates in meaningful and coherent cognitive judgments (ibid., 140, 147). On Johnson's somewhat unorthodox reading of Kant, the integration of empirically derived concepts and pure *a priori* concepts (the basic building blocks of Kant's description of human understanding) is achieved via the imagination.

Though Johnson praises Kant for recognizing how important the imagination is, he also complains that Kant retains an objectivist's tendency to "see reality as divided into two radically different and irreducible realms . . . a material realm governed by strict deterministic natural laws . . . [and] a realm beyond the physical where freedom is possible" (ibid., 167). Johnson claims that this dichotomy ultimately makes it impossible for Kant to explain how imagination works and undermines the usefulness of Kant's entire critical philosophy. Instead, Johnson proposes to update Kant's description of imagination by rejecting its dualistic premises and substituting his own claim that cognitive activity is emergent from and dependent on the physical patterns of bodily movement. For Johnson, the so-called material (i.e., determined) and rational (i.e., free) realms are best seen as poles along a continuum rather than mutually exclusive realms. He begins by rehearsing the *reproductive, productive,* and *schematizing* function of the Kantian understanding of imagination in order to show how central imagination is to Kant's description of consciousness and understanding.

"As *reproductive*, [Kantian imagination] gives us unified representations (such as mental images and percepts) in time, and unified, coherent experiences over time, so that our experience is not random and chaotic" (ibid., 165). Given the dualistic premises of Kant's ontology, the objective material world cannot have "its own principles of organization within itself" (ibid., 148). A knowing subject must supply the organization. By generating such principles, the reproductive aspect of the imagination transforms our sensory input from an uncontrolled torrent into something with the potential for meaning.

Bringing order to sensory input is, of course, merely the first step in a Kantian description of cognitive experience. According to Johnson, Kant sees the *transcendental unity of consciousness* as an outcome of the *productive* function of the imagination. "As *productive* it [Kantian imagination] constitutes the unity of our consciousness through time" (ibid., 165). The productive function of the imagination makes it possible for us to have "objective, public, shared experiences," by providing us with the "ultimate conditions for objective experience," including such basic categories as time, space, and causality (ibid., 151). Johnson claims that these moves lead to a "momentous conclusion about the importance of human imagination, namely, there can be no meaningful experience without imagination, either in its productive or reproductive functions. As productive, imagination gives us the very structure of objectivity. As reproductive, it supplies all of the connections by means of which we achieve coherent, unified, and meaningful experience and understanding" (ibid.).

For the most part, the reproductive and productive functions of the imagination operate within very strict boundaries. Most of us would normally not consider these functions "imaginative" and instead see them as mechanical processes operating well below our awareness. Still, on Johnson's reading of Kant, these functions remain part of the imagination, albeit a strictly regulated part. Things get more complicated, however, when he turns to Kant's understanding of schematism and aesthetic judgment.

Johnson says that Kant portrays the reproductive and productive functions of imagination abstractly as a "basic synthesizing activity." In short, these functions describe *what* happens in the imagination, but they do not really explain *how* it happens (ibid., 152). For an explanation of *how* the imagination works, Johnson claims we must turn to Kant's description of the schematizing function of the imagination. According to Johnson, Kant uses his notion of schematism as a tool for bridging the gap that he presumes must exist between empirical data and *a priori* concepts. "The schematizing activity of the imagination, then, mediates between images or objects of sensation, on the one hand, and abstract concepts, on the other. It can accomplish this mediation because it can be a rule-following or rule-like activity for creating figure or structure in spatial and temporary representations" (ibid., 156).

As Johnson sees it, Kant wants us to understand the schematizing function as an act of imagination whereby empirically derived concepts are brought under the "rule" of *a priori* concepts such as time, space, and causality. The schematism can mediate between them because on the one hand it is empirically derived (e.g. the image of a dog) and on the other it is structured by pure *a priori* concepts such as time, space, and causality (e.g., thus producing the image of a dog at this moment of *time,* in this particular *space,* and *causally* related in specifiable ways). Without the schematizing function, this "third thing" mediating between the empirical and the pure, it is hard to see how pure *a priori* concepts govern empirically derived information.

After outlining the schematizing function, Johnson points to what he thinks of as a crucial equivocation in Kant's position. "It is not clear in Kant's account whether he wants to say that the schema is a 'procedure,' or whether he thinks that it is a 'product' of a process. He speaks both ways. Sometimes he describes it as a product or structure resulting from imaginative activity in which concepts get connected to percepts. (A142, B181) But he also describes it frequently as the procedure or rule at work in imaginative structuring (A140, B179)" (ibid.). It should not surprise us that Kant needs to equivocate on this point. We can see in Kant's equivocation an effort to deal with the central problem that has occupied this entire volume. When he describes the schematism as a product, he lines himself up with those who see a sharp distinction between knowledge on the one hand and action on the other. This view of the schematism risks viewing it as a fixed conceptual re-presentation of some aspect of the objective/material realm. The path from the claim that the schematism is a fixed product to a full-fledged representational theory of knowledge is clear and well worn. Nevertheless, by simultaneously describing the schematizing function as a process, Kant seems also to be among those who want to describe knowledge as an activity, a way of being in relation to things. When the schematism is seen as an imaginative *process*, then Kant's position is more nearly in line with what I have been arguing for throughout this volume.

The source of this equivocation, according to Johnson, is the sharp distinction Kant makes between empirically derived information and the pure *a priori* concepts of the productive imagination. Moreover, this distinction is linked to the assumption that there must be a clear demarcation between an objective material realm governed by unyielding natural laws and a nonmaterial subjective realm where freedom is possible. Both of these assumptions lead Kant into a difficult struggle to explain the relationship between pure *a priori* concepts and empirically derived concepts. By equivocating over his description of the schematism, Kant is seeking to avoid the pitfalls of a pure subjectivism on the one hand and a radical objectivism on the other.

When the schematism is described as a fixed *product,* it becomes that "third thing," containing *both* empirical and *a priori* elements, mediating between the empirical and pure *a priori* concepts. For example, I can be aware of a particular telephone when a schematism brings the empirically derived concept "telephone" under the rule of the *a priori* concepts of space and time. Viewed this way, the schematism is a product of my subjective activity (it is I who bring the empirical concept under the rule), but it is also a fixed representation of an actual telephone here on my desk, in my study. Johnson complains, however, that when we describe the schematism in this way it too nearly resembles an unchanging concept that transcends and represents aspects of the known world. Viewed this way, the schematism is fully immaterial, residing in a mind that is equally separated from the world that is known. This gives too much away to Kant's objectivist tendencies, ultimately undercutting the turn to the subject that is so central to Kant's critical philosophy.

We have seen throughout this volume why the objectivist instinct is a tendency "well lost." Taylor, Davidson, Rorty, Dennett, and now Johnson have all shown us how it is responsible for many of the conundrums that have occupied Western thinkers for the past twenty-five hundred years. The alternative view promoted in various ways by Wang

Yang-ming, Dewey, and Whitehead is that we view "knowledge" as an activity, a continual effort on the part of an organism to restructure itself and its world in accord with specifiable objectives. Johnson makes a similar suggestion urging us to avoid Kant's dilemma entirely by rejecting the original premise that causes the problem. If we let go of the sharp distinction between the objective-material-determined realm on the one hand and subjective-nonmaterial-free realm on the other, we can embrace Kant's insightful redescription of imagination as an activity. It is through the activity of the imagination that we transform ourselves from simple organisms with rudimentary mental structures and meaning systems into full-fledged subjects that "have" and "respond to" a world. On this view, there is a line of continuity linking the so-called material and subjective realms and no such thing as pure *a priori* concepts. This does not mean, however, that we are surrendering to a radical subjectivism where anything goes. Instead, Johnson argues, we can look to the ways in which the physical patterns within the material realm (in this case our very bodies) set the stage for and make possible higher cognitive experiences. The pure concepts that Kant was certain must be derived in some *a priori* fashion could easily be seen as the natural outcome of bodies operating in temporal, spatial, and causal systems. True, these concepts would no longer be pure, but that does not make them purely subjective either.

On Johnson's view then, the schematizing function in Kant's philosophy becomes the production of image schematas from the physical patterns that structure our bodily activities. Thus, via the process of metaphorical extension, physical patterns provide the basic structure for our understanding and in the process generate the "objective" rules that Kant came to designate as pure *a priori* concepts.

Of course, the transition from physical to cognitive activity is hard to describe with precision. Nevertheless, this is where Johnson's insistence on the existence of *nonpropositional experience* is so crucial. The imaginative moves that enable us to build cognition up from physical feelings must necessarily originate below the level of higher order concepts such as propositions. "In exploring the workings of the imagination at this most basic level, we are probing the preconceptual level of our experience at which structure and form first emerge for us" (ibid.). Johnson follows Kant in arguing that cognitive structure and form emerge for the first time via the imagination. Thus, both Kant and Johnson consider the imagination to be the source for the vague yet powerful feelings that provide the very backdrop that is necessary for the clear and distinct ideas that have so preoccupied modernist philosophy.

Johnson also goes on to point out how positioning the imagination in this way, as the crucial first step in the development of cognitive experience, could help Kant deal with another confusing aspect of his critical philosophy. In the third critique, Kant turns his attention to aesthetic judgments and creativity. He acknowledges that the imagination is capable of doing more than merely setting the stage for representative knowledge of an objective world. It sometimes generates creative and novel ideas that seem to have no precedent in our physical world. In this mode, the universal objective rules that control the schematizing function do not limit our imagination. Instead, aesthetic judgments appeal to what seem like nonobjective standards that cannot be universalized. For example, we often recognize our artistic geniuses by virtue of their capacity to create unprecedented standards for aesthetic experience. Johnson, however, presses Kant, arguing that were we to apply the criteria developed in the *Critique of Pure Reason,* this imaginative creativity would have to be considered irrational. The *Critique of Pure Reason* secures rationality and objectivity by the application of universal objective concepts or rules. In the *Critique of Judgment* by contrast,

> Kant is struggling to express a deep insight which the confines of his system seem to exclude, namely, he sees that there is a kind of *shared meaning that is not reducible to conceptual and propositional content alone.* He sees that there is a *preconceptual activity of imagination that is not merely subjective,* even though it is not objective in the strict sense of being conformable to public rules. That is, he sees that there is a rationality without rules, that is subject to criticism, and so is not arbitrary. He sees that there are *structures of imagination that can be shared by communities of people.* (Ibid., 161)

The essential phrase in Johnson's comment is the notion of a "rationality without rules." Ultimately, Johnson argues, Kant fails to hold together the insights of the first and third critiques because he is unwilling to concede the possibility that there can be a rationality without rules. Consequently, Kant fails to provide a completely unified theory of imagination.

> There seems to be a gap between the creative function, on the one hand, and the reproductive, productive, and schematizing functions, on the other. What connects them is that they all involve the structured ordering of mental representations into meaningful unities within our experience. But the freedom of creative imagination (the production of novelty) is not explicable solely in terms of the orderly reproductive and productive functions. Kant does not bridge this gap—it seems that it cannot be bridged within his system. He *describes* the operation of creative imagination but does not *explain* it. (Ibid., 166)

Johnson locates Kant's problem in two issues. First, as we have seen, Kant is struggling to explain how the imagination holds together both the formal *(a priori* pure concepts) and the material (empirical concepts). Second, he is trying to explain how the imagination can be simultaneously rule-governed (e.g., rational) and free (e.g., creative) (ibid.). Again, the way out of both problems is to give up the material/immaterial dichotomy that leads directly to the Kantian distinction between empirically derived concepts and pure *a priori* ones.

> What would happen if we deny the alleged gap between understanding, imagination, and sensation? What if, following the consensus of contemporary analytic philosophy, we deny the strict separation of the analytic from the synthetic, the *a priori* from the *a posteriori,* the formal from the material? If we regard these as poles on a continuum there is no need to exclude imagination from some supposed pristine realm of "cognitive content" or "objective structure." (Ibid., 167)

Positing such a continuum allows Johnson to argue, with Kant's support, that imagination forms the starting point for cognitive activity. It also enables Johnson to go beyond Kant by proclaiming that our imagination and the metaphorical process whereby physical patterns are extended and elaborated in new and productive ways is the creative starting point for rationality. Only by making such a move can we finally shake the vaguely platonic feeling that imagination is a failed form of rationality. Creativity is not irrational in the sense that it is opposed to rule-governed rationality. Rather, it is prerational, or better, it provides the essential background that is necessary for rational reflection. "Imaginative activity is absolutely crucial in determining what we will regard as meaningful and how we will reason about it. Instead of being nonrational, imaginative structures form the body of human rationality" (ibid., 169).

Johnson's reinterpretation of the Kantian project, his redescription of metaphor as the extension of bodily patterns, and his overall effort to provide us with an account of the "embodied basis of meaning, imagination and reason" all are useful markers on the path toward a nonrepresentational theory of knowledge that recognizes the unity of knowledge and action. In the penultimate chapter of his book, Johnson makes two statements that could serve as cornerstones for the argument I have been building:

> This particular formulation of the relevant notion of understanding as a way of "being in" or "having" a world, highlights the dynamic, interactive character of understanding (and meaning). Grasping a meaning is an *event* of understanding. Meaning is not merely a fixed relation between sentences and objective reality as Objectivism would have it. (Ibid., 175)

> Furthermore, a non-Objectivist cognitive semantics insists that understanding is not a transparent medium through which words map onto

the world. The apparent transparency of understanding is really only the pervasiveness of shared understanding in ordinary experiences within stable contexts. (Ibid., 178)

In Johnson's work then, we have an example of an analytic philosopher who has been motivated by insights in cognitive science and cognitive psychology to break through the limitations of the linguistic turn and use the organicist assumption that experience is broader than cognition to blaze a trail toward a nonrepresentational theory of knowledge. Johnson's work is important for my argument because it illustrates my claim that the quest for a nonrepresentational theory of knowledge is a point of intersection cutting across most philosophic schools as well as cognitive science and cognitive psychology. Moreover, we can see in Johnson's project an effort that goes beyond what was available in Wang, Dewey, and Whitehead. I read Johnson's use of contemporary cognitive science, along with his detailed analysis of the process of generating image-schematas, as an empirically based confirmation of the epistemological claims made by Wang and the early pragmatic and process thinkers.

Throughout this book, I have described the quest for a nonrepresentational theory of knowledge as the "holy grail" of contemporary epistemology. Moreover, I have been trying to explain how we can make progress if only we allow ourselves to recognize some of the radical implications of insights given to us by Wang Yang-ming, John Dewey, and Alfred North Whitehead. In the *High Road around Modernism* (1992), Robert Neville has argued that the problem with contemporary epistemological reflection is modernism itself. To avoid modernist pitfalls he looks to thinkers who he claims were untouched by the flawed modernist agenda. Among the most prominent figures that he cites are Wang Yang-ming, Dewey, and Whitehead. I would like to end this book by looking to Neville's project in an effort to catch a glimpse of what things might look like were we to allow these three thinkers to play a critical role in shaping our understanding of knowledge.

AXIOLOGY AND KNOWLEDGE

There is no need to begin by arguing that Neville's positions intersect with Dewey, Whitehead, and Wang, as I have in my discussions of Taylor, Davidson, Rorty, Dennett, and Johnson. Neville regularly appeals to all three. Instead, my focus will be on the new directions his thinking takes. In 1995, Neville brought to a close a three-volume effort to present a reconstructed understanding of thought and thinking titled an *Axiology of Thinking*. Written over a fourteen-year period, all three volumes are designed to develop and defend the thesis that "thinking is primarily valuing, not mirroring form nor making moves like a computer and that there are four main families of thinking that do this: imagination, interpretation, theorizing and the pursuit of responsibility" (Neville, 1981, 216–17). *The Reconstruction of Thinking* (vol. 1, 1981) explores imagination, *Recovery of the Measure* (vol. 2, 1989) deals with interpretation, and *Normative Cultures* (vol. 3, 1996) is devoted to the analysis of theory and responsibility. In reviewing Neville's argument, I will consider each volume in turn. My description, however, will have to be relatively cursory. Neville's project is extraordinarily complex as it simultaneously explores ontological, cosmological, and epistemological questions. My goal in this section is to provide an accurate outline that gives readers a sense of the creative possibilities that emerge when the pragmatic, process, and Confucian traditions are used as a resource for confronting contemporary philosophic problems.

In *Reconstruction of Thinking,* Neville begins by pointing out that the classical Greek philosophers believed thinking to involve "appreciation, valuing, and being reasonable about both the intrinsic and the extrinsic worth of things" (1981, 6). He complains that much of our confusion regarding value and its role in epistemology stems from the fact that we have lost touch with the awareness that our experiences are *always* infused with a qualitative dimension. While acknowledging that the fact-value dichotomy contributed to the development of certain kinds of mathematical and scientific reasoning, Neville points out that it also led us to believe that reason is essentially deductive and that values are a subjective imposition onto a purely mechanistic world. Consequently, our innermost qualitative responses to each other, the world, and ourselves were set apart from the world and labeled unreal. Valuative feelings were contrasted with so-called objectively determined facts of the matter.

Neville, of course, is not alone in thinking that we have been led up a blind alley with respect to value theory. This was precisely the point that we saw Charles Taylor developing in *Sources of the Self.* Both Taylor and Neville defend the objective reality of value. Unlike Taylor, however, Neville is a naturalist whose Confucian, pragmatic, and process commitments put him in a position to argue that human values can be continuous with and an extension of the values inherent in all things. For this reason, Neville begins well ahead of Taylor. Readers will recall that though Taylor makes a strong phenomenological case for the objective reality of values (we really can't imagine a world where they are not real), he does not set his claims within a broader cosmological or metaphysical context. Consequently, his challenge to philosophers who posit a sharp distinction between the material realm and the realm of values is not as strong as it could be. Neville, by contrast, challenges mechanistic materialism directly by positing an alternative metaphysical and cosmological framework that renders plausible his claim that human values are emergent from and continuous with values inherent in nature.

As we saw in our discussion of Whitehead's organismic cosmology, the claim that there are values inherent within nature sounds to modernist ears like an outrageous lapse into premodern obscurantism. To defend himself against such charges Neville must present more than a theory of knowledge. He must follow Whitehead in undertaking a "systematic philosophy." At a time when interest in systematic philosophy is in almost total eclipse, Neville is one of a very few philosophers who defend the claim that we have a responsibility to think systematically. He argues that since philosophic theories are always nested within one another, it is irresponsible to act as if one's epistemology is not tied to one's metaphysics, ontology, and cosmology. For example, when Newtonian physics depicts time and space as empty moments and empty containers, respectively, it creates a favorable context for the assertion that values are merely human projections, no matter how real they seem to us. According to Neville, late modern rejection of value talk is a testament to the power theories have over our lives. The only way to change our understanding of value is to rethink the metaphysical and cosmological assumptions that led us into this confusion (1981, 33–50).

In the early chapters of *Reconstruction of Thinking* Neville draws heavily upon Dewey, Whitehead, Paul Weiss, and key Confucian thinkers (e.g., Hsun Tzu, Chu Hsi, and Wang Yang-ming) to develop an *"axiological* cosmology" that he claims should stand in place of the mechanistic models handed down by Newton and elaborated by contemporary scientists. An axiological cosmology describes the being of each thing as an expression of value. Neville builds his cosmology upon the basic organismic assumptions that we have been discussing throughout this volume, but he also shifts the focus just a bit. He argues that we understand ontology best when we see it through the lens of value. In a sense, for Neville value is a more abstract category than organisms, since it is the one thing that all organisms pursue.

In Neville's axiological cosmology the final real things are patterned integrations of *essential* and *conditional* features. An entity's conditional features stem from its relationships with other things. Its essential features are the unique way in which the conditional features are drawn together into a singular harmonic unity. Neville calls the patterned integration a harmony, and every harmony is the actualization of some value. Viewed this way *everything* is an instance of value. Value replaces Aristotelian substance and Newtonian matter. Moreover, according to

Neville, the components of every harmony (the essential and conditional features) are themselves harmonies. In short, the cosmos is harmonies/values all the way down.

Within Neville's system, cosmologies that describe matter as valueless bits of concrete reality are useful abstractions though hardly to be given pride of place as the ultimate description of the final real things. They make it difficult to explain the transition from material to organic entities and, most important, from organic activity to human experience. The main advantage that an axiological cosmology has over mechanistic alternatives is that it can be truly comprehensive. Neville's cosmology (like Whitehead's, Dewey's, and Wang's) fits the inorganic, organic, and human within a single comprehensive scheme, thereby avoiding all of the dichotomies that have made it so difficult for us to understand ourselves and our relationship to the things that make up our world.

With his axiological cosmology on the table, Neville has a context for defending his thesis that *thinking* is valuation and that thinking occurs in the modes of imagination, interpretation, theory, and responsibility. Neville takes these four modes from Plato's metaphor of the Divided Line. Indeed, the whole *Axiology of Thinking* is a creative updating of Plato's metaphor. Neville associates each mode of thinking with a "normative measure," an ideal form of order that each mode aims to realize. Imaginative thinking, for example, is the mode of thinking through which we engage the world in the quest for *beauty*. Interpretation involves testing whether our images are *truthful* relative to the world. Theoretical thinking aims to establish *unified* perspectives from which to discern what is *important* in a given situation. Finally, thinking in the mode of responsibility measures our actions against the human quest to embody a *good* and *moral* life. In sum, beauty, truth, unity, and goodness are universal norms against which we measure our imaginative, interpretive, theoretical, and moral thinking. Of course, it would be wrong to say that each norm applies only to its corresponding mode of thinking. All four norms apply in different ways to all four modes of thinking, and together they constitute what Neville calls the "norms of rationality."

Unlike those who would portray beauty, truth, unity, and goodness as subjective impositions on a valueless world, Neville's axiological cosmology allows him to argue that they are objectively real. Of course, Neville is not suggesting there exists a single transcendent beauty, unity, truthfulness, or morality that every being strives to attain. Plato's Form of the Good, Wang Yang-ming's *liang-chih,* Taylor's hyper-goods, and Neville's norms all point to the sense that we aspire to vaguely common goals, which are specified differently according to our situations. For

Neville, as for the others, thinking is more about *creating* specific instances of beauty, truth, unity, and goodness than finding them in some universal or transcendent form.

In the latter half of *Reconstruction of Thinking* Neville develops a detailed analysis of imagination that resonates quite well with what we have just seen in Johnson's work. Like Johnson, Neville begins by making it clear that he is using the term *imagination* to point to nonpropositional synthetic activities that necessarily precede and form the basis for higher-order cognitive experience. Likening his starting point to Kant's, Neville says that imagination is a "synthesis of otherwise merely causal components into a unity whose parts potentially have a meaningful relationship to each other" (1981, 17). Though this may sound complicated the point is actually quite basic. For there to be any experience at all, he claims, there must be organization of a purely causal flow into a coherent unity of some sort. At minimum then, this organization would be the creation of a vague but still distinct "background for focused attention" (ibid.). Without such a background, of course, there could be no field against which to construct cognitive experience. Neville's claim, however, is that the background is also a *constructed* field, something established by the creative imagination. This is the same basic point we saw Johnson making via Kant. In short, for Kant, Johnson, and Neville, there would be nothing but mere flow without the imagination. The imagination sets boundaries, lifts up patterns, and uses other techniques to define a field of experience. Put another way, it takes imagination to have any experience at all.

While the link between Neville and Johnson on this point should be clear, it is also important to see how their focus is different. Johnson describes imagination as a process of metaphorical extension whereby we establish the experiential field or background against which cognitive knowledge stands out. In describing this process, he focuses our attention on the creation of image schematas via metaphorical extension. Neville, who is also interested in describing *how* we establish the experiential field, is primarily concerned to remind us that imaginative syntheses are best viewed as *acts of valuation*. By synthesizing the causal flow in one particular way, we are necessarily opting for one synthesis over alternative imaginative syntheses. This is a point that is different from but compatible with Johnson's detailed description of the process of metaphorical extension.

Neville claims that beauty is the principle norm for imaginative synthesis. Imagination then is always an act of selection from among an indeterminate number of options in the pursuit of beauty. In the imaginative moment, there is not yet sufficient distance from alternative imaginative options to raise questions about accuracy, truth, or falsehood. Instead, Neville claims our imagination opts for whatever promises the greatest intensity of experience (to use a Whiteheadian phrase). Thus, according to Neville, our primordial response to the world is aesthetic rather than cognitive. With Dewey, Whitehead, and Wang, Neville claims that the higher levels of human cognition are dependent upon and emergent from a more primordial qualitative response to the world. This claim does not reduce cognition to aesthetics, but it does render clearer why attempts to cut values out of epistemology are doomed to fail.

Both Neville and Johnson are making the basic Kantian point that our own subjective activity (in this case imagination) is necessary for us to "have a world." Like Johnson, however, Neville rejects Kant's claim that we must appeal to a transcendental perspective to avoid radical subjectivism. There need be no transcendental explanation because Neville's axiological cosmology does not posit an ontological divide between the so-called material and immaterial realms. In this way, we can see how Neville's axiological cosmology preserves the line of continuity between percept and concept that was so central to Johnson's position. As we have seen with Johnson, when we deny this basic Kantian premise, the need to posit a dichotomy between empirical and pure *a priori* concepts disappears as well. Therefore, Neville would have no difficulty following Johnson's instinct to locate the imagination largely within the realm of non-propositional experience. From within the context of Neville's axiological cosmology, *all* things are already instances of value. Imaginative synthesis, operating below the level of cognition, is merely a particular example of the very same processes that constitute everything else. "The glory of the imaginative base of human culture is that it allows for the creation of values far more subtle and complex than that achieved by nature without imagination" (Neville, 1989, 18). Human imagination is, therefore, emergent from and dependent upon those values achieved in nature.

The rest of *Reconstruction of Thinking* explores the role imagination plays in higher-order cognitive activity. Drawing heavily from the language and structure of Whitehead's description of the "higher phases of experience," Neville develops sustained analyses of imagination's role in perception, beauty, form, and art. He also spends considerable energy exploring the role religion plays in cultivating imaginative contexts that are rich enough to sustain complex human experience. All of this is an elaboration of Neville's main thesis that "imaginatively synthesized images are what allow for the engagement of the world that we know as experience, rather than as other kinds of responses we know as the collisions of vectors of force or chemical transformative processes"

(1995, 217). In short, imagination is the uniquely human trait that transforms merely organic activity into human experience.

In *Recovery of the Measure: Interpretation and Nature*, the second volume in the series, Neville examines thinking in the mode of interpretation. In contrast to imaginative thinking, where the quest for beauty largely overrides issues of veracity, interpretative thinking is a "special quality of imaginative activity" that aims primarily at ascertaining the degree to which our images are faithful to that which they represent (ibid.). In short, just as beauty was the norm for thinking in the mode of imagination, truth is the norm for thinking in the mode of interpretation. The key, however, is to recognize that Neville sees interpretation as a natural extension of the imaginative faculty. It is not as if each mode is completely distinct from the other. Quite the contrary, they lead into and blend with one another, something that will become clearer as we proceed.

Some might see in Neville's approach to interpretation a fatally flawed effort to restore the representational theory of knowledge and the correspondence theory of truth. But Neville uses Peirce's semiotics to strike a delicate balance between his appreciation for pragmatic perspectivalism (with its concomitant rejection of the spectator theory of knowledge) and his Weissian sense that ultimately the world is the *measure* of the veracity of our thoughts. The central thesis of *Recovery of Measure* is that "truth is the properly qualified carryover of the value of a thing (or situation, or state of affairs, or fact, or any complex harmony that might become an object of interpretation) into the interpreting experiences of that thing. The achieved value in the thing is always a measure of the interpretation, and the dyadic character of the truth relation is thus preserved" (1989, 65).

In this way, Neville replaces correspondence theories of truth, where the focus is on the "replication of form," with a theory that focuses on causality and the carryover of value. Following a path originally marked by Whitehead, Neville says: "Carryover itself means that the value achieved in the thing not only enters into the constitution of the interpreters but is objectified in their experience" (ibid.). Where Whitehead used the metaphor *flow of feeling* to describe the basic cosmological movements, Neville opts for Peircian metaphor *flow of interpretation*. Both, however, could also epitomize their systems with the phrase *flow of value*. In this context Neville's understanding of what it means to think truthfully can be defined as taking up and including in the subject a value already achieved in that subject's objective world. The key to defending this thesis is Neville's insistence that interpretation *is not* a purely cognitive activity. Following Peirce and Whitehead, Neville makes interpretation a cosmological category attributable to *all* things.

For Neville, every *thing* is a perspectivally shaped interpretation of that which is included in its own constitution.

By making interpretation and value cosmological categories, Neville has the tools he needs to fight materialists (and Johnsonian objectivists) who describe causality in purely physical terms and thereby reduce value to an epiphenomenon. Neville's battle, however, is not just with mechanistic materialists. He also struggles against hermeneuticians and deconstructionists who seek to make *textual* interpretation and *conversation* the central metaphors for describing our cognitive relationships with each other and the world around us. In making this point Neville complains: "Compared to stars, seas, and mountains, to food, safety, and sociality, a text is effete body; compared to sensitivity, creativity, will, and passion, text-interpreting is effete mind. Deconstructive postmodernism reduces mind and body to the metaphors and tools of the academy, depriving the academy of its robust natural cultural context in the process" (1989, 13–14). This statement captures much of what Neville is afraid we lose if we allow the metaphor of textual interpretation to dominate our self-understanding. He argues we should stand with the early pragmatists who thought of themselves as scientists. "Whereas the root of hermeneutics is interpretation of texts, the root for pragmatism is experimentation" (ibid., 49). We engage in experimentation to test the usefulness of our theories regarding one another, the world, and ourselves.

Neville's position blends a realist's appreciation for the need to check our images against nature (via inquiry and experimentation) with the contemporary hermeneutical assertion that experience takes place only within interpretive settings that are not capable of mirroring nature. By arguing that truth is the carryover of value, Neville is trying to have things both ways, and for the most part he succeeds. With the hermeneuticians, he acknowledges that cognition does not give us direct or immediate access to nature. It is only via our imaginative activity that we "have a world." The world we "have," however, could never be identical to the "world-in-itself." Our knowledge is always rooted in subjective activity.

Having determined, however, that there is no such thing as a direct or immediate cognitive apprehension of nature, Neville is not willing to surrender nature's sovereignty over cognition. It cannot all be just a matter of interpretation. The images generated by the imagination do sometimes fail to carry over the actual values inherent in things. In those instances, nature brings us up short. No amount of interpretation will put bread on the table when there is none. To maintain his realist's credentials Neville argues that in most instances the imagination does not create its images out of whole cloth. Instead, our imaginations truthfully interpret the world when we draw the raw material for the images directly from the harmonic unification of values already achieved in the actual world. In other words, our images are truthful when they carry forward aspects of the world as it is. Therefore, though it may be true that we can't step outside of imagination to "know" the world directly, imagination can, via Neville's axiological cosmology, make use of real values, real things, as the raw material for its own constructive processes.

Interpretation is our way of winnowing images that are false from those that are more nearly in line with the actual values already achieved in nature. Neville avoids the negative effects of representationalism because his axiological cosmology makes thinking an *activity* rather than a mirror. Echoing Dewey, Whitehead, and Wang Yang-ming on this point, Neville rejects representational theories that present mind as a disembodied container of ideas and images. He describes all thinking (including interpretation) as the *active* attempt to incorporate past values into one's own self-constitution. Imagination and interpretation are never passive. By operating within the context of a cosmology that sees all things as the active incorporation of past harmonies into new harmonic entities, Neville frees himself (and us) from the problems that have haunted modernist philosophy. Thinking is a species of the same cosmic activity that underlies all things.

Neville realizes that a full defense of his position requires more than the axiological cosmology laid out in *Reconstruction of Thinking*. The central chapters in *Recovery of the Measure* contain a full-blown philosophy of nature that presupposes the axiological cosmology but goes beyond it to include discussions of such key issues as identity, value, harmony, time, temporality, space, motion, and causation. Neville needs this philosophy of nature to fill in the details that link his broad cosmological claim that all things are instances of value, with his specific claim that truth is the carryover of value from an object into the interpreter's own constitution. It is the details of this "middle level" theory (middle because it is less abstract than the axiological cosmology but still more abstract than theories about human behavior) that provide the ultimate rationale for the claims outlined above.

The last section of *Recovery of the Measure* brings the discussion back to interpretation in general and human interpretation in particular. With the full weight of his axiological cosmology (which accounts for why things are ultimately instances of value) and philosophy of nature (which describes how it is that thinking is an activity and that truth could be the carryover of value) behind him, Neville outlines a theory of human interpretation that rejects modernist claims that mind is outside of nature and that values are mental projections. In developing his theory of interpretation, he claims that it is "a mistake to build a theory of meaning on a theory of communication, because that makes it seem as if people were separate enjoyers of private meanings that then have to be communicated." For Neville, all meaning is "set within causal networks including non-cultural nature as well as other people and human artifacts such as symbols and language" (1989, 251). These networks precede and create the context necessary for any particular experience to be meaningful. We do not have experiences and then find ways to integrate them with the rest of the world. Rather, experience is always *embodied* (emerging within bodies that are physically interconnected with broader environmental networks) and *encultured* (located within particular cultural networks at specific times and in specific locations).

Philosophers who have taken the linguistic turn, and who model mind on language, focus too much attention on what Neville calls the "cultural side" of network meanings. While important in itself, such an approach underestimates the importance of the *physical* networks that embody and give meaning to thought. This, of course, is Johnson's main point. Moreover, those who reduce mind to language necessarily lose touch with what Neville calls the "content meaning" of interpretive thinking. From the perspective of linguistic philosophy, it is sometimes difficult to explain the connection between language and the world, as is shown by the crisis in objectivist philosophy as described by Johnson. In describing the advantages of his position Neville says: "Here is the payoff for joining a naturalistic metaphysics and cosmology to the theory of interpretation. The theory of natural harmony articulates a pattern of connections universal to all things to which reference can be made. . . . This is a wholly non-idealistic way of saying, with Peirce and Derrida, that everything is a sign or text" (ibid., 268).

Neville's position is nonidealistic because his axiological cosmology mandates that each thing includes within itself the actual values inherent in those things that are causally related to it. In this way, though everything is potentially a sign capable of re-presenting its causal ancestors to later interpreters, those entities serving as signs are not "mere representations." They carry within themselves the *content* of that which they signify. This content meaning is then transferred yet again into new interpreters as the process continues.

In sum, having made the case earlier that *nature* is a "flow of interpretation," Neville puts himself in a position to claim that *human* interpretive activity is a heightened, more complex version of what is already going on throughout nature. Of course, all of this must be seen from the perspective of Neville's claim that cognition is always an *act of valuation* rather than the passive replication of static forms. "Just as a sign is an interpretive activity, so its contents are sub-activities within the same process" (ibid., 269).

So far we have seen how Neville's axiological cosmology, theory of imagination, and analysis of interpretation (including the philosophy of nature) all support his claim that thinking is primarily an act of valuation rather than a conceptual mirroring of an objective world. It remains for us to examine his claim that the final two modes of thinking (the theoretical mode and the mode of responsibility) are acts of valuation as well.

Following a line of reasoning laid down by Peirce, Dewey, and Whitehead, Neville portrays theoretical thinking as a way of carrying forward the processes begun in imagination's pursuit of beauty and interpretation's pursuit of truth. Theory is "a special kind of interpretation that attempts a synoptic view of its subject matter in order to provide orientation for practical (and other) activities" (Neville, 1995, 217). Theoretical thinking brings together the many strands of our imaginative engagement with the world and settles them within *unified* perspectives that rank the *diversity* of things in an order of *importance* that shapes our choices and enjoyments. "So unity, diversity, and importance go together, and perhaps importance should be given pride of place. For it is importance that guides the structuring of theories so as to respect diverse singulars and attain unity of vision" (ibid., 31). Theory arises out of the need to "unify a diversity of interpretations. Diverse objects are present for theory only when they are (potentially or actually) interpreted. Therefore theory can be viewed as a synoptic vision that encompasses many interpretations" (ibid.).

With Neville's axiological cosmology as background, we can see the development from imagination to interpretation to theory as a natural outgrowth of the organic need to ensure that our actions are both *coherent* and *effective*. The key struggle in theoretical thinking is maintaining a proper balance between the quest for a unified vision that brings coherence and order, with an appreciation for the intrinsic value of the diverse elements contributing to our experience. Without the unifying effect of theoretical thinking, we are at the mercy of conflicting interpretations and have little ability to focus or direct ourselves. But unity itself is not sufficient. To be effective our theories also have to be sensitive to the objective reality of the actual values already present in our world. Otherwise, our unified synoptic vision would be nothing more than a "castle in the air."

Neville points out that contemporary criticism of theoretical thinking stems from our tendency to opt for unity of vision over an appreciation for things in their diversity. Many consider theory to be nothing more than a disguised version of the will-to-power. For example, Nietzsche and his followers argue that those who appeal to theory to justify their actions are usually guilty of bad faith. Such arguments typically subordinate competing interpretations (including alternative cultural assumptions about reason itself) to personal ambitions even as they point to a "nonexistent" universal reason and "so-called" objective values to justify their positions. Nietzschean mistrust of theory moves directly from this rejection of objectivist faith in universal reason and universal values to a pessimistic portrayal of any effort to construct a "synoptic vision" that integrates competing interpretations into a coherent point of view. Without universal reason or transcendent values to direct the process, all unifying visions seem reductive at best and often totalitarian in their implications. From the Nietzschean point of view then, all rankings of importance are subjective impositions rather than accurate responses to what is objectively real.

While acknowledging that theories can sometimes be self-serving in this way, Neville rejects the assertion that *all* theoretical reflection need be guilty of such distortions. Drawing upon his axiological cosmology, Neville counters Nietzsche's unmasking of modernism's self-deceptions with his own nonmodernist portrayal of the world as the "flow of interpretation." Things become what they are by incorporating within themselves the value that has already been accomplished. Neville's axiology, drawing as it does on process, pragmatic, and Confucian themes, is unlike anything Nietzsche and his followers criticize. It is not a mechanistic world of independent bits of matter all "known" from the disembodied perch of universal reason. Instead, Neville's ontology is relational. All things move together, and each individual thing is itself profoundly dependent upon its relationships with the things that make it what it is. Knowing (or thinking) occurs within this ongoing flow. Everything contributing to the process is itself the actualization of something intrinsically valuable. Value pervades the system and contributes to all aspects of it. Consequently, Neville can legitimately claim that theoretical thinking is directed by more than self-interest alone. When done well, theoretical thinking *is* capable of picking up, carrying forward, and building on the values already accomplished.

As Neville noted above, to understand theoretical thinking, we must come to grips with what we mean by importance. We engage in theoretical thinking to resolve problematic situations. The resolution comes in part by prioritizing competing interpretive demands. In some sense then, a theory is a potential order, a way of placing each thing somewhere in a hierarchy of values that give it meaning and structure from the point of view of the theory. Importance, however, is located in more than just the theory's own rankings. Each element ranked is itself a harmony of elements, containing its own hierarchical rankings, its own importances, which may or may not be registered by the theory. A good theory must do more than merely place things within the theory's hierarchy of importances. It must be capable of taking into account the importances of the things that it is designed to handle. "The defining hypothesis of the theory of importance to be expressed here is that importance is the value things have in site. The relations of things to and within their sites structure the various kinds of importance that have been identified, and these various kinds mark out most of what is meant by *importance* in commonsense usages as well as the kinds relevant to theorizing about things" (ibid., 48).

Neville uses the term *site* here to make the point that the harmonic integration that makes something what it is is itself a determinate set of relations to the things that make up its world. Each thing's importance, its value, its very being, stems directly from its relationships and how they are structured. As a result, theoretical thinking must blend the quest for a synoptic vision (a unified hierarchical ranking of things/values) with an effort to appreciate what makes each of those things *valuable* (their sitings).

Neville's theory of importance goes beyond those who complain that all theories contain distorting values and biases. They do, but that claim does not get to the heart of the problem. A good theory, according to Neville, constructs "within itself a field of sites, a theoretical field capable of representing the various sites of importance of the things in its subject matter" (ibid., 55). A good theory is able to suspend its own developing valuative framework in order to *appreciate* what it is that makes the things under discussion valuable in themselves. This involves an ongoing comparative process. "Comparison now takes on an unusual dimension. The usual dimension is that comparisons find something in common between the things compared and also something that differentiates them relative to what they have in common. But what they have in common from the standpoint of a theory might be something imposed by the theory, with differentia relative to this, that is not at all important to the compared things in any of their own sites of importance" (ibid.).

As the theory compares its own developing agenda with the existing agendas of its components, the theory changes and grows increasingly sophisticated. The possibility that theory might engage in this ongoing self-corrective process is what most critics of theory miss. By assuming that all theories have no mechanism for reevaluating basic orienting assumptions, these critics legitimate the claim that theory is ultimately nothing more than an expression of the will-to-power. This description of theory might make sense if we lived in a world where values were simply imposed from the outside by the subjective will. But when the world is value-filled, as is the case for Neville, theoretical thinking can be both value-laden and yet not totalitarian. When properly cultivated, it can engage in the kind of comparative reflection that enables it to take the intrinsic value of things into account as it shapes and reshapes the hierarchical rankings in its own system of importance.

Neville's theory of theories extends beyond the points made above to include a detailed analysis of *how* we cultivate theories that strike the proper balance between a unified synoptic vision and an adequate attunement to the intrinsic values of the things subsumed under the theory itself. His argument has two steps that I will refer to only briefly.

The first step describes how theories relate to one another. Typically, we think that our theories are nested within one another along the lines of subsections in a long mathematical equation. On this view, a specific claim that a chair is brown (for example) can be seen as subordinate to a more general theory about the interaction of light and matter. The theory of light and matter would itself be subordinate to still more general cosmological and metaphysical theories. Viewed in this way, the line from the most specific to the most general theories seems two-dimensional and direct. Following Peirce, Neville replaces this two-dimensional metaphorical representation of theories with a three-dimensional model that has theories interacting with one another at various levels of vagueness and specificity (ibid., 67). Some of our theories operate at the same level of specificity and compete with one another (e.g., Freudian versus Jungian psychology). Others are less specific (Neville's technical term is *logically vague*) and capable of being compatible with both. Whitehead's organismic cosmology, for example, is logically vague with respect to the psychological theories of Freud and Jung. Both might be true as far as Whitehead is concerned.

The corrective process, which is what is really at stake in this section of Neville's argument, operates up, down, and across the system of theories. We swim in a sea of theories, some of which are subordinate to one another, others of which are competing with one another, all of which are liable to correction and improvement as we view things from one theoretical point of view, then another, and then another. When confronted by competing theoretical claims, we do not just appeal to the empirical evidence to settle the question. It is all much more complicated. We have to be "standing somewhere," theoretically speaking, in order to see how two theories contradict one another and what of importance is at stake. We are able to negotiate among competing theories only from the point of view of yet another theory, which is itself logically vague (and therefore compatible) with respect to those that are under discussion. Moreover, this corrective process is multidirectional. Theories that are more abstract are themselves liable to modification or correction by those that are more specific. If, for example, Whitehead's organismic cosmology were to be viewed as incompatible with both Freudian and Jungian psychology, that would be evidence against the adequacy of Whitehead's metaphysics, not the other way around.

This whole section of Neville's argument is designed to drive home the point that we are not locked into the values embedded in our theories. We are capable of correcting them, and do so as we struggle to formulate theories that provide a synoptic vision. Ultimately, however, Neville acknowledges that theoretical thinking will always be selective in its emphasis and unable to take full account of the infinitely dense cluster of value inherent in each of the individual things that it subsumes. However, recognition of this fact need not lead us back to Nietzschean pessimism about theory. Instead, Neville ends his discussion of theory by pointing out the extent to which theory depends upon and gives way to *metaphor*. Neville's final word is that theoretical thinking must have enough humility to acknowledge its limitations. Good theories are tempered by a *pious deference* to the things themselves. We rely on metaphors to point vaguely toward the infinite value embedded in the things that make up our actual world.

At this point, we find ourselves brought back around to Johnson's claim that at its base, cognitive activity is tied to a process of metaphorical extension. According to Johnson we move from the bodily patterns learned from birth to the full-fledged cognitive patterns that are the basis for all thought, theory, and knowledge. Neville's theory of theories must also give priority to metaphor because the things that theories are designed to interpret are themselves *infinitely* dense actualizations of value. Johnson appeals to metaphor as a way of describing how our cognitive life is dependent upon and emergent from our physical interactions. Neville's speculative ontology, cosmology, and metaphysics provide the necessary theoretical background to Johnson's phenomenological and empirical arguments. Working directly from data in cognitive science and cognitive psychology, Johnson provides us with an empirical rationale for overturning the objectivist position. Neville, by contrast, draws upon Dewey, Whitehead, and Wang to construct a new theoretical vision free from the objectivist associations that Johnson criticizes so thoroughly. Neville can achieve this because the traditions he appeals to are, for the most part, not subject to the errors inherent in the modernist philosophical assumptions that are essential to the objectivist position (Neville, 1992).

When I began this discussion of Neville's *Axiology of Thinking*, I noted that the whole project was designed to defend the thesis that "thinking is primarily valuing, not mirroring form nor making moves like a computer and that there are four main families of thinking that do this: imagination, interpretation, theorizing and the pursuit of responsibility" (1995, 216–17). The final section of the *Axiology of Thinking* contains a discussion of the mode of thinking that involves the pursuit of responsibility. Most will consider it obvious that the pursuit of responsibility is more "valuing" than "mirroring." Nevertheless, there has been a tendency in the West to make moral reflection subordinate to the so-called purer forms of cognitive activity, such as theoretical knowledge. In a reversal of these classical patterns, Neville makes pursuit of responsibility the *culminating moment* in the process of thinking. While Plato and Aristotle both ranked theoretical thinking as the highest mode of human cognitive activity, Neville argues that the pursuit of responsibility should be given pride of place and that it is best if we see the pursuit of responsibility as a form of practical reasoning.

Responsibility, Neville argues, only becomes possible when creatures are capable of imagination, interpretation, and theoretical construction. Imaginative envisagment makes it possible for us to feel and appreciate the potentialities embedded in paths different from those that serve our own narrow self-interest. Interpretation is the process whereby we sort out which imaginative possibilities carry forward the values inherent in what has already happened. Theoretical construction is the way we integrate competing interpretations into a unity that is sophisticated enough to take into account the diverse (and sometimes conflicting) perspectives of its constituent elements.

According to Neville, we wake via these modes of cognitive activity to find ourselves already enmeshed in an intricate matrix of obligations that are the essential ingredients of our own status as human beings. "To be a human being with any powers of control or influence at all is to be obligated with regard to doing the best in those matters that can be affected. *Perhaps no other generalization about the human condition is more important than this, that to be human is to lie under obligation*" (ibid., 143; italics added). Most creatures pursue what seems immediately good with whatever energies they have and without regard for any point of view other than their own self-interest. Human beings, however, via imagination, interpretation, and theory, become capable of appreciating that they are always obliged to pursue a course of action leading to the "best possible outcome" even when such actions are contrary to their own self-interest.

The capacity to pursue responsibility is so important to Neville's understanding of human beings that he makes it *the* distinctive feature that separates us from the rest of the animal kingdom. "So far as we know, no other creatures are obligated, and if there are such on other planets they are obligated because, like human beings, they can do something about the normative consequences of their behavior and know they can do it" (ibid., 143).

In adopting this position Neville is *following and generalizing* a line of argument implicit in Dewey and explicit in George Herbert Mead's writings. Mead argues in *Mind, Self, and Society* that symbolic gestures and language are essential ingredients in the creation of self-conscious experience and that these traits distinguish humans from all other animals (Mead, 1974). Read with Neville's arguments in mind Mead seems to be claiming that symbolic gestures and language are what make it possible for us to experience the world from another's point of view. This capacity creates the need for what Neville describes as imagination, interpretation, and theorizing. Neville agrees with Mead's claim that human cognitive activity separates us from the rest of the animal kingdom. However, he reverses the order, arguing instead that imagination, interpretation, and theory are what give rise to language. In other words, these capacities are what make it possible for us to experience the world from another's point of view. Language is a product of imagination, interpretation, and theoretical thinking. This is why Neville claims that along with the emergence of language, we wake to find ourselves enmeshed in a matrix of social obligations. The obligations are real because they form the felt background (rooted in imagination, interpretation, and theory) that makes language and self-consciousness possible.

One of the advantages of Neville's description of the pursuit of responsibility is the way it integrates a strong sense of our *individuality* (we are responsible for the particular harmonic integrations we pursue) with a deep appreciation for the extent to which we (like all creatures) derive our very being from our *relatedness*. As we have seen earlier, relational ontologies such as Dewey's and Whitehead's have often been cited as weak when it comes to articulating how the individual emerges as a distinct unit, separable from the "flow of things." Here I find Neville's relationalist sensibilities tempered nicely by Wang Yang-ming, who encouraged his students to see thinking as an act of spiritual cultivation whereby they learn to take responsibility for their contribution to the whole of things. Both Wang and Neville see individuality and responsibility as *achievements* rather than starting points. We do not begin as individuals seeking to relate to the world. Instead, our individuality and our sense of responsibility emerge as our cognitive activity becomes capable of appreciating and taking into account points of view other than our own. We literally *become* responsible by integrating competing interpretations into what we take to be the best possible harmonic order we can muster. On Neville's view then we are never solipsistic individuals seeking desperately to overcome our cognitive isolation from one another.

As a way of demonstrating some of the practical outcomes of his axiology of knowledge, Neville builds from his discussion of responsibility a critique of the social contract theory. Whereas early modern thinkers such as Hobbes and Locke saw humans as discrete individuals (rather like Newtonian bits of matter) whose self-directed tendencies are brought under control by a rationally constructed social order, Neville argues that our individuality emerges from our relatedness, a relatedness that obligates us from the beginning to pursue what is best quite apart from our own self-interest. Neville reverses the assumptions of the social contract theory, arguing that human beings begin their lives fully obligated to one another at all levels. "Within the social contract suppositions is the notion that there are no moral norms save those constructed in the civil society itself, either in its sovereignty or in explicitly legislated duties and rights" (ibid., 148). Hobbes and Locke portray early humans as originally independent and completely free individuals who opt to establish some degree of security by voluntarily subordinating themselves to a social contract whose only justification is that it is in everyone's self-interest. Those areas of life not regulated by the social contract remain essentially private and free from any obligation whatsoever.

Neville complains that one of the chief problems with the social contract theory is that it cannot deal adequately with the extraordinary complexity of human social life, nor does it have a way of explaining how we are to behave when the social order breaks down. "Not only are moral norms relatively few on this conception, leaving a wide range of un-normed free and private behavior but, when civil society breaks down the norms disappear completely" (ibid., 149). Since the only justification for feeling obligated by a social contract is its ability to ensure one's own self-preservation, these obligations seem to vanish at times when society cannot protect us. Consequently, the social contract theory makes it seem as if there are no norms to guide us during times of crisis. Such a view could make sense only if we concede that self-interest is the only ultimate value worthy of motivating humans. Moreover, that claim rests ultimately on the assumption that we are independent, atomic units, who only acquire our "relationships" as secondary characteristics.

All of this seems a muddle from the point of view I have been developing throughout this text. Following the lead of Whitehead, Dewey, and Wang Yang-ming, Neville reminds us that our lives are ontologically dependent upon the relationships that constitute us. These interdependencies entail an extraordinarily complex set of obligations that permeate just about every aspect of our lives. By contrast, the social contract theory, with its atomic description of individuals, is too simple, too mechanical, too lacking in nuance to serve as a theoretical model for understanding human social order and the obligations that we feel toward one another. Recognizing this leads Neville to reverse the social contract assumption, arguing that "*In a pure state of nature, each person would be responsible for everything.* The function of civil society, on my contrary hypothesis, is to sort the obligations into channeled offices of responsibility for the sake of effectiveness" (ibid., 151).

From Neville's point of view, our humanity is rooted in the ability to feel and respond to obligations that go beyond our own self-interest. This is what he meant when he described thinking as an act of valuing rather than a mirroring of forms. We experience a world permeated by values, all of which we constantly weigh and sort as we struggle to determine what is the best course of action among those options before us. The task of managing our moral obligations would be overwhelming were it not for the fact that we find ourselves thrown into a social order that parcels some of our responsibilities to others, thereby relieving us to concentrate on fewer matters. For example, on Neville's model all human beings begin with a basic obligation to care for one another. In most instances, however, the children's responsibility to care for their parents is deactivated. We do not expect young children to take care of their parents except in the rudimentary ways that involve learning how to be intimately responsive. Young children are generally not responsible for feeding, clothing, and protecting their parents. And while exceptions can be imagined (e.g., child actors who become the family breadwinners or stressful situations where children are pressed into labor to secure sufficient resources to sustain family life), they make the point by demonstrating how unusual circumstances might rearrange which responsibilities are left active and which are deactivated. Here we can see how in times of stress our obligations to one another might even increase rather than decrease. Of course, the whole system is often reversed later in life when parents may no longer be able to care for themselves and it is the children, now grown, who are obliged to ensure their parent's caretaking.

Neville's axiology of knowledge leads him to let go of the most basic assumptions of the social contract theory. From his point of view, a *private life* is an accomplishment rather than a starting point. "Privacy is the high achievement of a successful society, not the natural state. Privacy only occurs when the obligations are so parceled out that the individuals have free time and space left over from fulfilling the obligations for which they have been made specifically responsible" (ibid., 151). Readers will recall how in chapter 8 I was critical of Rorty's attempt to set up a dichotomy between what he called our "public" and "private" realms. My objection then was that Rorty could not really account for how the two realms related to one another. His desire to protect the integrity of our private lives seemed to blind him to the ways in which that very privacy was dependent upon and emerged from public obligations to one another. My guess is that for all his criticisms of modernist epistemology, Rorty remains in some small way committed to aspects of the social contract theory. Neville, of course, turns things upside down, arguing that in our natural state we are neither free nor fully individualized. Instead, we awake to find ourselves obligated to one another and thereby socially determined in ways that could seem oppressive. A healthy social order structures itself in a way that permits each of us some measure of a private life, where our obligations to one another can be deactivated, and where we are free to pursue whatever strikes our imagination as valuable. Since it is hard to overestimate the intrinsic value of such an achievement, we have a tendency to speak of it as if it were a "natural right" built into what it means to be human at all. But the fact that we treasure our privacy does not mean that we understand how we achieve it. Neville's approach seems far more plausible, and it has the advantage of highlighting how difficult it is to create and sustain a social order that permits its members a measure of genuine freedom. Viewed another way, Neville's *Axiology of Knowledge* helps us to see privacy and freedom not as a given but as an achievement, which we are all responsible for sustaining.

FINAL WORDS

The goal of this chapter has been to provide readers with examples of two contemporary thinkers whose work seems headed in a direction that will move us forward in the quest for a nonrepresentational theory of knowledge. By now, the basic themes of this volume should be familiar, minimizing the need for an extensive conclusion. I will be quite brief in summing things up.

I have been arguing, with the help of Wang Yang-ming's *chih hsing ho-i,* that the best way to make progress in the quest for a nonrepresentational theory of knowledge is to begin by recognizing that knowledge and action are really one thing. Wang's slogan points to the need to shift our basic metaphors away from those that present knowledge as the static replication of forms and toward those that present knowledge as a way of forming relationships with the things that make up our world. In part 1 I cited Taylor, Davidson, Rorty, and Dennett as examples of contemporary philosophers who are pursuing (for various reasons) a nonrepresentational theory of knowledge. I also argued that their success was limited because each failed to question the basic metaphysical and cosmological assumptions that make the representational model plausible. Throughout my discussion of these thinkers, I tried to show that Dewey, Whitehead, and Wang each had something to contribute to the conversation, arguing that at key points they could help resolve seemingly intractable problems.

Having established the basic problem in part 1, and having justified my desire to include Dewey, Whitehead, and Wang in the conversation, part 2 was designed to lay out the central claims of these three thinkers. In each case I tried to show how their organismic and relational metaphysical claims led directly toward a nonrepresentational theory of knowledge where it was easy to see that knowledge and action were one thing.

Part 3 began defensively by responding to the objections of Richard Rorty, who finds organismic cosmologies old fashioned and "well lost." I argued that contemporary evidence in cognitive science and recent insights into the functioning of the human brain make the organismic model even more plausible. At a time when the empirical evidence presses us to see a direct connection between physical movements and cognitive activity, the panpsychists have the advantage over those who perceive a gap to exist between perception and cognition. Ultimately, as we have just seen, I turn to Johnson and Neville to help explain how knowledge can be a form of action. Though only Neville appeals directly to Dewey, Whitehead, and Wang, I have argued that the plausibility of both Neville's and Johnson's descriptions of knowledge rests in part on organismic and relational assumptions.

While it may at first sound relatively easy to shift the metaphors we use to describe knowledge, I hope this book makes the point that it is not. Such a shift requires that we rethink the most basic assumptions that we have made about minds, bodies, and their relationship to one another. This has entailed that we engage in metaphysical and cosmological speculations, despite the fact that much twentieth-century philosophy was dedicated to demonstrating that those forms of philosophic reflection are ultimately useless. By calling on us to look back to Dewey, Whitehead, and Wang Yang-ming, I hope to spark an appreciation for what they have to offer to contemporary discourse among those who would normally not be inclined to look their way. In the case of Dewey, in particular, I wanted to provide a counterbalance to those (like Rorty) who hope to benefit from Dewey's theory of knowledge while ignoring the metaphysical assumptions that made it plausible.

I call this section of the last chapter "final words," but I want to end by saying that I view this book as a starting point. I have attempted to lift up a point of intersection connecting the disparate projects of Taylor, Davidson, Rorty, Dennett, Johnson, and Neville. My hope is that by doing so I will have made it easier for followers of each to see how their work connects fruitfully with followers of the others. There seems no doubt that our basic understanding of knowledge is undergoing a tremendous transformation. The time has come to let go of old paradigms and old battle lines. We can find what we have been looking for by fitting contemporary discoveries in cognitive science into an organismic cosmology and a relational ontology. The philosophers whom I have looked to for help in this project are Dewey, Whitehead, and Wang Yang-ming. Of course, we should include many others in this conversation as well. My hope is that this volume will encourage others to do just that.

NOTES

INTRODUCTION

1. Throughout this book, I refer to Cartesianism rather than Descartes. I do so because there is a substantial debate over whether the Cartesian tradition accurately represents Descartes's positions and their consequences. My aim is to avoid that debate, focusing instead on consequences that stem from the way the Cartesian tradition has portrayed Descartes's positions.

2. For examples of two different accounts of the development of our current conceptions about selfhood see Charles Taylor, *Sources of the Self: The Making of Modern Identity* (1989) and Richard Rorty, *Philosophy and the Mirror of Nature* (1979). While Taylor and Rorty differ over many issues, both agree that there is nothing "natural" or "given" about the way we conceive of ourselves and our relationships with the world.

3. Along these lines, readers should note Steve Odin's efforts to draw out linkages between process, pragmatist, and other Asian intellectual traditions. His *Process Metaphysics and Hua-yen Buddhism* (1982) and *The Social Self in Zen and American Pragmatism* (1996) form a very helpful background for what I hope to achieve in this volume.

4. See David Hall and Roger Ames, 1987 and 1995. Robert Neville's work is permeated by his encounter with Chinese, pragmatic, and process thinkers. Among those works that deal with Confucian and pragmatist philosophy are 1981, 1982, 1987, 1989, 1991, 1992, 1996. See also Odin (1982, 1996) and Berthrong (1994, 1998).

CHAPTER 1

1. John Teehan raises these issues in an article titled "In Defense of Naturalism" (1996). He argues that Taylor's complaints against naturalism do not apply to Dewey's naturalistic philosophy. He goes on to claim that in the arena of moral philosophy, Dewey and Taylor have much more in common than Taylor realizes.

2. Though Taylor jumps straight to Augustine, there are many who have pointed to St. Paul as an important figure in the construction of human interiority. See Thomas J. J. Altizer, "Paul and the Birth of Self Consciousness," in his *History as Apocalypse* (1985, 63–79).

CHAPTER 3

1. This is, of course, a highly disputed issue. Those who call for a general theory of religion typically do so in an effort to adapt the study of religion as closely as possible to a mode of inquiry that mimics the natural sciences. Those who oppose such reductionisms, do so on the grounds that religious beliefs and practices arise out of a nexus of human structures that cannot easily be accounted for by focusing on a single perspective or two. The theorists respond that failure to develop a theory of religion prevents us from making any progress in understanding religion, and actually allows for the smuggling of inappropriate theological assumptions regarding the nature of the "sacred" into what should be a nontheological form of discourse.

2. It is probably important to point out that Dennett notes how this description of replicator's "intentions" is an anthropomorphic projection, rather than a literal description of their feelings!

3. A fuller discussion of the distinction Dewey draws between organic and inorganic entities can be found in chapter 6.

4. It is perhaps worth noting that Dewey's close friend and colleague George Herbert Mead originally suggested this line of explanation in the early twentieth century. In *Mind, Self and Society* (1934), Mead argues that self-consciousness emerges when gestures originally designed to stimulate a response in another organism begin to stimulate the same response in the gesturer. Mead calls such gestures "symbolic." He goes on to argue that symbolic gestures are the basis for all linguistic activity. Once such linguistic structures are in place, it becomes possible for an organism to stimulate itself. As Mead sees it, we literally gain self-consciousness by entering into conversations with ourselves. All of this points, Mead claims, to the conclusion that selfhood and consciousness are *products* of social activities, rather than starting points for social interactions.

CHAPTER 4

1. This interpretive demarcation between two important dimensions of the multi-valent term *li* is not meant to exclude other meanings. A. S. Cua makes a point of exploring all of Wang's binomial uses of *li* (e.g., *T'ien-li, i-li*) in order to nail down more clearly all that the term implies to Wang (Cua, 1982; 2001).

2. Though generally appreciative of Wang's theories, Robert Neville warns that this metaphor is dangerous, tending as it does to provide some legitimating language for different forms of totalitarianism. While I would argue that Wang has other safeguards built into his thought to prevent such dangers, I agree that the warning is well worth noting, since it is easy enough to lift such a metaphor out of context and apply it inappropriately.

3. This will become especially clear in this discussion of Wang's understanding of *ch'eng* (sincerity) and the link between *hsin* and *Li*. This sense of continuity is at the heart of Confucian naturalism. From this perspective naturalism is not so much a denial of spiritual or supernatural planes but a reaffirmation of continuity between the human and nonhuman realms.

4. This perspective helps to make sense of those puzzling passages where Wang seems to argue for an extreme form of idealism. If, as I am claiming, Wang is citing a continuity between *Chung-yung's* metaphysical understanding of *ch'eng* as primordial creativity and the *ch'eng* of *hsin*, then all things emanate from *hsin* because *hsin* is the locus of creativity within the human spirit. He is not arguing that things are "purely cognitive constructs." Rather, he seems to be pointing in the opposite direction, claiming that nothing exists outside of *hsin*, because a *hsin*, which is ultimately a *ch'eng* will, is tied to and therefore part of all that is. Some might reply, however, that sincerity is something attained rather than inherently present within the mind/will. But Wang seems to argue otherwise when he says: "Sincerity is sometimes interpreted as a task rather than as a state of mind. Sincerity is the original substance of the mind. To try to restore this original substance is the work of thinking how to be sincere" (1963, 78). Ultimately, Wang ties sincerity to principle and *liang-chih*, making explicit the metaphysical implications of his understanding of the term. "Sincerity is a true principle. It is innate knowledge. The true principle in its wonderful functioning and universal operation is spirit" (ibid., 225).

5. In *The Unity of Knowledge and Action* (1982), A. S. Cua addresses the identification of *hsin* and *li* from a different direction. He agrees that it is not an isomorphic linkage. Instead, he interprets it as a "quasi-identity" which is best understood in light of a number of other identifications that Wang develops. In addition to the *hsin/li* identification, Wang also identifies *Tao* with *T'ien*, *hsin* with *Tao* and *li* with ritual propriety *(li*)*. Cua sees these as quasi-identities, where each amplifies a different aspect of *Tao*. He calls them "amphibious terms." As identifications, the terms do not conflict because they present complimentary manifestations of the universal *Tao* from different perspectives. For Cua the identifications can be translated into "*Tao* is manifested in Heaven; Mind manifests *Tao*; Mind manifests *li*; ritual propriety manifests *li*." I find Cua's analysis quite illuminating and take it as indirect support for my own interpretation of the identification as functional rather than isomorphic. My only caveat stems from Cua's tendency to underplay the metaphysical implications of Wang's identifications. He specifically sets aside consideration of Wang's identification of *liang-chih* with *Tao* because it goes beyond the focus of his investigation. However, this identification provides the most direct evidence for the metaphysical interpretation I am pressing. As will be shown below, understanding *liang-chih* is a crucial requirement for grasping all of the implications of *chih hsing ho-i*. I am convinced of this despite the fact that Wang formulated the doctrine of *liang chih* long after *chih hsing ho-i*. As I see *liang chih* it is the completion of a line of thought that began for Wang in the enlightenment that brought forth *chih hsing ho-i*.

6. For a contrasting interpretation critical of the position Wang takes, see Cua, 2001.

7. It is important to note that while Wang sees *Chung yung* as a significant authority, he was willing to criticize concepts within it. In the passage cited above he goes on to reject foreknowledge, though the Chung-yung promotes it. To seek foreknowledge, according to Wang, is to lose touch with one's *liang chih*, "for *liang chih* knows only the incipient activating force of the present

moment." Foreknowledge seems to entail the development of a cognitive awareness of the future in abstraction from one's act of being in the present. For Wang, *liang-chih* represents our primordial reaction to things in the world, and therefore excludes the possibility of foreknowledge. To want foreknowledge is to be worried about "advantages and disadvantages" rather than responding unselfishly to things. I am grateful to A. S. Cua for alerting me to the ambiguity entailed in using this passage.

CHAPTER 6

1. In the preface to *Creative Synthesis and Philosophic Method*, Charles Hartshorne writes: "Philosophy has two primary responsibilities: to clarify the non-empirical principles and to use them, together with relevant empirical facts, to illuminate value problems of personal and social life" (1983, xiv). I will be arguing that Whitehead's cosmological description of experience makes it difficult to see how we could know anything "non-empirically." Once this is recognized, a pragmatic reading of Whitehead's philosophy becomes plausible.

2. Some might complain that this chapter also suffers from an overreliance on process neologisms. Since my hope is that it will serve as something of a bridge between the two philosophic traditions, I can't avoid using process language, but nor can I allow myself to be limited by it. I am painfully aware of the fact that those who are not "initiated" into the process tradition may find this chapter somewhat forbidding. Moreover, I suspect that traditional process thinkers will want more detailed argumentation of issues I touch on only briefly. In short, my guess is that everyone will find something to complain about!

3. It is worth noting here that this approach differs significantly from Dewey's starting point, where experience is more fundamental than subjects and objects. For Dewey, subjects and objects represent one way in which the overall unity of experience can be analyzed, or divided. Technically speaking, however, experience does not belong to the subject any more than it belongs to the object. Both are constituents in the interactions that make experience possible.

CHAPTER 7

1. In an important early article that in many ways anticipates concerns articulated in his critique of Dewey, Rorty argues that by including within his philosophy things that are beyond the realm of experience (e.g., actual entities), Whitehead effectively surrenders the most important aspect of Descartes's legacy and returns to a premodern dependence upon vacuous explanatory categories. While he acknowledges the value in Whitehead's emphasis upon the fact that all knowledge is constructed perspectivally, Rorty agrees with Sellars and other early ordinary language philosophers that we can avoid the felt need to appeal to undescribable entities through "a more careful deployment of our ordinary resources for describing mental acts" (Rorty, 1963, 134–57).

CHAPTER 8

1. David Hall has taken the lead in pursuing a philosophy inspired by process thought, Deweyan pragmatism, and postmodern aspects of Richard Rorty's work. See his *Richard Rorty: Prophet and Poet of the New Pragmatism* (1994). With respect to the issues raised in this chapter, it is also interesting to note that Hall is one of the pragmatists whose work has been most influenced by Taoism (1982a; 1982b).

2. It is important to note that though this chapter focuses on the relationship between Taoist and Confucian thought, most scholars acknowledge that Buddhism played an equal or even larger role in the transformation of medieval Confucianism into the Neo-Confucian tradition. Though I do think that scholars sometimes underplay the influence of Taoism on Neo-Confucianism, I do not want to suggest that this transformation took place only because of what Confucians learned from Taoists.

3. This is extraordinarily important for our discussion of Richard Rorty, who wants to retain the label of pragmatist while introducing a conceptual dichotomy between public and private reflection. For Rorty, attempts to integrate these two spheres of human activity are foolish remnants of older epistemological assumptions about the structure of knowledge. As he sees it, the public and private spheres have an independent status and independent criteria for evaluations. Rorty's willingness to adopt this radical dichotomy stems partly from his willingness to forgo the Deweyan demand that we set our understanding of human beings within a wider understanding of their physical and biological context. From the Deweyan perspective, this context provides the rationale for integrating public and private life as fully as possible. In addition, this physical and biological context provides the anchor (though not the foundation) for a genuinely pragmatic theory of value.

4. Chinese divination techniques sometimes give Western interpreters the impression that the culture presumed there was a "plan" on the order of a modified form of Calvinistic predetermination. This is a misunderstanding of the practice much like the wild misinterpretations of Calvin's doctrine of predestination. Richard Smith points out that divination is a way of trying to anticipate tendencies in a situation so that the diviner will know how to act wisely, rather than an attempt to describe a predetermined future. See Richard J. Smith (1991).

5. As we saw in chapter 5, the Principle of Nature is near Plato's Form of the Good insofar as that is kept distinct from Plato's doctrine of the forms. The doctrine of the forms is far too rigid and fixed to provide a useful analogy to Wang's dynamic understanding of principle and the Principle of Nature. However, Plato's Form of the Good does not suffer from that same rigidity. It is, by definition, the dynamic source of all harmonization and is in that sense analogous to Wang's understanding of the Principle of Nature and by extension his understand if *liang chih*.

6. Wang spotted remnants of this position in Chu Hsi's understanding of principle, knowledge, and *ko wu*. This is true despite the fact that Chu Hsi had accepted Chou Tun-i's identification of *T'ai-chi* and *wu-chi*. The whole point of Wang's identification of *li* with *hsin* was to eliminate the notion that the world

is constituted by a single transcendent order and open the Confucian discourse to our responsibilities as creative agents who should be engaged in the creation of value in partnership with Heaven and Earth.

7. Philip J. Ivanhoe (1990) flirts with this reading of Wang. At one point, he says that Wang believed in "an original, pure and fully-formed inner nature, hidden beneath an impure physical nature" (47). This pure inner nature, however, should not be confused with an *a priori* structure. As I read it, Wang tries to make clear that *liang chih* represents an indeterminate creativity that we share with Heaven and Earth. It is not that we have a fully pre-formed moral mind capable of applying a fixed set of transcendent principles to any concrete situation. Rather, humankind awakes to find itself already in the process of creating new harmonies, and it is that indeterminate capacity to create new harmonies that he is trying to capture in the phrase *liang chih*.

8. By "intellectualist" I am again referring to Dewey's comment that philosophers often fail to recognize the naturalist position because they take higher-order cognitive activities to be a basis or starting point for knowledge, rather than the product of precognitive organic activities (Dewey, 1958, 21).

CHAPTER 9

1. Johnson makes it clear that he designed his book to address "philosophers, linguists, psychologists and social scientists trained in, or influenced by, Anglo-American analytic philosophy." He goes on to point out that this means he cannot appeal directly to phenomenologists who are regarded by many in these traditions as "muddle-headed and inaccessible." I believe this also explains Johnson's failure to appeal to the classical pragmatists who are often assessed in this manner (1987, xxxvii).

2. On this point Johnson begins by citing Ulric Neisser, who says: "The schema is not only the plan but also the executor of the plan. It is a pattern *of* action as well as a pattern *for* action" (Johnson, 1987, 21; Neisser, 1976, 54).

WORKS CITED

Alexander, Thomas. *John Dewey's Theory of Art, Experience and Nature: The Horizons of Feeling*. Albany: State University of New York Press, 1987.

Altizer, Thomas J. J. *History as Apocalypse*. Albany: State University of New York Press, 1985.

Bernstein, Richard J. *Praxis and Action*. Philadelphia: University of Pennsylvania Press, 1971.

——. *Beyond Objectivism and Relativism: Science, Hermeneutics, and Praxis*. Philadelphia: University of Pennsylvania Press, 1983.

Berthrong, John H. *All under Heaven: Transforming Paradigms in Confucian-Christian Dialogue*. Albany: State University of New York Press, 1994.

——. *Concerning Creativity: A Comparison of Chu Hsi, Whitehead, and Neville*. Albany: State University of New York Press, 1998.

Boisvert, Raymond D. *Dewey's Metaphysics*. New York: Fordham University Press, 1988.

Chan, Wing-tsit., trans. and comp. *A Source Book in Chinese Philosophy*. New York: Columbia University Press, 1963.

Cheng, Chung-ying. *New Dimensions of Confucian and Neo-Confucian Philosophy*. Albany: State University of New York Press, 1991.

Ching, Julia. *To Acquire Wisdom: The Way of Wang Yang-ming*. New York: Columbia University Press, 1976.

Cua, A. S. *The Unity of Knowledge and Action*. Honolulu: University of Hawaii Press, 1982.

——. "Between Commitment and Realization: Wang Yang-ming's Vision of the Universe as a Moral Community." In *Confucian Spirituality,* ed. Tu Wei-ming. New York: Crossroad/Herder & Herder, 2001.

Davidson, Donald. "On the Very Idea of a Conceptual Scheme." *Proceedings of the American Philosophical Association* 17 (1973–74).

——. "The Myth of the Subjective." In *Relativism: Interpretation and Confrontation,* ed. Michael Krauz. South Bend: Notre Dame Press. 1990.

de Bary, Wm. Theodore. *Neo-Confucian Orthodoxy and the Learning of the Mind-and-Heart*. New York: Columbia University Press, 1981.

Dennett, Daniel C. *The Intentional Stance*. Cambridge: Massachusetts Institute of Technology Press, 1987.

——. *Consciousness Explained*. Boston: Little, Brown and Company, 1991.

Dewey, John. Human Nature and Conduct. New York: Henry Holt and Company, 1922.

——. *Experience and Nature*. New York: Dover Publications, 1929/1958.

——. *Art as Experience*. New York: Paragon Books, 1934.

————. *Logic: The Theory of Inquiry*. New York: Henry Holt and Company, 1938.

Frank, Manfred. *What Is Neo-Structuralism?* Trans. by Sabine Wilke and Richard Gray. Minneapolis, University of Minnesota Press, 1989.

Frisina, Warren G. "Metaphysics and Moral Metaphysics." *The Journal of Chinese Philosophy* 13, 1986.

————. "Relational Ontology from a Cross-Cultural Perspective." Ph.D. dissertation, University of Chicago, 1987.

Hall, David. *Eros and Irony*. Albany: State University of New York Press, 1982a.

————. *The Uncertain Phoenix*. New York: Fordham University Press, 1982b.

————. *Richard Rorty: Prophet and Poet of the New Pragmatism*. Albany: State University of New York Press, 1994.

Hall, David, and Roger Ames. *Thinking through Confucius*. Albany: State University of New York Press, 1987.

————. *Anticipating China: Thinking Through the Narratives of Chinese and Western Culture*. Albany: State University of New York Press, 1995.

Hartshorne, Charles. *Creative Synthesis and Philosophic Method*. Lanham: University Press of America, 1983.

Ivanhoe, Philip J. *Ethics in the Confucian Tradition: The Thought of Mencius and Wang Yang-ming*. Atlanta: Scholars Press, 1990.

James, William. *Pragmatism*. Cambridge: Harvard University Press, 1978.

Johnson, Mark. *The Body in the Mind: The Bodily Basis of Meaning, Imagination, and Reason*. Chicago: University of Chicago Press, 1987.

Kraus, Elizabeth. "Existence as Transaction: A Whiteheadian Study of Causality." *International Philosophic Quarterly* 25 (Dec. 1985).

Kuhn, Thomas. *The Structure of Scientific Revolutions*, 2nd ed. Chicago: University of Chicago Press, 1970.

Lakoff, George, and Mark Johnson. *Philosophy in the Flesh: The Embodied Mind and Its Challenge to Western Thought*. New York: Basic Books, 1999.

Lao Tzu. *Lao Tzu*. Tr. D. C. Lau. Baltimore: Penguin, 1963.

Mead, George Herbert. *Mind, Self, and Society from the Standpoint of a Social Behaviorist*. Chicago: University of Chicago Press, 1934; 1974.

Mote, Frederick. *Intellectual Foundations of China*. New York: Alfred Knopf, 1971.

Needham, Joseph. *Science and Civilization in China*. Cambridge: Cambridge University Press, 1956, vol. 2.

Neisser, Ulric. *Cognition and Reality*. San Francisco: W. H. Freeman, 1976.

Neville, Robert C. *The Reconstruction of Thinking*. Albany: State University of New York Press, 1981.

————. *The Tao and the Daimon*. Albany: State University of New York Press, 1982.

————. "Wang Yang-ming and John Dewey on the Ontological Question." *Journal of Chinese Philosophy* 12 (1985).

————. *The Puritan Smile*. Albany: State University of New York Press, 1987.

————. *Recovery of the Measure: Interpretation and Nature*. Albany: State University of New York Press, 1989.

―――. *Behind the Masks of God*. Albany: State University of New York Press, 1991.

―――. *The High Road around Modernism*. Albany: State University of New York Press, 1992.

―――. *Normative Cultures*. Albany: State University of New York Press, 1996.

Odin, Steve. *Process Metaphysics and Hua-yen Buddhism*. Albany: State University of New York Press, 1982.

―――. *The Social Self in Zen and American Pragmatism*. Albany: State University of New York Press, 1996.

Robbins, J. Wesley. "Donald Davidson and Religious Belief." *American Journal of Theology and Philosophy* 17, no. 2 (May 1996): 141–55.

Rorty, Richard. "The Subjectivist Principle and the Linguistic Turn." In *Alfred North Whitehead: Essays on His Philosophy,* George L. Kline, ed. Englewood Cliffs: Prentice-Hall, Inc., 1963.

―――. *Philosophy and the Mirror of Nature*. Princeton: Princeton University Press, 1979.

―――. *Consequences of Pragmatism*. Minneapolis: University of Minnesota Press, 1982.

―――. *Contingency, irony, and solidarity*. Cambridge: Cambridge University Press, 1989.

―――. *Objectivity, Relativism, and Truth: Philosophical Papers*. Vol. 1. Cambridge: Cambridge University Press, 1991.

―――. "Dewey between Hegel and Darwin." In *Modernist Impulses in the Human Sciences 1870–1930,* Dorothy Ross, ed. Baltimore: Johns Hopkins University Press, 1994. Also found in *Rorty and Pragmatism,* Herman J. Saatkamp, Jr., Nashville, Vanderbilt University Press, 1995.

Rosenthal, Sandra. *Speculative Pragmatism*. Amherst: University of Massachusetts Press, 1986.

Schwartz, Benjamin. *The World of Thought in Ancient China*. Cambridge: Bellknap Press of Harvard University Press, 1985.

Sleeper, R.W. *The Necessity of Pragmatism: John Dewey's Conception of Philosophy*. New Haven: Yale University Press, 1986.

Smith, John E. *Purpose and Thought*. New Haven: Yale University Press, 1978.

Smith, Richard J. *Fortune Tellers and Philosophers: Divination in Traditional Chinese Society*. Boulder: Westview Press, 1991.

Stuhr, John. "Experience as Activity: Dewey's Metaphysics." Ph.D. dissertation, Vanderbilt University, 1976.

Taylor, Charles. *Sources of the Self: The Making of Modern Identity*. Cambridge: Harvard University Press, 1989.

Teehan, John. "In Defense of Naturalism." *The Journal of Speculative Philosophy* 10, no. 2 (1996).

Tu Wei-ming. *Neo-Confucian Thought in Action: Wang Yang-ming's Youth (1472–1509)*. Berkeley: University of California Press, 1976.

―――. "The Unity of Knowing and Acting: From a Neo-Confucian Perspective." In *Humanity and Self-Cultivation: Essays in Confucian Thought*. Berkeley: Asian Humanities Press, 1978.

———. *Confucian Thought: Selfhood as Creative Transformation*. Albany: State University of New York Press, 1985.

———. *Centrality and Commmonality: An Essay on Confucian Religiousness*. Albany: State University of New York Press, 1989.

Varela, Francisco J. *Ethical Know-How: Action, Wisdom and Cognition*. Stanford: Stanford University Press, 1999.

Varela, Francisco J., Evan Thompson, and Eleanor Rosch. *The Embodied Mind: Cognitive Science and Human Experience*. Cambridge, MA: MIT Press, 1991.

Wang Yang-ming, *Instructions for Practical Living*. Trans. Wing-tsit Chan. New York: Columbia University Press 1963.

———. *The Philosophical Letters of Wang Yang-ming*. Trans. and annot. Julia Ching. Columbia: University of South Carolina Press, 1972.

Whitehead, Alfred North. "Analysis of Meaning." In *Essays in Science and Philosophy*. New York: Philosophical Library, 1948.

———. *The Function of Reason*. Boston: Beacon Press, 1929/1958.

———. *Symbolism: Its Meaning and Effect*. New York: G. P. Putnam's Sons, 1927/1959.

———. *Science and the Modern World*. New York: The Free Press, 1929/1967.

———. *Adventures of Ideas*. New York: The Free Press, 1933/1967.

———. *Process and Reality*. Corrected edition, ed. David Ray Griffin and Donald W. Sherburne. New York: The Free Press, 1978.

Wu, Kuang-ming. *Chuang Tzu: World Philosopher at Play*. Chico: Scholars Press, 1982.

INDEX

Accuracy, and subjective aims of
  inquirers, 132–133
Action as completion of knowledge,
  75, 77
Activity
  defined by Dewey, 105
  imagination as, 212
  linked to tranquility, 174–175
  thinking as, 223
Aesthetic knowledge, 119, 123,
  131–133
Aesthetics
  and Dewey's understanding of
    value, 169–170
  Kant's discussion of, 213
  Neville's discussion of, 220
Alexander, Thomas, 104
Ames, Roger, 171
Anthropology, Taoist, disagreements
  with, 167, 171, 173–174, 181
Anti-representationalism. *See*
  Nonrepresentational theory of
  knowledge
Appearance and reality, distinction
  between, 149, 151, 153
Aristotelian portrayal of imagination,
  208
Aristotle, on theoretical thinking, 230
Augustine, on self-reflection, 20, 22, 24
Autonomy in disengaged self, 22–23

Beauty discussed by Neville, 218–219
Being, dynamic character of, 78–80
Being-standpoint, 172
Belief systems
  derived from language, 31–32, 182
  described by Rorty, 39
  as product of inquiry, 108

Bernstein, Richard J., 5–7
Biological activity. *See also*
    Organic/replicator systems
  consciousness emerging from, 115,
    200
  inquiry in, 108–109
  and intellectual activity, 111–112
  and language development, 116,
    169
Bodily activity
  and dualism between mind and
    body, 73–74
  and embodied experience, 224
  generating image-schematas, 198
  mental activity emerging from,
    143, 160
  and problems with disembodied
    concepts, 197
Brain. *See* Mind/brain
Buddhism affecting Neo-
  Confucianism, 166, 241

Cartesian tradition
  characterization of knowledge in,
    6, 9–10, 18
  disengagement in, 21–24
  focus on individual in, 6
  representational theories in, 2, 43
  separation of knowledge from
    action, 1, 21–22
  subjectivity in, 34
  visual metaphors in, 54
Causal efficacy in experience,
    described by Whitehead, 26, 33,
    36–37, 95, 128–130, 134, 157,
    198, 206
Chan, Wing-tsit, 83, 84
Chang Tsai, 79, 80, 98, 164

and cognitive activity, 33
consciousness as outcome of,
    54–55, 111–115
embodied, 224
enculturated, 224
explained by Dewey, 33, 95,
    102–106, 118, 156, 158, 168
as inquiry, 108
interactions in, 101, 118, 127
and language acquisition, 115–118
movement of matter in, 49
noncognitive or primary, 106–108,
    126, 151
nonpropositional
    described by Johnson, 198,
        199, 206, 212
    imagination in, 219, 220
prereflective response in, 94–95,
    212
primordial awareness in, 94,
    96–97
as product of situations, 104, 155,
    167–168, 186, 190
relationship to nature, 102, 104
reporting and descriptions of,
    47–48
    paradoxes in, 51–52
and sensitivity to sociality, 120
subjectivism in, 34
as tensional situation seeking
    equilibrium, 103–106, 109,
    118, 158
as trait in organic systems, 156
Whitehead's understanding of,
    123, 127–131
    causal efficacy in, 26, 33,
        36–37, 95, 128–130, 134,
        157, 198, 206

Fantasy compared to genius, 190
Feelings
    noncognitive, 157
    physical
        about past experience, 132
        and emergence of cognition,
            212
    qualitative and valuative, 26

Feminism, contemporary philosophy
    of, 160
Foreknowledge rejected by Wang,
    239–240
Frank, Manfred, 147
Freud, Sigmund, Rorty's use of, 39,
    41, 188–189

Genius compared to fantasy, 190
Gestures, symbolic, and linguistic
    activity, 115, 120, 231, 238
Goodness
    discussed by Neville, 218–219
    inherent in human nature, 95–96
    innate awareness of, 18
    orientation to, described by
        Taylor, 13, 14

Habits
    challenging of, 115, 121
    as learned responses, 62–63, 109
Hall, David, 171, 241
Hartshorne, Charles, 4, 124
Heaven as creative source, 171–173
    humans as partners with, 176,
        177, 183, 207
Hegel, Georg, 147
Heidegger, Martin, 187
Historical events, and belief systems,
    39
Historicism
    and Dewey's philosophy, 155–156
    Rorty's views on, 147–148,
        150–151
Hobbes, Thomas, on social contracts,
    232
Homeric tradition, emphasis on living
    of life, 20
Hsin (heart-mind)
    identified with *Li,* 84, 90–93, 99,
        175, 238, 239, 241–242
    and interdependence of subject and
        object, 82
    link to dynamic universe, 80
    as locus of creativity, 92, 239
    as locus of will, 88–89, 90, 93
    relation to *liang-chih,* 97–98

and connectedness with the whole
of things, 28
crises engendered by, 25
and partitioning from external
world, 19–27, 54
Interpretative thinking, 218,
221–225, 230
and Neville's flow of
interpretation, 221, 224, 226
Intuitive judgment described by
Whitehead, 132
Ivanhoe, Philip J., 242

James, William, 147, 150
Johnson, Mark, 143, 160–161,
196–215
The Body in the Mind, 196–197,
199
comment on rationality without
rules, 213
compared to Dewey, 199
compared to Neville, 219
compared to Whitehead, 199
on continuity of activity in bodily
experience, 198–199, 208
critique of Rorty, 196
description of understanding,
206–207, 214–215
image-schematas of, 198,
206–207
patterns in, 198, 199, 200–201
imagination discussed by, 207–214
meaning described by, 201–202,
214
metaphors described by, 205–207,
214, 229
on nonpropositional experience,
198, 199, 206, 212
objectivism discussed by, 195–198,
229
position compared to *liang-chih,*
199, 204, 206
reading of Kant, 208–214
Judgment
intuitive, described by Whitehead,
132
negative, 136

Kant, Immanuel, 188, 202
on empirical and *a priori* concepts,
211–212
Johnson's reading of, 208–214
Knowledge
aesthetic, 119, 123, 131–133
as agent of change, 114–115, 121
as beginning of action, 75, 77
changing descriptions of, 3, 6
cognitive, affectional content of, 96
in community experiences, 5–6
as form of action, 4, 110,
118–119, 123, 168, 204
in Whitehead's philosophy,
124–131, 137
hypothetical, 120, 123, 133–137
as ideas imposed on passive mind,
23–24
and imagination, 208
innate, 88. *See also* Liang-chih
(innate knowledge)
as interactional pattern, 101
mentalistic definition of, 6, 9
moral, 76–77
as movement, 89
nonrepresentational theory of, 9, 10
search for, 3–4, 5, 11, 234–235
practical, 75–76
and *chih hsing ho-i,* 74–75
as product of inquiry, 108, 119
purely cognitive forms of, 75, 96
sense data theories of, 125–126
in social activity, 120
spectator theory of, 168, 182, 221
Wang's understanding of, 75,
176–177
Ko wu (investigation of things)
dualism illustrated in, 91, 92
and internalization of *li,* 90, 91
and renovation of oneself, 76, 100
Kraus, Elizabeth, 127
Kuhn, Thomas, 3

Lakoff, George, 161
Language
analysis in critique of subjectivism,
35